IF ONLY YOU KNEW

The hidden truths and the hidden dangers.
Your health, your choice. Be informed.

First Edition

by

Andrew D. Lewis

B Pharm (hons) LCPH (UK)

If Only You Knew

Acknowledgements

Thanks to my wife Sue for her patient listening ear and her encouragement to write this book. She has been a constant source of support over the years I have been studying the information in this book. I express my love and gratitude for her being in my life.

I thank my parents Ron and Jean for bringing me into this world so that I could write this book.

Thanks to Julie my neighbour and friend for her advice and help with the finer detail of presenting the book for e-publication; and thanks to my Son in Law Pete for help with the cover.

 Thank you to my brother, Stephen, for his valuable editing and ideas for how I could improve certain aspects of the book.

My gratitude goes to all the people and institutions I have quoted and referenced in this book. I thank them for their dedication and for providing knowledge, which will serve the enquiring mind on the road to empowerment.

Finally I acknowledge all those brave pioneers of human endeavour, past and present, who have had the courage and strength to step outside of the constraints of conventional thinking and begin to formulate a new world view so that humanity might change its current destructive course and one day come to realise a new worldview which is based in balance, harmony and peace.

Dedication

This book is dedicated to my family and friends to be an aid for them to make more informed choices in their daily living and interaction with the world around us.

I also dedicate this book to my broader human family so that they may become aware of information that would ordinarily be out of their field of reference.

<u>Disclaimer</u>

The information contained in this book is not intended to be a substitute for appropriate, qualified medical advice. There is no intention to treat or diagnose disease. The information is for educational purposes only.

Any action taken by the reader as a result of what they read in this book is solely their own responsibility, particularly in relation to changes in medication. Always consult your health care professional for advice.

****

Responsibility of course is a big issue in our society and we are only too willing to accept government dictates as to what constitutes a healthy life style, what is good and nutritious for us to eat and what is the best medicine to help us to live longer. Proper advice should lead to informed consent. There will always be conflicting information and it is our choice as to what we believe to be true. The law only interprets what is written by the law givers. Just because something is written in law by man neither makes it true nor valid. For example; legally defined limits for toxins in our food does not make them safe.

Why do we so readily accept 'the official line' on something? Is it because we are constantly drip fed the ideas through the media? We are exposed on a daily basis to newspapers, TV, radio, advertising boards, magazines etc. We are conditioned from an early age not to challenge authority, not to challenge the experts. The experts know best, don't they? They and they alone understand the latest ideas on health and well being which, if you follow the history of medicine, change on a very regular basis. When you seek medical or nutritional advice from your doctor are you given a disclaimer? No, yet medicine and so called nutritional advice is responsible for hundreds of thousands of deaths world wide as we shall see.

__Table of Contents__

If Only You Knew

If Only You Knew

__FOREWORD__

Why did I write this book?

I have been studying health information for many years, this includes what would be considered both conventional and alternative and also some ideas that many would consider unorthodox in any realm of medical health.

When I got my first iPad and had information literally at my finger tips, my ability to assimilate and research information became quite an easy task. No longer did I need to boot up the PC and spend hours in isolation in an office situation; I could browse information while I was drinking my morning coffee before starting my daily tasks.

One day I was thinking about all the knowledge my brain had accumulated and thought I should write it down for the benefit of friends and family who often asked for information on health issues. This was my initial impetus but after writing the book I realised that in actual fact anyone who was not aware of what is happening in the medical and food industries could benefit from the information.

Two web sites that I consulted quite regularly and which the reader will be directed to many times are _http://www.thennt.com_ and _http://www.greenmedinfo.com_. Studying the information on these sites really opened my eyes to the poor efficacy of conventional medicine in treating chronic disease and the evidence base for alternatives which were often more effective but without the inherent side effects associated with conventional therapy.

The information of course is not hidden and is readily available for those who care to seek it out; in reality few people would choose to do this because of many different factors which may deter them.

So the reason I wrote this book is to convey in a relatively short space, enough information to allow you the reader to get an overview of the overwhelming amount of information that may be relevant to your health and well being.

We all take for granted that the information we are being given by recognised authorities is true and accurate; the question arises however 'what is true in this context?' I hope these pages will shed some light on the issues and allow you the reader to make more informed choices.

<u>Chapter 1 – INTRODUCTION</u>

When I was approaching the start of my university education I had no idea what I wanted to study. One day my father came home and suggested applying for pharmacy. He'd seen the local pharmacist as someone who was successful in life and enjoyed a reasonable standard of living. Something most parents want for their children.

I wasn't given much real guidance at school and had no personal inspiration and since chemistry was my favourite subject at school my studies in pharmacy began. I completed my pharmacy degree in 1974 and became registered to practice in 1975. The word practice is interesting; we use this word to describe a professional operation. Do we ever become really competent or are we only ever practicing? Maybe we are, after all to get a degree the minimum pass mark is around 40%[1]. Is this why a medical diagnosis often approaches that level of accuracy in general practice?

> *In one study 55.3% of physicians were able to accurately diagnose easier cases but the number able to diagnose more difficult cases fell to just 5.8%[2].*

If you have a difficult case you might want to get a second or even third opinion!

Pharmacy of course, is a scientific discipline where everything is determined by experiment (supposedly). Experiments in the physical sciences tend to have a definitive outcome and end point; biological systems don't always follow the ideas of mechanical systems and hence we have to employ the use of statistics to evaluate the effectiveness (or not) of any drug treatment. We will look at this aspect later in the book. Have no fear it will be simple stuff that most people should be able to understand.

I remember when I was in my first work placement coming across the concept of homoeopathy and thinking 'how could this work? There's nothing in it'. Later on in life after having broadened my horizons in terms of my general education I thought that I should look into homoeopathy and so embarked on a four year part time course. This was truly life changing in terms of increasing my understanding of the capacity of the body and mind to heal given the appropriate stimulus. One of my first experiences was a personal one which is always the best of course.

I had been laying a wooden floor so had been kneeling quite a lot. At some point I had become aware that my right knee didn't feel quite right. The following morning when I awoke my knee had swollen considerably. Being on my homoeopathy quest I thought to myself "I'll take a remedy". I decided to take a dose of Silica 30C (can't quite remember why!). My wife, being a physiotherapist, strapped my knee and off I went to work in the pharmacy. When I got home that evening my knee was much worse and the inflammation had started tracking down the facia between the muscles. The remedy had done absolutely nothing and I was disappointed to say the least. By this time my right knee was about 50% bigger than my left knee. I reassessed the case and decided on another remedy Apis 30C. I took a single dose and sat back and waited. My wife and I were sat together watching TV (and my knee!). Within half an hour of taking the remedy my knee had reduced in size to almost normal. I was stunned and thought to myself "I don't know anything in conventional medicine that can do that".

After completing the course I had come to the realisation that there is more to medicine and indeed the human being than is portrayed in the conventional view. Conventional medicine has an extremely closed view of health and sickness. The body is compartmentalised into systems and named diseases. Diagnoses are made so a treatment can be prescribed. Conventional medicine doesn't ask the question; why is someone ill or expressing a certain symptom picture? Symptoms are just a nuisance to be suppressed at all costs and no-one thinks about the consequences of suppressing the symptoms.

When you start looking at things from a different perspective you get an enthusiasm to want to know more. I went on to study nutrition and nutritional healing.

It's rather concerning that most conventional medical training, including pharmacy and other professions allied to medicine, has very little teaching on nutrition. I'm talking about detailed training on how the body relies on having certain nutrients in the right place to perform its day to day activities. Many medicines are indeed anti-nutrients in that they caused depletion of vital molecules the body needs, more of that later. The conventional system doesn't think that what you put in your mouth is important nor does it seriously regard toxic exposure problematical unless it is of an acute nature. Most of our toxic exposure is low level, chronic and insidious; the effects build up over time and exposure is often difficult to pin point.

One of the main purposes of this book is to help you to start to think about what you put into your body and how that might affect your health and not to just blindly accept what you are told by the experts. True choice is about having all the facts that are available, about knowing what questions to ask your health professional, about being empowered and not succumbing to victim mentality. After all it is your body and it's the only one you have in this lifetime!

When someone has a so called terminal condition they are often told by their doctor that there's nothing more that can be done for them; what this means is there is nothing more they can offer within their paradigm. Some people will choose to go home, get their affairs in order and dutifully die according to the prediction. Other people have a stronger desire for life and don't accept the doctor's terminal prognosis. These people become self empowered and choose to take a different path, they do their own research, change their mind set or experience a profound shift in consciousness. These people often achieve an improvement in their quality of life and extend life well beyond the doctor's prognosis. We always have choices, even though sometimes we think not, because the choices are often not ones we are ready to make.

In this book I want to stimulate the reader into thinking of possibilities by providing information that may help you to be more empowered. When you become informed from your own efforts and have the awareness that what's being offered may not be in your best interests you may decide to make other choices. When you have more information about a particular treatment option you become more aware of the issues and are more able to make decisions that are right for you. A famous scholar once said:

> **"I cannot teach anybody anything. I can only make them think"**
>
> Socrates

Medical education does not provide doctors with the 'all seeing eye'! Remember the 40% pass mark quoted before. Despite the libraries full of medical knowledge we are only just scraping the surface of the knowledge of what makes the human instrument function at a fundamental energetic level. The medical literature only concerns itself with the physical structure of man. Psychiatry which supposedly is focused on the mind aspect of our being often relies on unproven theories of chemical imbalance and uses powerful psychotropic drugs to numb the mind/brain into submission.

Have you ever asked yourself; where is the mind? Is it an organ in your head? Is it physical? What happens when you go 'out of your mind'? What or who tells you to change your mind?

Our current medical paradigm has only been around a short time in the history of humanity and as we'll see later the effectiveness of this system is neither guaranteed nor is it free of inherent danger. New knowledge only slowly percolates into clinical practice so your clinician may not be aware of the latest research. If you want to be more informed about the decisions you make regarding your health then you are unlikely to get the full picture from your regular medical practitioner. Most doctors only get information on which their prescribing is based, from sources which promote a certain ideology.

If you are able to weigh up the pros and cons and to ask questions of the health practitioner you will gain more control over the decisions you make. Don't expect them to know all the answers, they surely won't. There is now a wealth of easily accessible knowledge and alternative viewpoints and all it takes is the desire to investigate.

Taking responsibility for your own health and well being will bring a powerful feeling of control into your life. Starting to truly think about things and ask the right questions such as, "why is my immune system not protecting me from these bacteria?"

A doctor needs to make a diagnosis in order to be able to prescribe a drug to deal with the symptoms. What if the symptoms were an expression of your body trying to heal? Other systems of medicine do indeed take that view and try to encourage the body in its own healing endeavours. The body is, in essence, self healing. Diet and life style and mental attitude have much to do with our ability to perform this function

Over the course of my career in pharmacy the number of drugs prescribed for an individual has increased at an alarming rate. People are not seen as being in a diseased state but rather having a number of diseases and thus being prescribed drugs for each of these diseases and may be drugs for the side effects of other drugs. We have even created disease states which are really just a natural function of ageing, menopause for example.

We are led to believe that drug development is scientific. Nearer to the truth is that drug discovery can be rather hit and miss and is more often than not a lucky strike when a new compound is developed. Large automated machines are used to produce and identify potential drug molecules. Many compounds are synthesised but few are promising. Often drugs are brought to market for a side effect that is discovered during trials. Viagra is such an example. This drug was originally being developed for heart disease; many of the male trial members however reported the interesting side effect of having more or better erections; hence a new treatment was born!

We are influenced by constant propaganda to have the belief that taking medication is necessary if we want to extend our lives and live healthily. Nothing is further from the truth. The reason we need pills is to suppress the symptoms of a body out of harmony with its natural way of being and expression. The reason the body is out of harmony is because of numerous factors which we will explore.

Our current popular science is unfortunately deeply entrenched within a mechanistic rut. This is the reason why governments only fund mechanistic based medicine; they get their advice from mechanistically thinking scientists! We forget that the government is elected to represent the people and therefore the people must demand change if we are ever to change our medical paradigm which is clearly not working even though the marketing would have us believe otherwise.

Recall the words of Mahatma Ghandi:

"When the people lead the leaders will follow".

This book is aimed at those individuals who have the desire and courage to face and oppose the growing control over our health and well being and indeed freedoms in general. With knowledge and information it is possible to question the accepted view point and discuss the relative and absolute benefits or harms of a particular treatment, procedure or food product you might ordinarily assume to be safe. Most people accept that if the government says it is O.K. then it must be. This, for the most part, is a very naive assumption particularly when you become aware of the vested interests of the people advising the government.

None of the information in this book is new and I take no credit for it. It has been compiled from various sources and can be researched and verified by anyone who cares to take the time. My greatest wish is that it will help the reader to be more able to make informed choices regarding their own health and well being, about the medicines and foods they allow into their body and the procedures they subject themselves to. I hope each reader will become one of the growing numbers that the government will eventually have to follow.

My intention is not to give masses of data to support a particular argument or idea but just to provide enough information and references to give people ideas and motivation to look at things for themselves. Many of references come either directly or indirectly from officially recognised sources such as the Cochrane database or National Institute of Health (NIH) and allied sites.

When speaking to many medical professionals keep in mind that they may firmly believe that what they've been taught at medical school and subsequently reinforced by the drug companies is the absolute truth. They 'know' how the body works and that drugs and surgery are the only answer. They have a vested interest in the current paradigm and just because that paradigm is widely accepted it doesn't make it true or the only one.

We knew about the role of fruit and vegetables in health at least a hundred years before it was accepted by the medical people of the time. They just could not accept that something in a lowly lemon or orange could cure that most deadly disease of scurvy. This was a long time before vitamin C was discovered as the curative agent. We used to think the earth was flat and at the centre of the solar system. The list goes on. Science has this wonderfully repetitive notion; "we used to believe that was true but now we know this is true"; this and that of course are constantly changing but the truth never changes. Humility is needed to recognise that the knowledge base we have is incomplete and full of holes.

Where do doctors and other medical professionals get much of their drug education from? The answer is from the very companies that are selling the drugs. They provide lavish seminars to introduce and market the products; incentives used to be freely offered to prescribe the product. This is less evident since industry regulation has been enforced but the cynic in me feels it probably still goes on in more covert ways.

If drug companies are educating the doctors, the information is hardly likely to be unbiased, is it? I'm sure the research scientists are working conscientiously in their own way, however the boards of directors of these companies are more likely to be focused on company profitability, the bottom line and share holder dividends. We have had many scandals where drugs brought to market are withdrawn because people are dying or where drugs are inappropriately marketed.

Doctors, in good faith, accepting the information as factual and basing their prescribing on it, can easily be misled unless they do their own research; most don't because of time constraints and obtaining truly unbiased information can be difficult. An example of this is the high profile influenza vaccination which is being recommended for almost everyone now. The Cochrane database, the gold standard for medical research, says that the vaccine is of no conclusive benefit in the elderly and for the average healthy adult, between 30 and 100 people would need to be vaccinated to prevent one case of flu. Does that seem like a good deal to you? A flu vaccine can have a good efficacy and produce antibodies to the virus strain in the vaccine, but it may not be effective i.e. prevent you getting flu. It is on the basis of efficacy that it is promoted. There are over 200 strains of viruses which cause flu or flu like symptoms, the vaccine has only 3 or 4 strains which may be one of the reasons for its poor track record.

Remember this; all truth passes through three stages.

1. It is ridiculed

2. It is violently opposed

3. It is accepted as being self evident

(Arthur Schopenhauer, German philosopher 1788 – 1860)

Our medical system is supposedly evidence based yet the evidence is often flimsy. The evidence lies in the statistical analysis of the data. If the effect is greater than that expected by chance (or placebo) then it is said to be significant. The fact that relatively few people may benefit is of little consequence. We will see how the data is taken and used to market products in a positive way giving the impression to the untrained eye that many will benefit. For example TV advertising gives the public the impression that pain killers work for everyone. Statistics are used to manipulate data to give a positive appearance. Trial data supplied to licensing authorities are provided by the very companies who make the product; this is hardly independent and devoid of vested interest.

I find it interesting that of all the things we give our money for, medicine is the only commodity that comes without a guarantee. Any other product or service comes with some sort of guarantee which gives the consumer a right of redress if the product or service is poor quality or doesn't perform as expected. As we will see later our medical system is directly responsible for many deaths which is just attributed to 'the cost of doing business'.

We have been conditioned to accept a set of beliefs as being true. As time progresses these beliefs become an accepted reality just because they were adopted sometime in the past.

> *"We must not believe in a thing said merely because it is said; nor traditions because they have been handed down from antiquity; nor rumours, as such; nor writings by sages, because sages wrote them; nor fancies that we may suspect to have been inspired in us by a Deva (that is, in presumed spiritual inspiration); nor from inferences drawn from some haphazard assumption we may have made; nor because of what seems an analogical necessity; nor on the mere authority of our teachers or masters. But we are to believe when the writing, doctrine, or saying is corroborated by our own reason and consciousness. "For this," says he in concluding, "I taught you not to believe merely because you have heard, but when you believed of your consciousness, then to act accordingly and abundantly"*

THE LORD BUDDHA

One of the purposes of this book is to challenge some of the beliefs with which you have been conditioned and in challenging those beliefs you will be in a stronger position to make better informed choices.

One important thing that differentiates us from animals is our ability to think. Animals may appear to think but in reality they just follow patterns of programmed behaviour, remember Pavlov and his dogs? Humans are also subject to programming and marketing experts use this with great prowess which is the reason why they have large advertising budgets.

If you give some serious thought to the matter it would appear that modern society is being geared up to reduce our ability to think, some might call it a 'dumbing down'. In the work place we have standard operating procedures so everyone has to do it according to a written directive, no need to think. In the medical professions we have best practice so that the same treatments and protocols are used, goodbye individuality, no need to think about the treatment, it's all decided for you. On the weather website we are told how many layers of clothes to wear just in case we can't work it out ourselves! Technology does everything for us; we rely on calculators to do the simplest of mathematical functions, no need to use our brains. We have more and more laws, rules, regulations and surveillance which control our freedoms; all in our best interests of course!

Many things we are subjected to in daily life affect our ability to think: mercury in our teeth, fluoride in the water, bromine in the bread (affects thyroid function), poor blood sugar regulation, too much stress and noise pollution, intoxication with alcohol and drugs, subconscious programming by television and other media, laws which tell us apparently what is right and what is wrong.

I urge you to remember that if your doctor is unable to support you in your quest for health then you have the choice of looking for one who will. There are a growing number of professionals who are stepping out of the box and taking on board more holistic views.

This book is not intended to be light reading or to be of great literary merit; I did in fact fail school certificate English at 14! (I did however pass French and German; not sure of the implication!!)

The intention of the book is to give the untrained eye some insights into what is happening in conventional medicine and food industries and inspire them to take control of their own health. I have tried not to be too technical however some science is inevitable in a book of this nature. Please keep in mind that our current science may only be our best shot at this point in time; nothing should be taken as written in stone. We have to adapt to our current knowledge base and be prepared to change. We can only make choices if we have the information to assist us.

Medical science takes many years to adopt a new philosophy because of vested interests in the current paradigm and the unwillingness to think differently. Ignaz Semelweiss discovered that if Doctors washed their hands between dissecting dead bodies and delivering babies the number of deaths from puerperal fever could be reduced drastically. That may appear common sense to us now but in those days his idea was greeted with ridicule. He was committed to an asylum where he soon died after being beaten by the guards. This is an early example of medical arrogance which still occurs to this day in some form or other.

****

Much of the information presented in the book is based on data from the United States of America. I think it is reasonable to assume that the information is applicable to most western economies, to a greater or lesser extent. There are some notable exceptions; labelling of GMO foods for example. I leave it for the reader to decide if the information is applicable to their area of domicile. References were all good at time of publishing however due to the dynamic nature of the internet they cannot be guaranteed to be functional. The astute reader will be able to find their own references.

References

1. http://www.nottingham.ac.uk/academicservices/qualitymanual/assessmentandawards/degree-classification.aspx
2. http://archinte.jamanetwork.com/article.aspx?articleid=1731967

<u>Chapter 2 - RESPONSIBILITY & EMPOWERMENT</u>

When we look back in history there has always been someone to take care of our health needs. In the distant past we had the wise ones and healers who were knowledgeable about herbs and things from the natural world .The shamans of American Indian society or the priest physicians of ancient Egyptian culture are such examples. Every society had its own particular version of 'healer' and knowledge of the healing arts was passed down from practitioner to apprentice by oral tradition.

By contrast our modern day medical education is the domain of the university where those with a suitable inclination and high school exam grades can pursue the study of a formal, structured degree. It is interesting and even concerning that in order to be accepted into medical school in this day and age a calling is not sufficient; you generally have to get straight 'As' in all your exams. This academic focus on student recruitment, in my opinion, might not be the best way to select people who have a genuine calling and who have all the qualities needed to serve their fellow man: compassion, devotion, honour, integrity, respect, humility and openness to name a few.

There have always been different approaches to our understanding of the human body and mind and how it should be coaxed or cajoled back to health. Here in the western world we adopted the reductionist mechanical view point which grew out of Newtonian physics and tends to view the human body as a set of machine parts to be treated individually as if they are not connected. Within the current medical paradigm therefore, we have drugs for our blood pressure, drugs for our aches and pains, drugs for constipation, drugs for anxiety, drugs to counter the side effects of other drugs and so on. The list is long! The drug paradigm alas, does little to address the underlying cause of illness; it merely suppresses the symptom expression of that underlying cause.

Traditional Indian and Chinese medical systems have an entirely different view of the human structure. In these systems we are considered to be an integrated whole of mind, body and spirit which constitute the energetic structure of the human being. The premise is that when we are healthy the vital energy, flows harmoniously within our structure. This life energy has been called by many names, prana, chi, orgone and vital force to name a few; any disease (read – dis-ease) is due to an imbalance or blockage in this energy flow. It could be compared to having a blockage in the fuel line of your car, the fuel, or energy, cannot get to where it's needed and the car becomes 'sick' and doesn't work properly.

The body is an orchestra which in health has harmonic resonance; it is 'in tune' so to speak. When a part of the body becomes diseased it goes out of tune, it is resonating at a discordant frequency, like a badly tuned piano, the result is the symptoms we call disease. The disease symptoms are the expression of the underlying discordance, they are not the cause, although symptoms as we know often lead to discomfort.

Frequency and vibration are interesting in the context of health. Most people associate frequency and vibration with sound. Science is now achieving a greater understanding that all phenomena, including our physical body, are expressions of frequency, vibrations at different rates. There is no such thing as solid matter; it is merely an illusion of our sensory system or systems of measurement. There is a duality within our reference framework, what you see or more accurately, what you detect is what you get. If you set up an experiment to detect particles then particles appear; if you set up an experiment to detect waves (frequency vibration) then waves are observed.

When you are ill there is an imbalance in the body-mind complex for whatever reason; the goal of the physician should be to rebalance the system and restore harmony. Traditional Chinese medicine (TCM) has been in existence for several thousand years unlike the western system which is relatively young by comparison. In the Dynastic era when the physician was summoned to the emperor he was only allowed to take the pulses at the wrist, ankle or foot and from this he was able to determine the imbalances and apply corrective procedures. If he got it wrong his head was soon parted from his body!

You can see from these few short paragraphs that there are different philosophies and we do have a choice as to how we view ourselves and the world in which we live. Are we essentially a complicated biological machine or are we something more in line with the eastern holistic idea of body, mind and spirit? A quantum physicist would have no problems with the energetic view of the human; everything is seen as a sea of energy in which we all have our own little niche. The choice is yours based on your own understanding and intuition, your own knowledge and feeling. It is said that it takes between 50 to 100 years for an alternative belief system to be accepted (paradigm shift); and as our current medical system is deeply in the mechanistic paradigm we shouldn't expect any change to occur soon. Vested interests, secrecy and corruption are some of the most powerful factors holding back new approaches to health and indeed many other aspects of human advancement. On a positive note, the advent of the internet has greatly improved the dissemination of non orthodox information and more and more people are choosing to question the current ideas on health and well being.

Over the last 100 years or so the world has become a very different place with the continual progression of the technological age. You are subjected to so many different things that can have an impact on your health and well being: the stresses of modern life, chemical exposure, electromagnetic fields, GM foods, foods with little nutrition, drug treatments and medical procedures just to name the more obvious.

Your health status is being determined by a set of biological tests which say you are above or below the normal reference, whatever normal means. Often these values are arbitrary and constantly change so as more people are brought into the prescribing process. Blood cholesterol is a good example of this; the accepted 'norm' for this has been gradually lowered over the last few decades and more and more people are being prescribed cholesterol lowering drugs. Who is behind this? Are people living longer because of this? We will look at this topic in much more detail later on.

Do we truly have a health care system? The answer is definitely no, it is a sickness management system. Here I am talking about the chronic diseases which afflict mankind: heart disease, cancer, diabetes, hypertension, arthritis etc. There are no cures for these diseases within the current paradigm only drugs to manage the symptoms. Do the drugs work? You can make up your own mind based on the information to be presented.

Can you honestly expect the doctor to know everything about all the possible ramifications of the toxic modern world in which you live? He/she has too many patients to deal with to spend the time researching each individual person and so there is what is called 'best practice' i.e. everyone is treated according to standard guidelines regardless of individual circumstances, which in essence become irrelevant. The doctors supposedly practice evidence based medicine yet more and more we are seeing medicines prescribed for "off label" use which has little evidence in terms of good clinical trials. One such example is the use of quetiapine in sleep disorders. Quetiapine is a powerful antipsychotic used in schizophrenia and other mental disorders. It is being used in low dose for sleep issues despite, at the time of writing, having no approval for this use.

If your doctor doesn't have time to assess all the ramifications and options for you as an individual then who does have the time? In a modern world time is often in short supply and we rely on professionals to have the answers. Unfortunately real life is not a reflection of what happens on TV in the medical shows. There are frequent headlines around the world which show a health system in turmoil. If you are really interested in your own health and wellbeing then the only person that can make time to come up with some answers is you; it's simple to accept the easy option and follow the expert's advice and instructions but as you read later this may not be to your best advantage.

There are instances in medical history when the doctors have said they can do no more, they have nothing more to offer. The majority of people may accept their fate; but there are cases where that is not so and individuals have found solutions against all odds. Lorenzo's oil is one example where people with no medical back ground used insight and determination to discover something that medical science with all its available resources was unable to, or had no desire to, achieve. In the event the discovery of Lorenzo's oil did not help the individual, who had adrenoleucodystrophy (ALD), because the disease had progressed too far; it has however been highly beneficial to many others when it is given early in the disease process. The story was made into a film called 'Lorenzo's Oil'.

When you start to take responsibility for your own health and begin to educate yourself and not just blindly accept information that is given, you will be in a stronger position to question treatments and even offer some of your own knowledge. You will start to make choices based on your own understanding together with advice given by professionals. When you become educated about food choices you will begin to think more carefully about what you put into your mouth.

Education used to be a privilege of the few but with our current technologies, that is no longer true, all it takes is time and motivation.

I believe, along with many others, that the role of the doctor should be to support you in your own informed choices and accept that they don't have all the answers; there should be respect for your choices and not disdain, as is often the case. The word doctor is derived from the Latin word 'docere' meaning 'to teach'; so a doctor's role is surely to advise you how to become healthy and stay healthy, not just to diagnose disease states and prescribe drugs. A doctors training is concerned with diagnosis of disease and the prescribing of corrective measures which as stated previously address the symptoms and not the cause. Unless a doctor has a much broader education, and some indeed do, it is not possible to provide all the information regarding your individual health status.

In your search for knowledge it is important to realise 'the truth' is propagated by the existing educational system and paradigm shifts are rare. For a long period in history the Earth was thought to be flat and at the centre of the solar system. Anyone who suggested otherwise was a heretic and risked imprisonment and/or torture. Doctors used to be involved in cigarette advertising proclaiming how healthy they were. We now know the truth the tobacco industry was aware of even in the early days. Advertising and marketing people know the power of the doctor in promoting products and this is why they use this powerful psychological image whenever and where ever possible.

At the end of your research you may not find a definitive answer but you will more than likely know what to avoid and what may be helpful. You will be in a stronger position to determine which advice to accept and which to reject. I hope the information in this book will be a starting point on the path to your greater understanding and empowerment. Let's begin by considering how much say you can have or not in controlling your own decisions regarding your health.

Chapter 3 – INFORMED CONSENT

What is informed consent?

Do you know your rights when you go to see your doctor or any other practitioner for that matter?

Do you care?

Do you consider that a medical treatment, even the simplest such as a flu jab, could cause harm?

If you ordinarily don't consider these questions then maybe now is a good time to start.

When you give informed consent you are saying that you are aware and understand all of the ramifications of the treatment and that you voluntarily agree to the treatment; you realise the potential risks and what the chances are that you will actually get any benefit from the treatment. There should be no duress or coercion i.e. intimidation or threats. You have the absolute right to autonomy over your own body; you can say no without any reprisals.

To put this more concisely, when any medical intervention is offered be it a surgical procedure, a drug intervention, hands on treatment from a physiotherapist or chiropractor etc., you have a right to be informed about:

- *Any risks the treatment may have: side effects, drug/drug interaction, drug/food interactions, alterations in bodily function and even the possibility of death.*
- *Any negative impact if you decline treatment.*
- *The absolute benefit of the treatment: i.e. the chance that you will actual receive a positive outcome. (The difference between absolute and relative benefit is explained later on.)*

A knowledgeable therapist will also be able to advise you of any alternative choices within or outside their field of expertise.

It is your body and/or your mind which may be affected by a medical intervention. You have absolute authority over these two aspects of your being and it is the practitioner's legal and moral duty[1] to supply you with all the information you need to make an informed choice. The information should be given to you in a clear, concise, easy to understand format free of medical jargon.

Often in the heat of the moment, when you are under stress and not thinking clearly, you may make choices without the level of understanding you need to be truly informed. Having the attitude of 'doctor knows best' can lead to health problems you didn't expect. You have to remember that your family doctor is a general practitioner, not an expert. Even experts get it wrong. It has been shown that 1 in 12 diagnoses were incorrect at autopsy[2]! If you have a problem which is difficult to diagnose then there may be only a 6% chance that your diagnosis may be accurate[3].

When you go to see a doctor for a check up and for example your blood pressure is elevated the doctor may discuss the need for drug intervention.

Are you told about:

- *The **absolute** benefit of the treatment?*
- *The potential side effects or harm potential?*
- *How much longer you can expect to live by having the treatment?*
- *The chance that the treatment may shorten your life?*
- *Any drug/food incompatibilities you should be aware of?*
- *Definate negative health effects if you do nothing?*
- *Other available options either conventional or alternative?*
- *Lifestyle and nutritional choices that may benefit your condition.*

It's probably fair to say that most doctors won't be aware of options outside of their own remit. However they could be with a little research on their part, continuing professional development as it's known in the jargon. After all, their patient's best interest should be their focus of attention; I'm sure you agree.

It is natural to worry about your health and trust that the doctor knows best, after all it is their job; what they've been taught in medical school however may only be a small part of the knowledge that is available. The doctor may not be aware of the statistics behind a particular treatment. Often a relative benefit ratio is used and not an absolute ratio. This will be discussed later, it is important to know the difference. New knowledge takes quite a long time to percolate down into the educational system and clinical practice. Remember the vitamin C story mentioned previously.

It is well known in the medical community that drugs can have harmful effects, yet these properties are rarely given the importance and attention they deserve and as we will see drug related death is a big issue. Drug reactions may be acute requiring an immediate remedial response or they may have a more chronic effect over time and lead to gradual deterioration in health or even sudden death.

It is reasonable to assume that medicines are safe because the regulating authorities have deemed them to be so. Safety is a relative issue and is determined by a group of 'experts' who assess the data given to them usually by the drug manufacturer. The information is rarely independent! There have been many cases over the years of drug withdrawal because of unacceptable levels of fatalities. A relatively recent example is Vioxx, an anti-inflammatory, which caused thousands of deaths worldwide from heart problems; this effect should have been foreseen because of the drug's basic mode of action[4].

Be aware that much of a doctor's postgraduate education on drug therapies will more often than not be supplied by the drug manufacturer at a nice venue where food and drinks are provided. You might ask if this scenario is likely to provide an unbiased learning opportunity. Drug companies are interested in making a profit and therefore are unlikely to focus on any negative aspects of therapy. If you think you can get an unbiased opinion from your friendly pharmacist, be assured that they attend the same drug company promotional seminars and are educated using the same information base.

It is common for drugs to be used for non licensed conditions i.e. the use is not specified in the drug data sheet. An example of this is quetiapine, an antipsychotic used in the treatment of schizophrenia and bipolar disorder which is commonly used for sleep disturbance although this is an unlicensed use and has little clinical data to support that use. We also do not know how quetiapine really works; we do know it can have some pretty serious side effects[5].

Drug trials may be carried out in a specific age group and the results extrapolated to other age groups. This is very true of many drugs used in the elderly which have never been tested in this age group and any benefits shown in the trials may not be valid in elderly patients.

These are just some of the things to think about. The only real things that separate humans from animals are spoken language and our ability to think. Are you truly encouraged to think about your treatments? How many doctors are really happy with in depth questioning about their diagnosis and treatment plan? Doctors like patients to do as they're told, be compliant and not ask questions with which they are uncomfortable and to which they may not know the answer. The experts can do our thinking for us and take away our need for self responsibility. I hope this book will stimulate you to think more about the choices you make.

When you visit your doctor/therapist next time here is a list of questions you might consider asking before agreeing to a particular treatment. Any medical intervention should involve concordance and not just compliance to the medical prescription. Concordance is a state of agreement which you cannot have without informed consent. Compliance is doing as you're told!

- *Is the treatment proposed absolutely necessary?*
- *What are the consequences of not having the treatment?*
- *How safe is the treatment?*
- *How much experience do you have of using this treatment?*
- *What are the possible serious side effects of the treatment?*
- *How common are these side effects?*
- *Are any side effects reversible if the treatment is stopped?*
- *Might the treatment affect other aspects of my functioning?*
- *Has this drug been evaluated in my age group?*
- *Is the treatment proposed within the products data sheet or is it an unlicensed use?*
- *Is there a chance, no matter how small, that the treatment may lead to my early death?*
- *Are there any issues with this treatment and other medicines or supplements I am taking?*
- *Do you know any alternatives to what you're proposing?*

With regard to the second point, bear in mind that for an acute situation there are only two possible outcomes if there is no intervention. You will recover or you will die. For the vast majority of acute conditions, given the appropriate supportive therapy and time, you will recover. Acute life threatening situations are one area where modern medicine excels. These situations are fortunately, relatively rare and for the most part are dealt with in a hospital A & E department.

If a condition becomes chronic then ideally the intervention should improve the disease state without compromising your health in other ways.

If the intervention is intended to be preventative then the outcome surely must be extended life. Is it sufficient to alter a biological marker (e.g. blood pressure), which drugs do, if your life expectancy and/or quality of life are not enhanced in any significant way?

References

1. http://www.ncbi.nlm.nih.gov/pmc/articles/PMC2840885/

2. http://jama.jamanetwork.com/article.aspx?articleid=196684

3. http://archinte.jamanetwork.com/article.aspx?articleid=1731967

4. http://www.uptodate.com/contents/cox-2-selective-inhibitors-adverse-cardiovascular-effects

5. http://www.medicinenet.com/quetiapine/article.htm

<u>**Chapter 4 – DO DRUGS WORK?**</u>

We know that drugs (mostly manufactured chemicals) have an effect on biological systems. Biochemical processes are altered by drug action; whether that action is appropriate or necessary is a question to pursue and furthermore whether an improvement in quality of life and/or an extension of life beyond what would be normally expected is likely.

In the emergency room and in trauma situations there is absolutely no doubt that drugs and other interventions can be life saving. Fortunately most of us rarely if ever experience those situations.

Much of the drug use in the western world is centred on so called preventative medicine. With this in mind we might ask the question; is this use justified in terms of reversing disease progression or prolonging life; that is preventing a fatal event? This encompasses one of the basic tenets of evidence based medicine in the form of improved outcome. If a treatment does nothing more than alter a biological parameter without extending life then is it useful?

Another major area of drug use is in treating infections. Antibiotics have been used and abused and we are now rapidly entering a time when we will have no useful antibiotics. As we'll see later antibiotics are totally unnecessary for many of the minor infections we succumb to and prescribing for these conditions merely add to the burden of antibiotic resistance.

There is a great deal of fear constantly being drip fed into your subconscious mind by the medical/pharmaceutical propaganda machine. If you don't partake of a particular treatment be it a flu vaccine or so call preventative treatments then you will surely die. Your consciousness is being manipulated to follow a particular course of action without questioning. Fear is a great motivator to do or not to do something. Irrational fear drives people to do things they would not normally do or not do things they want to. Fear of being different or not conforming to what's considered normal (whatever normal is!). Fear of being reprimanded for being non-compliant. Who is in charge of our bodies and minds?

For those of you who are interested in how this manipulation can occur then watch the YouTube video 'The Century of Self'.

https://www.youtube.com/watch?v=eJ3RzGoQC4s

This video is about how a man called Edward Bernays, a nephew of Sigmund Freud, manipulated public opinion and became one of the main players in the birth of consumerism.

If you are aware of how effective or not a treatment is for a particular situation then you can choose whether to partake or not and whether you might choose to pursue an alternative course of action.

The question of whether drugs work or not is really determined by how we interpret the word 'work' and how we classify what a drug is.

If you have a deficiency of an essential nutrient such as a vitamin or mineral then chances are that if you don't replace it your health will be severely compromised or you may die. The question is, are nutrients drugs? I would say no, even if they are artificially produced. Ordinarily you obtain nutrients from your foods; alas many foods nowadays are high in macro-nutrients (carbohydrate, protein and fats) and low in micro-nutrients (vitamins, minerals, antioxidants etc.). Vitamins may be synthetic and minerals may be formulated in a way that is not best for utilisation by the body. So I personally would not consider replacement of an essential nutrient drug therapy. A doctor may have a different view of course.

Sometimes your body may stop producing an essential substance such as thyroid hormone, thyroxine. From a conventional standpoint synthetically produced thyroxine would be given to substitute for the deficiency. An alternative practitioner might ask the question; why is there this deficiency? Why is there insufficient thyroid function? It may be possible to correct it and get the gland to function normally again. In this situation you are given what is in essence a natural substance. This type of intervention is only replacing the natural missing substances and again I would not consider it drug therapy in the true sense of the word.

With most other types of drug treatment, whether it is acute, chronic or preventative, the drugs that are given are synthetic, they are not found in nature. Efficacy (how effective they are) is determined by statistical analysis. You must have heard the term *'lies, damn lies and statistics'* (Benjamin Disraeli), well read on.

Statistics are used to see if the drug response is significantly better than giving placebo (no active ingredient). With any intervention the placebo response can be up to 60%[1] i.e. up to 60% of people will show a positive benefit from taking a non active pill. The placebo effect is influenced by various parameters and it is not the purpose here to go into this, just to say the effect is rather large and considered somewhat of a nuisance by medical researchers. There has been research that has shown that even a sham operation, where the patient is cut open and then sewn back up with no other action, provides a positive benefit. Equally the nocebo effect is the opposite and if you believe it to be harmful then it can be. This also applies to diagnosis!

'Statistically significant' means is that a mathematical formula is used to see if the drug response is greater than that due to chance when comparing it with placebo. So say in a trial there are two groups of 1000 people in each; one group is given a sugar pill and another is given the test drug. Usually neither the test subjects nor the researchers know which is placebo and which is the test drug; this is called a double blind trial.

In the placebo group say 30% show a positive effect and in the test group 40% show a positive effect then this would show a statistically significant benefit over placebo. There are mathematical calculations performed on the data to come to this conclusion. But as you can see from the figures the test drug is only benefitting 10 people out of a hundred. You have to treat 100 people to benefit 10. In practice the numbers are often lower than this so you might have to treat 100 people to benefit 2 or 3!

A concept which is being used more commonly nowadays is called <u>Number Needed to Treat</u> (NNT); this is the number of people who need to be treated in order to prevent one additional bad outcome. The ideal NNT is 1 which means that for every person treated there is a positive outcome. The higher the number the less effective is the treatment. We will look at some examples later on when we investigate specific intervention therapies.

The amount of money spent on prescription drugs worldwide is large, very large! In 2014 it was in the region of 1 trillion dollars; that's 1 with 12 zeros after it[2]; pharmaceuticals are big business, no question about that; but is it money well spent? Let's pursue the original question of the chapter title by looking at specific drug therapies and how effective they are.

<u>Antibiotics</u>

How did antibiotic therapy come into being? The answer is firmly seated with Louis Pasteur, the father of the germ theory. The theory basically encompasses the idea that it's the germs that are the problem and we must do all in our power to control and kill them. So over time, as a direct consequence of this theory, we have had the development of vaccines, antibiotics, antiseptics and sterilising equipment. Of course there's no doubt that bacteria are implicated in the disease process but do they cause the disease or are they there because of the disease?

One might ask, 'How did the human race survive this far?' We have in our bodies more than 700 species of bacteria. There are at least 1.5 kilograms of bacteria in our colon and there are 10 times more bacterial cells in our body than there are human cells[3]. Bacterial cells are much smaller than human cells.

Bacteria are everywhere in their trillions; why are we not all dropping down dead? The answer is our inborn capacity to keep things in balance and requires an optimally functioning immune system together with a balance of all the microbial life within us. Balance is an important word; many modern day influences in our lives serve to disrupt the balance which in turn causes ill health.

Antoine Bechamp[4], a contemporary of Pasteur said exactly that, in French of course! If your immune system is healthy, disease causing bacteria will be kept in check and live harmoniously with the rest of your so called 'good bacteria'. A large part of the immune system is concentrated around the gut. This should be no surprise if we think about it. The digestive tract is essentially a tube from one end to the other which is in contact with the outside world. Entry of pathogens is always a possibility and having a good level of immune function in this area would be protective to the organism as it prevents the entry of potential pathogens into the blood circulation and thence to bodily tissues and organs. Interestingly a large part of immune function is associated with the probiotic bacteria which inhabit the digestive tract and airways also known as *'the microbiome'*. These organisms normally keep potential disease causing organisms in balance.

Even if pathogens should manage to enter the body in spite of the physical barrier of the gut lining and the probiotic helpers, the body is able to mount a powerful defence if the immune function of the blood and lymph is in order. There are many things in the modern life style which compromise our probiotic flora and our body's ability to mount an adequate immune response, antibiotics, other drugs, stress, sugar, alcohol to name a few. People who are immune compromised are very susceptible to opportunistic infections and have to be given antibiotics all the time.

Returning to Louis Pasteur, on his death bed he renounced his theory and said it was the terrain (i.e. the body) that was important and not the germs. All that we do with our modern diets and life style is create the soil in which the pathogenic (disease causing) bacteria thrive. An acidic, low oxygen environment is exactly right for such growth.

The renunciation by Pasteur was far too late, the system had taken hold of his theory and the antibiotic and vaccine era had begun[5].

In the pre-antibiotic era, when there was poor housing and sanitation issues, normally benign diseases could become killers; improve these living conditions and people strengthen their immune systems and the diseases go away as will be seen later on.

Antibiotics have often been prescribed for viral infections for which they have no benefit; this only serves to add to the problem of antibiotic resistance. The medical logic may be to prevent bacterial complications, a precautionary measure which is not necessary in most cases; the antibiotics are merely having a placebo effect.

Most common infections will resolve without any intervention, the benefit of antibiotic therapy in these situations is dubious. Historically, antibiotics should have been reserved for use only in life threatening conditions such as meningitis or pneumonia. In these conditions they can be life saving; however due to excessive and inappropriate use, antibiotics are becoming less effective in these conditions and we are fast approaching a time when antibiotics will not be effective at all. Even now in practice, higher doses are being given for longer periods and in more inventive combinations of different drugs.

Antibiotics are used in animal farming in much larger quantities than in human medicine; this is adding tremendously to the resistance problem and of course contamination of our food supply.

The Cumbrian health authority in the UK has published a guideline for antibiotic prescribing[6]. If you are generally healthy then common conditions such as: sore throat, tonsillitis, sinusitis, otitis media(infection of the middle ear), bacterial conjunctivitis and acute bronchitis do not routinely need antibiotic treatment. There are many natural substances which can help with these common conditions.

 Let's look at a selection of definitive evidence in relation to antibiotic (and antiviral) use.

The figures in the following table are all taken from a source of information I will often reference, http://www.thennt.com, this site references information from prestigious sources such as the Cochrane database, the gold standard of independent medical research. The table shows the number of people having no benefit and the percentage of people harmed. The number needed to treat (NNT) is the number of people who are given medication for 1 person to show outcome benefit and the number needed to harm (NNH) is the number of people treated to show harm to 1 person. The infinity sign (∞) is used where no one had benefit.

Treatment	% with zero Benefit	% Harmed	NNT	NNH
Acute bronchitis in adults[7]	100	2.6	∞	37
Animal bites[8]	100	No data	∞	No data
Acute sinusitis[9]	94	12	18	8
Acute middle ear infection[10]	100	11	∞*	9*
Antivirals for post shingles nerve pain[11]	100	0	∞	∞
Tamiflu for influenza[12]	95	3	20	37

*1 in 16 had pain reduction after 2-7 days, 1 in 9 had diarrhoea.

With regard to the treatment of influenza the research says:

'Influenza is mostly a self-limited respiratory illness that lasts 7 days on average.'

When one takes a neuraminidase inhibitor (NI), e.g. Tamiflu, for treatment of acute influenza the review finds an average of about 1 day of symptom relief. Unfortunately this only applies to those with proven influenza infection who take the drug within 48 hours of the first symptom.

> *'...there is currently no good data to support the claim that NI's reduce influenza complications such as pneumonia, hospitalization, or mortality'.*[12]

From the examples quoted it is evident that antibiotic (and anti-viral) use for the conditions listed has limited benefit and indeed resolution would likely occur without treatment. This also applies to the conditions listed at NHS Cumbria as previously given.

Why are antibiotics being used as placebo? Is it because of the expectation that when you go to the doctor you receive a prescription for a medicine that will 'cure' you? When you get better is it because of the medicine or that the infection has just run its course? By taking unnecessary antibiotics your immune system may be compromised and the possibility of antibiotic resistance is increased. You are also exposed to the possibility of drug side effects.

The bottom line is that for simple non-life threatening infections antibiotics are neither indicated nor necessary. For more serious conditions the figures are somewhat better although as you can see there's no guarantee of success.

Treatment	% with zero Benefit	% Harmed	NNT	NNH
Respiratory infection in intensive care[13]	75	No data	18	No data
COPD exacerbation[14]	88	5	8	20

(COPD = chronic obstructive pulmonary disease)

Only one person out of 18 showed benefit from antibiotic treatment for respiratory infection in intensive care and 1 out of 8 for COPD exacerbation. This just emphasises the random benefit profile of any conventional drug intervention. You have no way of knowing if you will benefit just as you have no way of knowing absolutely if your horse will win its race. You look at the odds and decide whether you want to chance it or maybe do something else.

People have the expectation that when they take a drug they will receive a positive outcome with no negative effects. As you can see from the data this is clearly not the case.

Childhood Vaccinations

Vaccination for childhood diseases have been progressively introduced into immunisation schedules since the 1950's. Of course this is the time when antibiotics were coming on board in a more prolific way.

If we look at the incidence of infectious diseases in the 1900's there was a natural decline in mortality *before* the introduction of vaccines which specifically targeted the diseases. Let's look at some evidence from US statistics. The following graph clearly shows the decline in the incidence of some of the major childhood diseases well before the introduction of vaccines.

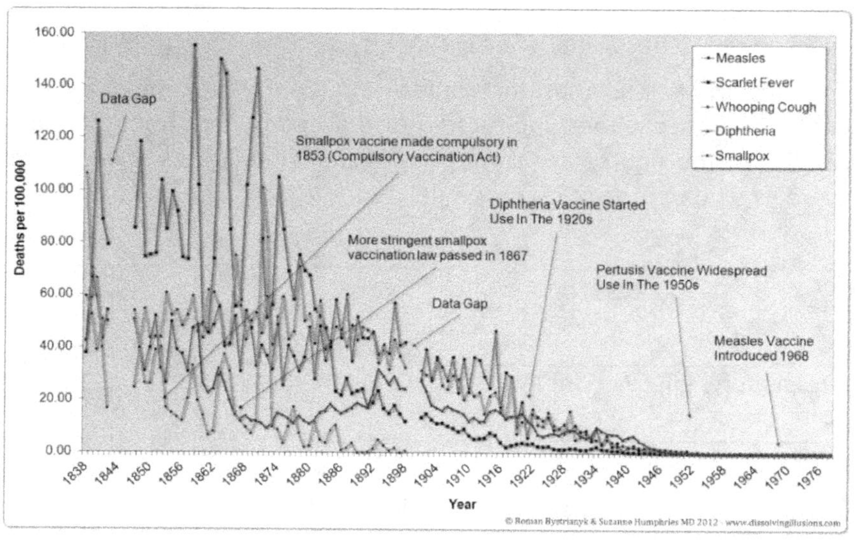

(Graph by courtesy of *www.healthsentinel.com*)[15]

We might wonder why the disease death rates were falling. If you consider the poor sanitation and housing conditions, poor hygiene and availability of good nutritious foods then we may have some indication of the reason. In any third world country it is a well known that when there are improvements in sanitation, a supply of clean water and good nutrition the disease rate declines markedly [16].

With any medical intervention benefits clearly have to outweigh the risks. In this section we are only concerned with whether the vaccines work or not. In the chapter on toxicity you will have the opportunity to consider the toxic side of childhood vaccinations.

Like most things in science and medicine there are always those for and those against. I have included a list of sites where you can get more information so you can make the right choices for you and your loved ones.

Vaccines do not confer lifelong immunity they have to be repeated many times throughout childhood and increasingly adulthood; when a vaccine is found to be less than effective the answer is to give more doses. Having the natural disease generally does confer lifelong immunity and helps to strengthen the immune response to non specific degenerative diseases. The natural disease is important in the developmental stages of the immune system.

When I was a child, I and most of my friends contracted measles, German measles, chicken pox etc. Yes it might have been uncomfortable to experience but it was something that was expected and dealt with. These diseases are hardly ever fatal, only in rare circumstances when there may be weakness due to a compromised immune system or malnourishment.

> *'With good nutrition, and good nursing, unvaccinated children are able to overcome measles and other natural childhood infectious diseases, with long-term benefit. Vaccines, in contrast, are not just un-protective, but their immune-sensitising effect changes a normally beneficial disease into a dangerous atypical form. It is time to heed what has been documented repeatedly for decades.'[17] - Dr Viera Scheibner PhD from the BMJ 20th January 2013.*

The top five vaccine companies in 2012 were Sanofi, Merck, GSK, Pfizer and Novartis[18]. Combined revenue from these companies amounted to over $21 billion dollars. That's a huge amount of money isn't it? Does that have anything to do with why companies lobby governments to introduce vaccine schedules[19]?

There have been many instances of outbreaks of disease in vaccinated populations. In one case there was a 98% vaccination rate yet there was a measles outbreak[20], how come? Whooping cough provides another example of an outbreak in vaccinated children[21].

When you allow your child to have a vaccine you expect it to prevent the disease and have no side effects, don't you?

At the end of the day you have to weigh up the pros and cons of vaccination. Do the perceived benefits out weight the potential risks? And consider the long term risks which are investigated in the chapter on toxicity. Ask yourself whether the information you are being given is unbiased. Is it appropriate that government bodies accept information from manufacturers as *being* unbiased and then use that information to direct so called medical excellence? Most doctors will just regurgitate the official message passed down from higher authority without question, 'get vaccinated or suffer serious consequences'. Is it appropriate and in the patient's best interest, that doctors accept this potentially biased information without personally investigating? Is this a dereliction of duty of care?

- *Ask yourself how dangerous are the common childhood diseases?*
- *What is the chance of serious consequences from contracting the disease?*
- *What is the chance of contracting the disease in an outbreak?*
- *What are the potential side effects of vaccination both acute and long term?*
- *In a democracy, should you have the right to choose what goes into your body and your children's bodies?*

More vaccine information at:-

http://www.vaccinationcouncil.org/

http://www.nvic.org/

http://healthsentinel.com/

<u>Drugs used in Cardio-Vascular Disease (CVD)</u>

In this section let's look at the two main areas of CVD, coronary heart disease (CHD) and strokes. Heart disease is the number one cause of death in the western world. The main classes of drugs used to try and prevent a heart attack and/or stroke are:-

- *Statins – to reduce cholesterol*
- *Anticoagulants (Blood thinners) – to prevent blood clotting*
- *Anti-hypertensives – to lower blood pressure*
- *Anti-arrhythmics – to regulate heart rhythm*

Let's first of all look at primary prevention of CVD, that is where there is no history of heart attack or stroke, the rationale behind this intervention is that the patient has 'risk factors'.

Risk factors are considered to include:-

- *High cholesterol, particularly LDL (more about fats and cholesterol later)*
- *Smoking*
- *Family history*
- *Sedentary lifestyle*
- *Alcohol*
- *Hypertension*
- *Obesity*
- *Raised blood glucose – diabetes.*

Drugs may be used to reduce some of these perceived risk factors. Now let's think about this a moment; if you're going to introduce a foreign synthetic substance, that may have potentially serious side effects, into your body to prevent a perceived threat to your health then:

- *What level of risk reduction would you be happy with to justify treatment?*
- *What level of benefit would you expect from such medication?*
- *What side effects would you consider to be acceptable?*

Before we look at some of the data we have to consider <u>*the difference between relative risk and absolute risk.*</u>

Relative risk/benefit is the figure the drug companies and your doctor are likely to use when explaining the benefits of drug treatment, you'll see why.

Let's look at a simple example. In a trial of a drug used for the prevention of 'cardiovascular events' such as heart attack, say 3 out of 100 (3%) people in the placebo group die and only 2 out of 100 (2%) in the drug group die the relative benefit is 33% .

3-2 = 1   1/3 x 100% = 33%

<u>Relative benefit of drug over placebo = 33%</u>

This looks quite good doesn't it? Maybe worth taking that drug you might think. The absolute benefit however is only 1%. Only 1 person out of 100 benefits from the treatment by not dying.

(3/100) – (2/100) =1/100 = 1%

<u>Absolute benefit of treatment = 1%</u>

Another way of looking at this is something called 'number needed to treat' or NNT. In this case the NNT = 100; which means 100 people need to be treated to prevent 1 death. Get it?

When your doctor tells you that a drug may reduce your chance of say a heart attack or stroke by 30% or whatever, then it might be prudent to ask if they are quoting relative or absolute values. If the number is high and appears impressive you can bet your bottom dollar that relative benefit is being quoted. Another way of looking at it is to ask yourself; what is the chance of me personally getting benefit? The answer is 1 in 100. In gambling terms that would be considered an outsider; wouldn't it?

Statins and low dose aspirin are the main stay of CVD prevention. Let's look at some actual data which can be found at http://www.thennt.com.

Aspirin used for the prevention of a first non-fatal heart attack has an NNT of 2000[22].So if you have some cardiovascular risk factors and you are given aspirin as a preventative then the chance of benefit to you as an individual is 1 in 2000. If you've already had a heart attack then the odds of benefit are improved to 1 in 50[23], these odds are somewhat better but still not great; are they?

A Statin given for 5 years as a preventative has an NNT of 104[24] for prevention of a first non-fatal heart attack; no-one however was saved from death. If you have a history of heart disease then the NNT is 83 for saving a life and 39 for prevention of a non-fatal heart attack. To put it more succinctly, if you have already had a non-fatal heart attack the chance of statins preventing a second fatal heart attack is 1 in 83. Millions upon millions of people are taking these drugs with only a small minority benefitting. Statins also come with inherent dangers: muscle damage, diabetes and cancer[25].

Aspirin has been prescribed for many years now as a preventative for heart attacks. The data indicates that it has almost zero benefit and the FDA has recently changed its stance on the use of aspirin in primary prevention of heart attack[26]. Statins appear more effective, even so, 98 % of people taking a statin to prevent a heart attack will not benefit.

Even in secondary prevention where you've already had an event, the chances of these medications benefitting you as an individual are pretty low. Statins prevent 12 deaths per 1000 people treated for 5 years and aspirin 3 deaths per 1000.

Unfortunately when medicines are prescribed, the focus becomes how the medicine affects a biological marker, not on whether it prolongs or saves lives. Statins most definitely lower cholesterol, aspirin most definitely reduces platelet stickiness to prevent blood clots but as we can clearly see from the figures the outcome benefit is poor. Many people have to be treated in order that a few will benefit; there is no way of knowing if you will be among the small minority of beneficiaries.

If you are taking beta-blockers as a first line treatment for the prophylaxis (prevention) of heart disease you might want to check out this link[27].

If you are taking calcium channel blockers you might want to check this reference[28].

Most of the major diseases which we are experiencing in the so called civilised world are disease of life style and food choices. We will look later at what positive interventions we can make ourselves to improve our longevity and enhance our well being and reduce our chance of having a cardio-vascular 'event'.

Antihypertensive treatment gives an NNT of 125; one person out of 125 people treated will be saved from dying from this intervention[28.1].

Anticoagulants for stroke prevention

Anticoagulants, as the name implies, stop the blood from coagulating or clotting. Blood clots are a big problem and can lead to heart attack, strokes and other medical emergencies. It would be an invaluable treatment if it worked for everyone at risk. From an NNT view point a figure of 25 is deemed to be quite respectable, however this means that only 4% of people taking this preventative measure will benefit; the majority, 96%, will receive no benefit[29]. If you are the lucky 1 out of 25 then great; odds are against that though, aren't they?

It would seem that the drugs do indeed lower the risk and from the statisticians point of view the risk reduction is significant. From the individual patients viewpoint it may not be so clear cut. Reducing the risk of having a serious event like a stroke by 4% may be considered good by the statisticians. Is that good enough for you?

Treatments used in cancer therapy

The only treatments that can be legally offered for cancer treatment in the western world are surgery, radiation and chemotherapy.

In 1971 President Nixon signed the National Cancer Act. This was considered to be the beginning of the 'war on cancer'. The word war is not used out of place as much of the pharmaceutical armamentarium used comes from the field of warfare. **Firstly radiation**, which will burn the tissues, will make you sick and make your hair fall out just like radiation sickness from nuclear fallout. **Secondly chemotherapy**, which was developed initially from mustard gas used in the First World War in the trenches with such devastating effect. These treatments are inherently deadly, they kill and maim just as in the battlefield and there is always collateral damage. This may appear a little emotive but it makes the point quite clearly if you think about it and I encourage you to do just that.

We cannot cure cancer with the conventional approach; we can only force it into remission. The word cure has been redefined to mean 5 year survival after initial diagnosis. If you die of cancer in year 6 then this is still considered a cure for the purpose of survival statistics. This redefinition is important for medical and political reasons. The professionals and politicians can say people are being cured by using this definition. According to the Oxford English dictionary the word cure in this context, means to eliminate (a disease or condition) with medical treatment. Forcing the disease into submission leading to temporary remission is not a cure in my opinion, what do you think?

In the US in 1971 the cancer death rate per 100,000 people was 163[30] and in 2011 the rate was 184[31] per 100,000. If you take the rate per 100,000 of population and multiply by the population of the respective years we get a figure for the absolute number of deaths.

1971 population = 207.66 million therefore number of cancer deaths = 338,486/year or *927 people a day.*

2011 population = 311.59 million therefore number of cancer deaths = 573,325/year or *1570 people a day.*

The death rates of people with cancer are likely to be under estimated as they don't include those that die from the treatment!

> ***'.....in this issue of the Journal, Welch and Black raise the concern that cancer death rates are systematically underestimated, in that many patients who die as a result of cancer treatment do not have cancer recorded as the underlying cause of death.'[32]***

The overall 5 year cancer survival rates between 1974 and 2007 apparently increased from 50% to 68%[33] that's an absolute improvement of 18% which seems good yet more people are dying of cancer per 100,000? Don't quite understand that! It's those lies, damn lies and statistics in operation maybe?

Earlier diagnosis because of mass screening programs will mean longer survival times although as we will see later, screening programs have their own down side in terms of false diagnosis and unnecessary treatments. As the population increases more people are dying of cancer. It would seem on the face of it that the war is lost despite the trillions of dollars that have been and continue to be spent. It would appear that the only people benefitting from this war, as in most wars, are the arms manufactures i.e. the pharmaceutical companies, medical imaging, radio isotope manufacturers and of course the medical practitioners. In 2010 the US spent $125 billion[34] on cancer treatments. Is it likely that a cure is going to be found? If it is then it is likely that a lot of people are going to be out of work and profit margins severely eroded. The political and economic ramifications of a cure are enormous.

Drugs used in pain relief

These drugs come in many guises:

- *Simple analgesics like paracetamol*
- *Opiods, synthetic morphine like drugs*
- *Opiates, morphine, codeine and related substances*
- *Disease modifying anti-rheumatic drugs (DMARDS)*
- *Non steroidal anti-inflammatories (NSAID's)*
- *Steroidal anti-inflammatories*
- *Centrally acting substances which modify neuro-transmitters in the brain*
- *Preparations applied to the skin*

How effective are these drugs at relieving pain? If you believed the hard sell in the adverts you would expect that if you were in pain and you took one of these substances your pain would dissolve away; if only it was that simple.

Pain is a very subjective experience. At one end of the scale there are those who are naturally hypersensitive to pain and at the other end those who have a very high pain threshold. Remember the placebo effect can be up to 60% and that alone can account for a significant level of relief.

The Bandolier website has much data on pain. On this site there is a summary of trials done to assess pain relief for moderate to severe pain[35]. Many of the more common pain relief drugs are listed. The outcome measure is a 50% pain reduction over 4-6 hours after the dose.

The most effective drug in the list is Etorcoxib 180mg or 240mg a NSAID showing 77% of people having 50% pain relief and NNT = 1.5. So for every 3 people treated 2 will get 50% pain relief. The least effective drug in the list is Codeine 60mg with 15% reaching the outcome measure and an NNT of 16.7 i.e. only 1 person in 16 will get 50% pain relief. Placebo got an 18% response in this data set. Interestingly

Codeine is widely prescribed in general practice. Most of the drugs listed had an NNT of between 2 and 8. Some people can't take NSAIDs and therefore their options of pain relief are more limited. In chronic pain many of the common pain killers are not effective and this is why the use of opiod drugs and drugs which act in the brain are being used in multi-drug combinations and in ever increasing doses.

Here is a selection of some of the drugs used in chronic neuropathic pain (pain of nerve origin). The NNT is the number of people who need to be treated for 1 to acheive 50% pain reduction.

Drug Treatment	**NNT**
Pregabalin for post herpetic neuralgia[36]	3.9 - 6.9
Gabapentin for diabetic neuropathy[36]	5 - 7.5
Carbamazepine for neuropathic pain[37]	1.3 – 2.2
Antidepressants for diabetic neuropathy[38]	3.4
Antidepressants for post herpetic neuralgia[38]	2.1

The NNTs are quite good for these drugs but as you can see there is no guarantee of at least 50% pain relief. These drugs may have a less than acceptable side effect profile certainly when taken over long periods of time in high dosage and multiple combinations.

Disease Modifying Anti-Rheumatic Drugs (DMARD's) used in the treatment of certain inflammatory states are essentially drugs which suppress the immune system. Methotrexate and TNFα inhibitors are commonly used in this type of therapy. TNFα inhibitors have an NNT of 4 or 5[39]. Remember NNT is number needed to treat for one person to achieve ACR50. A standard called ACR50 is used to determine improvement (ACR = American College of Rheumatology). The 50 refers to a 50% improvement in disease parameters. With these drugs 20% - 25% of patients will achieve ACR50.

N.B. TNFα inhibitor = tumour necrosis factor inhibitor e.g. Etanercept, infliximab, adalimumab

These drugs are powerful immune suppressants and the potential side effects are quite serious. When the immune system is suppressed the chance of infections and cancer is increased[40].

We have looked at a broad cross section of pain relieving drugs for which the general outcome measure is 50% pain reduction. From the referenced data it can be concluded that pain relief is not guaranteed even though some of these drugs have a good success rate. I think it fair to conclude that the drugs only partially work in some people for moderate to severe pain of non malignant aetiology. When deciding on choice the potential side effect profile must be considered, particularly for long term treatment.

Drugs for osteoporosis

The main class of drugs used for treating osteoporosis is the biphosphonates which include alendronate, etidronate and zoledronic acid.

Bone is a living tissue like the rest of your body; it is constantly being built up and old bone is broken down and removed. These drugs increase bone density by stopping the breakdown of bone by cells call osteoclasts and therefore you get build up of old bone.

Let's look at the World Health Organisation (WHO) definition of osteoporosis; please bear in mind that this is a definition and not an absolute reality. You also need to have a very simple understanding of some statistical terminology. Don't worry my understanding is pretty simple, never did like statistics!

In any population you can take a parameter, like height for example, and if you draw a graph showing on the vertical axis the number of people at a particular height then you get what is called a normal distribution. I will repeat that since it is important; <u>you get a normal distribution.</u> It's called a bell curve and looks like this:

Normal Distribution Curve

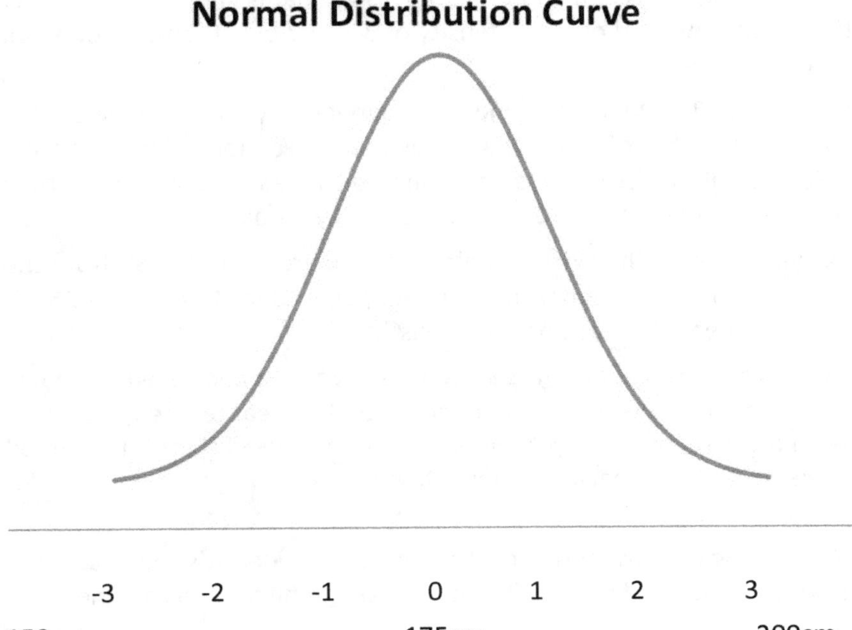

The spread from left to right represents the shortest to the tallest; the height of the curve represents the number of people in the sample at each height. The top of the curve is the mean height; in this example it is 175cm. The numbers on the bottom (-3 to +3) represent a statistical concept of standard deviation (SD) and as can be seen in a normal distribution most people are within 2xSD of the central value.

In a normal distribution you will inevitably get some people at the very bottom and some people at the very top and of course they are still within the normal range. In the example of height you get some people who are very short and some very tall.

The highest point in the centre represents the mean or average for the particular element of interest, in this case height. You can plot these Bell curves for almost anything, height, weight, blood pressure, bone mineral density etc. Are you with me so far?

Now we can look at the WHO definition of osteoporosis. Normal bone density is considered to be plus or minus ($\pm$) 1 standard deviation (SD) of the young (30 years) adult mean. This is what is known as a T-score. If a graph is plotted of bone density of 30 year olds then we get a bell curve as shown above.

If you are 30, 90 or anywhere in between, your bone density is compared to that of a young adult. Is that reasonable? Can we expect a 90 year old to have the same bone density as a 30 year old? They certainly don't have the appearance of a 30 year old!

Carrying on with the WHO definition; if you are -1 to -2.5 SD from the mean you have low bone mass (osteopenia) and if you are -2.5 SD from the mean you have osteoporosis[41].

There is a measure called a Z-score where you are compared to people of your own age, which to my mind (and other learned people) would seem more reasonable, yet this is not routinely used since it is deemed to be misleading because lower bone density is common in older people.

Most biological parameters decline as we get older, it's called aging, it is not a disease and it doesn't mean we are going to break a bone.

If you think about the definition closely it implies that any 30 year old adult who is part of the normal distribution and whose bone density is -1 or more SDs from the mean is either osteopenic or osteoporotic. The only way in reality to tell if your bones have reduced density is to measure bone density from early adulthood and follow it throughout life.

Because the drugs used cause the build-up of old bone then one of the side effects is brittle bone which can lead to atypical fractures and osteonecrosis (bone death) of the jaw[42]. Around 2% of people treated with intravenous biphosphonates will experience an atypical fracture.

This arbitrary definition of osteoporosis was set by the WHO in the 90's and is an example of manufactured disease created out of a normal ageing process. You only have to give it some thought and ask; why is an 80 year old person diagnosed as having osteoporosis when their bone density is less than a 30 year old? Also one might ask; is it reasonable to start an 80 year old on medication that will take several years to show benefit, if any?

If you have low bone mass as per the definition you are likely to be offered preventative treatment. Choose wisely!

Ageing is becoming a disease and of course if there is a drug to combat that then everyone's game, aren't they? One of the last prescriptions I dispensed was for a biphosphonate prescribed to an 84 year old lady; how did she get to 84 without breaking a bone? What was the rationale behind that decision to prescribe for someone in the latter years of life?

Spending on osteoporosis drugs is over $8 billion annually and of course there are the associated bone scanner sales. So ask yourself who is benefitting from this created medical condition?

For an in depth look at this subject see this reference[43].

Now to finish let's look at some NNT figures for some biphosphonate drugs. Remember NNT is the number of people that need to be treated for one person to benefit.

Prevention of hip fracture over 3 years[44].

Risedronate (Actonel): 77

Alendronate (Fosamax): 91

Zoledronic Acid (Reclast): 91

To prevent one hip fracture you need to treat between 77 and 91 people for three years.

Prevention of Vertebral fracture over 3 years[44].

Risedronate (Actonel): 15

Alendronate (Fosamax): 37

Zoledronic Acid (Reclast): 13

To prevent one vertebral fracture you need to treat between 15 and 37 people for 3 years.

Conclusions from a Therapeutics Initiative – evidence based medicine[45] show that there is little evidence for use of biphosphonates for the prevention of hip fractures in women, particularly where there is no history of prior fracture.

Of course no-one in the conventional medical field is promoting how nutritional factors can affect bone health and fracture risk or the well known fact that other drugs can cause mineral loss which will affect bone health.

<u>Treatment of hypertension</u>

Hypertension or high blood pressure is arbitrarily defined as being over 140/90. 140 is the systolic pressure when the heart beats (contracts). 90 is the diastolic pressure in between beats (no contraction). The values are in millimetres of mercury – mmHg.

Most people with high blood pressure are diagnosed with what is termed 'essential hypertension' which basically means unknown cause. It's interesting that doctors have been diagnosing hypertension for decades, and the incidence is escalating, yet we apparently have no idea what is causing it. I say apparently because the possible causes are seemingly not being taught in medical school and we will investigate them later.

In America 1 in 3 people suffer from hypertension[46]. One of the risks from hypertension is that blood vessels may rupture and cause a bleed in a vital area of our anatomy, particularly the brain causing a stroke. Knowing how effective a preventative strategy is will help us to decide whether to adopt it or look to for alternatives.

Mild hypertension is defined as having a BP between 140-159/90-99 mmHg. What is the evidence that treating mild hypertension is beneficial? The evidence is that it actually benefits no-one and indeed will cause harm to a significant number of patients[47]. If you are taking medication for mild hypertension you may want to discuss the benefits, or lack of benefit, with your doctor. If you decide to stop taking any medication then it should be done gradually under medical supervision.

Let's move on to more severe hypertension; where the BP is greater than 160/100; this is also known as stage II hypertension. In this category 1in100 people will avoid a heart attack, 1 in 67 will avoid a stroke and 1 in 125 will survive death by being treated[48]. Just to restate that; it is necessary to treat 125 people to prevent one death; will you be that lucky person?

Once you understand the data and realise that the benefit is are, in my opinion, marginal if you have severe hypertension and nonexistent if you have mild hypertension then you might want to consider other options for enhancing longevity. *Remember that the data here represents the number of people that need to be treated for 5 years to prevent one negative event.*

On thennt.com website the treatment of severe hypertension is given a green light which indicates it is worthwhile and of course it is to that one individual out of 100 or so but will it benefit you. That is the $64,000 question isn't it? There are other strategies that can help with hypertension as we will see later on.

Dyspepsia and GORD

Dyspepsia is a malfunction in the digestive process which leads to abdominal discomfort and pain. There may be bloating, nausea, vomiting and heartburn. It is very common in the general population.

GORD in an acronym for Gastro Oesophageal Reflux Disease which means the contents of the stomach, which is acidic, is regurgitated into the oesophagus; the acid from the stomach causes heartburn

Rightly or wrongly these conditions are often treated with proton pump inhibitors (PPIs).

That sounds very technical however what they basically do is block acid production in the stomach which will, to a greater or lesser extent, alleviate some of the symptoms, in some people.

Unfortunately, as with most drug treatments, the cause of the problem is not addressed; merely symptom alleviation.

Before PPI's came on the scene doctors of the 'old school' used to diagnose acidity problems as being due to too much or too little stomach acid. If you are producing too much acid then you may get reflux and heartburn symptoms in certain circumstances. If you are producing too little acid (and acid production declines with age) then your digestion will not work well and you may get bloating and pain and acid reflux. The reason you can get reflux if you have too little acid is that the sphincter which closes the top of the stomach is sensitive to the acidity level in the stomach. If there is insufficient then it remains open and allows reflux. Doctors used to treat excess acid with alkali mixtures and too little acid with an acid mixture. Seems logical doesn't it?

Now we're getting into NNTs let's look at some data.

For GORD the NNT is in the region of 3 to 4 for short term healing (8 weeks) and 2 to 3 for long term (1 year) [49].

These figures are relatively good but as you can see only around 1 in 3 will heal their oesophagus. Long term treatment with PPI's can have its own consequences which we will consider later.

For treating 'functional dyspepsia' which is a common use for PPIs (particularly now they can be bought over the counter) the NNT is around 10 [50].

Depending on the condition being treated between 3 and 10 people will take medication for 1 person to benefit. Is anyone even asking why people are having so many digestive problems?

<u>Flu vaccination</u>

We live in a world of influenza paranoia. Almost everyone is being targeted for flu vaccination. The people that used to be targeted when flu vaccines were first developed were the people who were likely to be more susceptible to the disease and one could reason that this was appropriate. Now the very young and the elderly are classed as 'at risk' no matter what their health status just because they fall in to that age group. People in between are being recommended to have it, 'just in case'.

In some places people are being denied the right to work if they don't get vaccinated. Surely an unvaccinated person is no risk to a vaccinated person are they? Or are they saying that if you get the flu you can pass it on to vaccinated people because the vaccine doesn't work? Well, of course the vaccine wouldn't work if you had flu of a different strain to that in the vaccine.

Flu vaccinations are being given by an ever increasing number of medical professionals, doctors, nurses, pharmacists. There is TV advertising, High Street banners, news papers and magazines. We are certainly being subjected to a massive media campaign and most medical professionals think it highly beneficial to get vaccinated.

There is a well know system used in manipulating public opinion it is referred to as 'problem, reaction, solution' [51]. The World Health Organisation (WHO) has done its best to create huge fear around so called flu pandemics. We have had 'avian flu', 'swine flu', 'seasonal flu' etc.

If a health crisis (= problem) like a flu pandemic is given high profile there will most certainly be a public outcry to do something (=

reaction); the government response is to offer flu vaccines and antiviral treatments (= solution).

The big question is does the flu vaccine work?

'Evidence based medicine' is the mantra of our health systems so what's the evidence? The seasonal flu vaccine is usually made up of three strains of virus out of the 200 or so strains identified [52]. How do they choose which ones to put in the vaccine? It's an educated guess based on various factors, the evidence here is the probability that the correct strains have been chosen.

Because it is often difficult to categorise absolutely a case of flu unless it is laboratory confirmed, the term, 'influenza like illness' (ILI), has been coined. So many cases of so called flu may indeed not be flu at all.

Back to the question of whether the vaccine works. The Cochrane collaboration which has been mentioned several times before has done some independent research on the subject.

Yearly flu vaccination is now recommended for a broad spectrum of individuals, children and adults alike. So how effective is the vaccine in these different groups of people.

In children under the age of six the NNT for the live attenuated vaccine is 6, as you now know this means the chance of benefit is 1 in 6. The efficacy of the inactivated flu vaccine in children under 2 years of age is no better than placebo and for children over the age 6 - 12, 28 individuals must receive the vaccine for 1 to benefit[53].

Are the figures any better in the adult population? Apparently not since around 71 people need to be vaccinated to prevent 1 case of confirmed influenza[54]. If you are paying privately for a flu shot you might want to consider whether it is money well spent.

The elderly have been and still are one of the largest groups targeted for flu vaccination, this is a worldwide phenomenon. Naturally this group of individuals is more likely to suffer complications of contracting flu such as secondary bacterial infections leading to pneumonia and death. Indeed it is thought that many of the deaths during the 1918 flu pandemic were in fact due to pneumonia; there were no antibiotics available then. The evidence for effectiveness in this group of people is inconclusive despite over 40 years of usage[55]).

Healthcare workers are now being almost forced to receive a flu vaccination or lose their jobs. The rational presumably is that if these individuals have the vaccine it will reduce the risks to the patients they are caring for particularly the elderly who are more susceptible to flu related complications. There is no evidence that this is effective; other measures including hygiene procedures are likely to be more effective[56].

For people with lung diseases such as asthma and chronic obstructive lung disease there appears to be a benefit in having the flu vaccine. However the benefit will not be universal as with all drug treatments it is a game of statistics. For other lung diseases such as bronchiectasis and cystic fibrosis benefit is not so clear[57].

In summary, from the evidence it seems that if you are healthy the benefit of having a flu vaccine is tenuous. For healthy adults the NNT to prevent one case of influenza is around 70.

Ask yourself the question; why are flu vaccinations so heavily promoted to healthy people when the evidence clearly shows they are of little benefit. Why is the fear mongering ramped up in times of so called pandemics? What is a pandemic? It is defined by the World Health Organisation when they see fit.

The controllers of large pharmaceutical corporations have a huge influence on political decisions and the fact that flu vaccines are big business,$1.6 billion dollars in the US alone, just might have a bearing on the situation; don't you think?

The number of worldwide deaths in the declared 2009 flu pandemic was estimated at between 151,000 and 575,000. The flu pandemic of 1918 killed between 50 and 100 million people, that's two orders of magnitude greater than in 2009. So was the 2009 outbreak really a pandemic or just a plain old epidemic. The word pandemic instils much more fear and panic than epidemic. Fear makes us do things we would not ordinarily do, like get a flu shot!

Antivirals for treating and preventing flu

Are antivirals such as amantidine and oseltamivir (Tamiflu) any better for treating and preventing influenza?

Amantidine has been in use for a long time as a treatment for Parkinson's disease. Its use as an anti-viral came later. Amantidine is no longer recommended for the treatment of influenza because resistance has developed [58 & 59].

The use of the neuraminidase inhibitor oseltamivir is now almost exclusive (excluding vaccination) in the drug treatment of flu. It is also widely used as a preventative strategy in times of epidemic/pandemic flu. If you are using this drug for treating flu you can expect the time period of your symptoms to be reduced by less than a day and any benefit from reduced complications is non-existent. As a preventative the NNT is 33; 33 people need to take the medication for 1 to benefit[60].

Conclusion - For the majority of healthy people the flu vaccine and/or antivirals are of very limited benefit.

<u>Actions which may help to prevent and combat flu and its complications</u>:

1. Follow the recommended sanitary precautions. Why?

Helps to reduce the spread of the virus to other people who may be immune compromised.

2. Ensure your vitamin D status is good. Why?

Vitamin D is important for a fully functioning immune system, among other things.

3. Avoid sugar. Why?

Sugar has an immune suppressing effect. It blocks the uptake of vitamin C into cells. Vitamin C is an important nutrient for optimal immune function.

4. Take high dose vitamin C and I mean high dose, up to bowel tolerance or use liposomal vitamin C which has a far superior absorption. Why?

Vitamin C is involved with phagocytosis, the process whereby cells engulf foreign invaders.

5. Take natural antivirals like garlic. Why?

Because they are indeed antiviral; there are many such substances in nature.

6. Reduce stress. Why?

Stress causes the body to produce cortisol which is immune suppressant.

7. Get adequate amounts of quality sleep. Why?

Poor sleep patterns disrupt normal immune function.

8. Meditate, it's good for improving health. Why?

Meditation can reduce negative thought patterns which compromise immune function.

9. Practice Yoga or Tai Chi. Why?

These disciplines reduce stress hormones and stimulate lymphatic removal of toxins.

Anti-depressants

Around 10% of Americans now take antidepressants; there has been a huge increase in prescribing over the last 20 years. If you are female and between 40 to 50 then you have a 1 in 4 chance of being prescribed these drugs[61].

In America (and New Zealand) drugs can be advertised directly to the public. This puts enormous pressure on doctors to prescribe drugs which the patients see on TV. Have no doubt that advertising influences people to almost demand the drugs they see presented before them. The top two U.S. drugs Cymbalta (duloxetine) and Lexapro (escitalopram) produced around $6 billion dollars in sales in 2011-2012.

How do you know if you're suffering from clinical depression? Remember being happy and sad is part of everyday life. How would we know happiness if we never experienced sadness? Many of us experience sadness in the course of our lives and that doesn't mean we are clinically depressed.

The Hamilton depression scale is a clinical tool to assess depression. It, like many such questionnaires, has a degree of subjectivity and doctor diagnosis is not a precise science and one research paper showed less than 50% diagnosis accuracy[62].

For serious clinical depression drugs may be beneficial but for the more frequent mild to moderate depression the case may be much less clear.

The chemical imbalance theory is one of those beliefs which is accepted in the medical community as being true. Let me tell you, *there is no evidence to substantiate this theory*. When drug companies found a substance that could affect serotonin then the modern treatment of depression ensued. Does that mean low serotonin causes depression? Various academics in the field think not [63 & 64].

The chemical which is supposed to be out of balance, serotonin, is a neuro-transmitter in the brain. It is a chemical messenger which facilitates communication between cells in certain areas of the brain. This chemical imbalance idea was propelled to the foreground with the development of SSRIs, Selective Serotonin Re-uptake Inhibitors. These drugs increase the level of free serotonin in the brain most definitely but do they help with mild to moderate depression any more than placebo? A review of 30 years of data came to the conclusion that the benefit is minimal to nonexistent[65] .

For more in depth information you may be interested in an article by Dr Jeffrey Dach with can be found at greenmedinfo.com[66].

My own personal observation is that these drugs are certainly being prescribed much more frequently and in ever increasing doses, commonly up to the maximum recommended doses and also in combination with other antidepressants. Taking SSRI's is not without problems and although the side effect profile is supposedly better than the older antidepressants there are many horror stories which you can research at http://www.ssristories.org/ .

This section wouldn't be complete without a look at NNTs :

> *SSRIs showed a clinical benefit for improvement in depression scores (NNT = 7; 95% CI, 7 to 8). More patients in the SSRI group withdrew from trials because of adverse effects........[67].*

This is a piece of research which shows a positive benefit for 1 in 7 patients given SSRIs. We will see in a later section that evidence of lack of benefit was suppressed by the industry and was only revealed after it was requested under the Freedom of Information Act.

<u>Endnotes</u>

In this chapter we have investigated some of the major classes of drugs used in medicine today. Some therapies are treatments and some are based around preventative intervention.

While I have given references to back up the data supplied I accept that other sources of reference may give different figures. The argument however will still hold valid that drugs don't work in most people. The same conclusion was made by Alan Roses, a senior executive of GSK pharmaceuticals, in 2003[68].

> *'The vast majority of drugs - more than 90 per cent - only work in 30 or 50 percent of the people," Dr Roses said. "I wouldn't say that most drugs don't work. I would say that most drugs work in 30 to 50 per cent of people. Drugs out there on the market work, but they don't work in everybody.'*

Of course the word 'work' is open to interpretation as we've seen! This is the standard that is accepted in medicine; *is this the standard that you find acceptable?*

A human being is an infinitely variable complex structure of mind, body and spirit. It is impossible to know who will benefit from drug treatment and who will suffer a side effect which in some cases may be lethal. As we will see later, prescribed drugs and other medical treatments do kill people. This may be inflammatory but it is a statistical reality.

- *When you are given a medicine or medical procedure do you expect it to work?*
- *Do you anticipate that it may cause harm?*
- *Do you consider the possibility that it could lead to your early demise?*

I suspect the answers for most people to these questions would be yes, no, no.

If you take your car into the garage to fix a problem and the mechanic says there's only a 30% chance I can fix it, would you accept that?

The problem is that the human body is not a machine and therefore the same principles of mechanical thinking don't work as we've clearly seen.

The emphasis for the future has to be prevention. Just as servicing your car regularly, ensures many years of care free motoring; looking after your body and mind will ensure many years of disease free living.

Much of the emphasis with preventative medicine is focused on manufactured diseases and conditions based on a false premise such as the fat hypothesis (see later). Many of our chronic conditions have an underlying inflammatory process which is a direct result of our diets and lifestyles; if we expect medicine to fix these issues then we will be waiting a long time.

This book is not meant to be an exposé of the pharmaceutical industry and medical establishment although it inevitably is. There are much better and more in depth exposés for those who care to search.

The sole purpose of this chapter is to impress upon the reader the way in which our current drug paradigm functions; so that you have an understanding of figures behind what is considered to 'work'. Surely before you choose a particular treatment you need to know what the potential benefits are, don't you? If you're told there is a 1 in 3 chance of the drug giving you an absolute benefit then you may choose to take it. At the other end of the scale where the odds are not so good like aspirin mentioned earlier 1 in 2000, you may choose not to take it. If you don't know the figures it's difficult to make an informed choice, isn't it?

Evidence based medicine simply means, that after statistical analysis, a benefit is shown which is over and above what can be expected from placebo. It is taken for granted that medicines only work in some people, not even the majority. Side effects and death are an accepted part of the system. Governments generally only fund (with your money) this conventional approach and an educated person might ask the question, why? The answer from the academics would be that there is no research or evidence base to substantiate the claims of alternatives while maintaining that their system is evidence based. They ignore the fact that drugs are being prescribed with greater frequency for off label uses where the evidence is purely anecdotal or is deemed by the doctor to be appropriate because they have the authority to prescribe in that manner.

You now understand the chance nature of medical treatments; of course this may also apply to alternative forms of healing, however, unlike conventional medicine alternative choices are much more likely to have a more acceptable safety record. Why do doctors pay such high malpractice insurance premiums? In the US the cost of malpractice insurance is between $20,000 and $200,000 per year depending on the area of practice and in which state the doctor practices[69]. This says a great deal about the dangers inherent in the medical system we currently operate and why doctor's fees are so high; you are paying the premiums! My wife has alternative medical indemnity insurance to cover her holistic skills; the insurance premium is around $100 a year.

You have learned a little about statistical interpretation of data sets. You know what an NNT is and how relevant that is to whether a treatment is worthwhile or not. I have not covered all areas of drug use but the same principles apply.

The crux of the matter is that we generally have to treat a lot of people for a few to get any benefit. The guarantees of benefit are pretty slim for chronic diseases. Surely there has to be a better way where the majority will benefit from the intervention and not the minority. How do we determine who will benefit from drug treatment? The answer is we can't and therefore everyone gets the same treatment. Does this feel right to you? Why are governments not putting more focus on poor quality nutrition and toxic exposure?

When taking drugs it must always be kept in mind that they may have side effects and can be potentially fatal in themselves. Many drugs used by the elderly have never been tested in that age group and they are the ones more likely to suffer adverse effects since liver and kidney function decline with age.

These are just a few examples of how drugs may or may not benefit the individual. If you are on medication and are unsure of the benefits or are concerned about side effects then do a bit of research. If you have your own computer and internet it's easy, if you don't then the library does. Discuss the pros and cons with your doctor and if the doctor isn't prepared to listen then maybe a change is indicated.

References

1. http://www.wrf.org/alternative-therapies/power-of-mind-placebo.php
2. https://www.rt.com/business/207255-usa-medicine-global-spending/
3. http://www.scientificamerican.com/article/strange-but-true-humans-carry-more-bacterial-cells-than-human-ones/
4. http://www.naturalnews.com/030384_Louis_Pasteur_disease.html
5. http://www.mnwelldir.org/docs/terrain/lost_history_of_medicine.htm
6. http://www.northcumbriaccg.nhs.uk/search-results.aspx?search_keywords=antibiotic+guidelines
7. http://www.thennt.com/nnt/antibiotics-for-acute-bronchitis/
8. http://www.thennt.com/nnt/antibiotics-for-animal-bites/
9. http://www.thennt.com/nnt/antibiotics-for-clinically-diagnosed-acute-sinusitis/
10. http://www.thennt.com/nnt/antibiotics-for-otitis-media/
11. http://www.thennt.com/nnt/antivirals-for-preventing-post-herpetic-neuralgia/
12. http://www.thennt.com/nnt/neuraminidase-inhibitors-for-influenza/
13. http://www.thennt.com/nnt/antibiotics-prophylactic-for-icu-respiratory-infections/
14. http://www.thennt.com/nnt/antibiotics-for-copd-exacerbation/
15. http://healthsentinel.com/joomla/index.php?option=com_content&view=article&id=2654:united-states-disease-death-rates&catid=55:united-states-deaths-from-diseases&Itemid=55
16. http://www.who.int/water_sanitation_health/en/
17. http://www.bmj.com/content/346/bmj.f245/rr/626008
18. http://www.fiercevaccines.com/special-reports/sanofi

19. http://www.wellbeingjournal.com/profits-not-science-motivate-vaccine-mandates/

20. http://www.ncbi.nlm.nih.gov/pmc/articles/PMC1646939/

21. http://healthimpactnews.com/2014/whooping-cough-outbreaks-among-vaccinated-older-children-increasing/

22. http://www.thennt.com/nnt/aspirin-to-prevent-a-first-heart-attack-or-stroke/

23. http://www.thennt.com/nnt/aspirin-for-cardiovascular-prevention-after-prior-heart-attack-or-stroke/

24. http://www.thennt.com/nnt/statins-for-heart-disease-prevention-without-prior-heart-disease/

25. http://www.thennt.com/nnt/statins-for-heart-disease-prevention-with-known-heart-disease/

26. http://www.bmj.com/content/348/bmj.g3168

27. http://onlinelibrary.wiley.com/doi/10.1002/14651858.CD002003.pub4/full

28. http://onlinelibrary.wiley.com/doi/10.1002/14651858.CD003654.pub4/full

   28.1   http://www.thennt.com/nnt/anti-hypertensives-to-prevent-death-heart-attacks-and-strokes/

29. http://www.thennt.com/nnt/warfarin-for-atrial-fibrillation-stroke-prevention/

30. http://gilbertling.org/lp2.htm

31. http://www.webmd.com/cancer/news/20110617/cancer-death-rates-us-still-dropping#1

32. http://jnci.oxfordjournals.org/content/94/14/1044.full

33. http://report.nih.gov/nihfactsheets/viewfactsheet.aspx?csid=75

34. http://www.ajmc.com/publications/evidence-based-oncology/2012/2012-2-vol18-n1/the-economics-of-cancer-care-in-the-united-states-how-much-do-we-spend-and-how-can-we-spend-it-better

35. http://www.bandolier.org.uk/booth/painpag/Acutrev/Analgesics/Leagtab.html

36. https://www.nps.org.au/radar/articles/pregabalin-lyrica-for-neuropathic-pain

37. http://www.bandolier.org.uk/booth/painpag/Chronrev/Other/Carbamazepine.html

38. http://www.bandolier.org.uk/booth/painpag/Chronrev/antidc/antidep.html

39. http://pubmedcentralcanada.ca/pmcc/articles/PMC2377247/

40. http://www.uptodate.com/contents/tumor-necrosis-factor-alpha-inhibitors-risk-of-malignancy

41. http://www.niams.nih.gov/Health_Info/Bone/Bone_Health/bone_mass_measure.asp

42. http://www.ncbi.nlm.nih.gov/pubmed/22753670

43. http://www.greenmedinfo.com/blog/osteoporosis-myth-dangers-high-bone-mineral-density

44. http://www.fpnotebook.com/rheum/pharm/Bsphsphnts.htm

45. http://www.ti.ubc.ca/2012/01/24/a-systematic-review-of-the-efficacy-of-%EF%BF%BC%EF%BF%BCbisphosphonates/

46. http://stateofobesity.org/hypertension/

47. http://www.thennt.com/nnt/anti-hypertensives-for-cardiovascular-prevention-in-mild-hypertension/

48. http://www.thennt.com/nnt/anti-hypertensives-to-prevent-death-heart-attacks-and-strokes/

49. http://www.bandolier.org.uk/bandopubs/gordf/gord.html#Heading23

50. https://www.cadth.ca/efficacy-proton-pump-inhibitors-adults-functional-dyspepsia-0

51. http://ethics.wikia.com/wiki/Problem_Reaction_Solution

52. http://www.cdc.gov/flu/about/season/vaccine-selection.htm

53. http://onlinelibrary.wiley.com/doi/10.1002/14651858.CD004879.pub4/abstract;jsessionid=89FE613D47CFA76E41DC94A551399E22.f02t03

54. http://onlinelibrary.wiley.com/doi/10.1002/14651858.CD001269.pub5/abstract

55. http://onlinelibrary.wiley.com/doi/10.1002/14651858.CD004876.pub3/abstract

56. http://onlinelibrary.wiley.com/doi/10.1002/14651858.CD005187.pub4/abstract

57. http://www.cochrane.org/CD000364/AIRWAYS_vaccines-for-preventing-flu-in-people-with-asthma

58. http://onlinelibrary.wiley.com/doi/10.1002/14651858.CD002745.pub3/abstract

59. http://onlinelibrary.wiley.com/doi/10.1002/14651858.CD001169.pub3/abstract

60. http://onlinelibrary.wiley.com/doi/10.1002/14651858.CD008965.pub4/abstract

61. http://well.blogs.nytimes.com/2013/08/12/a-glut-of-antidepressants/?_php=true&_type=blogs&_r=0

62. http://www.ncbi.nlm.nih.gov/pubmed/19640579

63. http://www.npr.org/blogs/health/2012/01/23/145525853/when-it-comes-to-depression-serotonin-isnt-the-whole-story

64. http://www.plosmedicine.org/article/info%3Adoi%2F10.1371%2Fjournal.pmed.0020392#s5

65. http://jama.jamanetwork.com/article.aspx?articleid=185157

66. http://www.greenmedinfo.com/blog/antidepressants-no-better-placebo-jama-study

67. http://aafp.org/afp/2010/0701/p42.html

68. http://news.bbc.co.uk/2/hi/health/3299945.stm

69. http://work.chron.com/much-doctors-pay-insurance-7304.html

Chapter 5 – ALTERNATIVE TREATMENT CHOICES

The scientific hype and constant exposure to advertising might lead us to believe that modern medicine has the answers for all your illnesses and providing you keep popping the pills your health may be assured.

The marketing has been aggressive and influential; claims are made which may be only a shadow of the actual reality as we've seen in the last section. We will see in a later chapter that modern medicine can be and for many is a life shortening experience. The Hippocratic idea of 'first do no harm' seems to have been relegated to the archives of medical history; it is clearly not a tenet that modern medicine can adhere to as there is implicit danger built into drug therapy and surgery which is accepted as part of the 'cost of doing business'. What was once a calling to serve humanity and relieve suffering has now become a multi-billion dollar industry with almost god-like status afforded the professionals who wield the power of life and death. Despite all this there is and always has been alternative choices, many of which have been subjected to ridicule and persecution by a system which is fearful of losing market share. Medicine is big business and anything which is remotely likely to challenge its authority is quickly and ruthlessly dealt with. Much of this activity never reaches the mainstream media since to do so would only draw attention to it.

Many people turn to alternative or complimentary medicine only after they've been given the 'sorry we can do no more for you' from the conventional system. Often their body and/or mind is in a depleted state of vitality which is not a good starting point for trying to restore health and vitality; in spite of this many do indeed achieve an improvement and even, dare I say it, cure. When asked to explain such responses the conventional reply is spontaneous remission!

Medical systems like Ayurveda and Traditional Chinese Medicine (TCM) have been in use for several thousand years; if they had no substance then they would have surely faded into insignificance over time. That has not happened. Unlike our current medical paradigm, these time honoured treatments involve the use of natural substances coupled with knowledge of the more subtle energetic nature of man.

Ideas encompassing the energetic nature of reality have been expanding over recent decades with quantum theory, string theory, M theory, quantum entanglement and other ideas starting at least to hit mainstream awareness, if not understanding. We know that matter has an illusory nature and doesn't really exist as a solidity; that is just an aberration of our senses. Some of these ideas may be alien to you and it matters not whether you understand what I'm referring to. The only thing to understand is that all is energy as summed up by one famous scientist.

> *"Concerning matter, we have been all wrong. What we have called matter is energy, whose vibration has been so lowered as to be perceptible to the senses. There is no matter." —Albert Einstein*

Many alternative approaches to dealing with sickness are often focused on the energy system and flow of that energy within the human instrument. The conventional view to this is often hostile and incredulous, when we talk of energy and energy fields we stretch the ingrained belief systems of a medical paradigm which is firmly in the camp of solid matter. Because of this when you start looking for alternative solutions to health problems and health maintenance it is highly unlikely that your doctor will be able to or want to advise you. Encouragingly however there are a growing number of professionals who are thinking and working outside of the conventionally accepted structure; they are developing a different understanding of health.

The purpose of diagnosis is so that you have a name to the disease; once you have a name you can prescribe a treatment. I remember attending a homoeopathy lecture in the UK where there was a 'test' subject who had her case analysed as part of the lecture. The lady had seen three specialists in the conventional field and received three different diagnoses and consequently three different treatments, none of which were effective.

Many systems of alternative medicine do not rely on a diagnosis; since the approach is holistic the 'name' of the disease is not important. Holistic simply means that the whole person is considered, not just the bit that apparently has the problem. The concept of whole person includes both body and mind; physical structure and mental and emotional aspects of being.

Symptoms are merely the manifestation of a diseased state of being; symptoms are not the cause of the condition. The chronic diseases from which an individual may suffer do not suddenly manifest, they generally develop over many years and show no symptoms until the homoeostatic (balancing) mechanisms of the body become overloaded and can no longer keep balance. We also have to consider the role of our mind and emotions in the aetiology of disease; this area of functioning is generally not considered by conventional medicine to be an influence in physical disease; physical disease has a physical cause. Of course some conditions definitely have a physical cause, if hit by a bus for example. However one might ask why were you standing in a place to be hit by the bus?

Your doctor's training includes very little about nutrition and more than likely nothing about the use of natural remedies. It is unlikely that toxic exposure, unless overt, will be considered as part of the causative factors and yet we live in a world of ever increasing toxicity as we will see later. It is not uncommon that drug use is based on unproven theory and/or unknown mode of action which is frequently the case in psychiatric medicine.

There are treatment modalities being used in other parts of the world to which we don't have general access in the western medical systems. People experience apparently miraculous cures which the medical system writes off as 'spontaneous remission' as if there's no reason for it. This is because the schools of medicine do not teach knowledge of the electro-dynamic nature of the human structure, the seen and the unseen; there is no place in modern medicine for the non-physical part of our beings which is considered the domain of religion: yet hasn't science become the new religion for many?

Researchers at the cutting edge of scientific thinking may be uncovering information that will allow us a new way of perceiving reality, yet this reality is not new to the sages in the eastern medical systems previously mentioned such as Ayurveda in India and TCM in China. In the Western world we have a concept of the human body/mind and its ability to heal which is clearly missing some areas of understanding.

When I was in pharmacy school we learned about the autonomic nervous system. This part of the nervous system is responsible for such things as regulating the heart beat and breathing; it affects blood pressure and bladder control and helps to provide more blood to our muscles so we can run when we are in danger. I was taught that this system runs automatically and functions mostly below our normal conscious control. *So how can a Hindu yogi slow his heart rate at will?* There is obviously more to it than we currently understand.

Nassim Haramein, a controversial figure in the field of quantum physics tells us quite clearly that the reality we live in is 99.9999% space. This is difficult for most people to comprehend as our senses give us a false impression of solidity as noted previously. We look for our answers in this very small part of reality (0.0001%) when according to Nassim we should perhaps be looking in the 99.9999% which is ordinarily inaccessible to our senses.

Dr Rupert Sheldrake PhD talks about morpho-genetic fields. In simple terms these are formative electro-magnetic fields on to which matter displays itself. One way to understand this is to remember the experiment we all did at school with a magnet under a piece of paper and iron filings sprinkled on top. The iron filings display the shape of the unseen magnetic field. So there is this idea of a field structure underlying our apparent physical substance and indeed the whole of the universe. These fields have been demonstrated with high voltage photography (Kirlian photography) where if you cut a leaf in two and take such a photograph you can see the whole leaf field still remaining. The subject of phantom limb pain is interesting; medical science says it is due to the severed nerve still sending signals to the brain, maybe. My wife, who uses Bowen therapy, once treated a man with phantom limb (leg) pain. She obviously couldn't treat the leg that wasn't there so she manipulated the space where the leg should have been. During the treatment the patient asked her what she was doing as he could clearly 'feel' something. His phantom limb pain went away. Could have been placebo of course, the patient didn't care his pain was resolved.

Science has, in recent years, been trying to convince us of the genetic nature of disease. The human genome project was going to provide all the answers and yet the results have thrown up more questions. They discovered that there weren't enough genes to account for the 70,000 proteins in the human body; the idea of one gene one protein was incorrect. The medical genetic boom has quietly receded into the background.

More and more evidence is being presented, from independent sources, regarding the epigenetic factors influencing our health. Epigenetics is a fairly new scientific discipline and is the study of how gene expression is influenced by external factors such as diet, lifestyle, toxicity etc.

Many researchers are exploring the nature of consciousness and how our conscious focus can affect our physical well being and disease expression; mind over matter so to speak.

Both the human body and nature as a whole have mathematically precise structure ordered into them. The golden ratio[1] and spiral structures, fractal geometry[2] derived from the Mandelbrot set which describes within its infinite structure all the seemingly random shapes in nature.

Once we start to realign our thinking and understanding to take on board the bigger picture of reality as alluded to in the few examples above then we can have an appreciation that the human condition is far more complicated than just the idea of a biological machine.

We are now beginning to have a greater understanding of the energetic nature of reality and this is where many of the systems outside of the current medical paradigm function. We call these systems alternative or complementary yet this is somewhat a misnomer as many of them have been around long before our modern system was developed. Let us have a quick look at a few of the alternative systems of treatment, some old and some relatively new. I say quick look because there are volumes of information on each of these subjects; the idea is just to acquaint you with other possibilities you might not ordinarily consider.

Acupuncture as part of traditional Chinese medicine (TCM) has been around for at least 3000 years compared to less than 100 years of our current paradigm. If acupuncture (and TCM) didn't work then, as I previously stated, it would have surely fallen into decline. Acupuncture involves the insertion of extremely fine needles into so called acupuncture points. The purpose being to affect the flow of energy in channels (meridians) which bring the body back to a more harmonious state of being. Symptoms are recognised as being an expression of disharmony in the body or mind. Interestingly acupuncture points have a lower electrical resistance to that of surrounding tissue which can easily be measured. Of course the practitioners of old knew where the points and meridians were without the aid of modern electronics. They also were able to diagnose the state of health or disease by just using pulses in the wrist. This was the only part of the Emperor they were allowed to touch.

SCENAR[3] (Self Controlled Energo Neuro Adaptive Regulator) is an instrument developed by Russian scientists which utilises acupuncture theory and dermographic (skin) associations to treat medical conditions.

SCENAR is a biofeedback instrument which 'talks' to the body and changes the dynamics of the disease condition to promote self healing. It helps to regulate the body's neuro-endocrine systems thus stimulating a healing response. The neuro-endocrine system is very important in homoeostasis, the body's self regulation. SCENAR was developed in the 1970's primarily for the astronauts to use in space. They never got into space with it due to curtailing of the space program; SCENAR is however used throughout Russian hospitals and clinics. More practitioners in the West are starting to use these devices. Case histories are available to view on the web site given[4]. SCENAR can be used in many conditions to achieve a drug free outcome. Personal devices can be bought so you can treat yourself and your family after you are satisfied with the medical diagnosis.

Homoeopathy has been around for over 200 years now. In this system of medicine a homoeopath will take an in depth case study of physical, mental and emotional symptoms. It will include disease symptoms; personality traits; likes and dislikes; how you are affected by external forces such as weather; hot and cold etc. It is truly a holistic discipline. The principle of homoeopathy is 'similia similibus curentur', like cures like. Remedies are 'proven' to ascertain a symptom picture and then diseases which give similar symptoms are treated with that remedy. This is a bit of a simplistic view but gives the general idea. It takes years of practice to become proficient in this discipline. The remedies are made in a very specific way involving sequential dilution and succession (forceful shaking). The argument from conventionally trained people is; how can it work when there are apparently no molecules of the original substance left in the final product? I must admit that when I was first working in pharmacy I had exactly that attitude. After studying the discipline and observing some remarkable effects my ideas were changed.

Water is the main component of any homoeopathic remedy. Water is unique, it has been called a liquid crystal and because of the geometry and electrical charge on the molecules within liquid water it is able to hold information, information from the original substance and yet have none of the toxicity of the original. How fantastic is that? Interestingly Hahnemann, the founder of homoeopathic medicine, knew that if you heated a remedy above 60°C it was destroyed; the liquid crystal structure of water breaks down around that temperature. Dr. Gerald Pollack of Washington University is a leading authority on water structure if you are interested in furthering your knowledge.

Herbal medicine has been in use for as long as there have been people on the planet earth. It is surprising that conventional wisdom doesn't accept anecdotal information as evidence yet the same argument we made for TCM applies.

If herbs did not have healing properties their use would not have continued, would it? Many pharmaceuticals have been derived from plant sources in the past. Herbs of course are part of our food; in the West we tend to use them more of a condiment than as a therapeutic agent. Traditional cultures use herbs and spices as an integral part of their culinary delights. Indian cooking for example does not use a pinch of spice but an appreciable quantity which when used on a regular basis will have therapeutic actions.

> *"Let food be thy medicine and medicine be thy food."*
>
> **Hippocrates**

Our intuition should tell us that we don't need double blind clinical trials to know whether our food, including herbs and spices, has a health effect for us. Even so there is a mounting body of evidence, for those who require hard facts, amassing on this subject[5].

It's fairly obvious if you think about it that your physical body is what you eat or more accurately what you absorb and assimilate into your tissues. Your body is an incredible, organized structure with an in built ability to adapt to difficult times. It can make do with poor nutrition or accommodate toxic exposure up to a point at which time it starts to deteriorate and symptoms begin to appear. The medical view within our current paradigm is that the symptoms are a nuisance and must be suppressed. What if the symptoms are the body's expression of a problem? If we choose to carry on in the same way without change then the symptoms will undoubtedly progress. Drugs will only suppress symptoms up to a point. If your blood pressure is not being controlled what happens? An increase in dose or the addition of more drugs to the schedule is the standard approach. The other option is to listen to your body and change what you're doing. Much of the food eaten by western cultures is full of calories but lacking the vital nutrients needed for a healthy existence.

It is vital that the nervous system in the body is operating at maximum effectiveness. It is responsible for communication within the body. We have something called the psycho-neuro-endocrine system which involves regulation of our day to day functioning. This interplay between our mind, nervous system and endocrine system is responsible for how well we are functioning, physically, mentally and emotionally.

Many modalities can address these areas of our function. Neurolink[6], Emotional Freedom Technique[7], Acupuncture, Bowen technique[8], SCENAR, hypnotherapy and homoeopathy are some of these. It's important to find the right therapy and therapist which suit your own personal way of being and with which you are comfortable.

If you have painful musculo-skeletal problems then there is physiotherapy, chiropractic, osteopathy, Bowen therapy. Your doctor will just prescribe tablets to 'dull the pain' or 'take the edge off'. Medication will not address the cause. I like to relate this comparison; when the oil light comes on in your car you have two choices. You can put some oil in i.e. treat the cause, or you can disconnect the bulb i.e. treat the symptom.

One of the main issues with any healing process is accepting responsibility for where you are at. You are the result of your choices even down to the choice to step out into the road and get hit by a bus. If you had expanded awareness you may have pre-empted the scenario. Life involves making choices; different choices will lead down different paths. How many times do you hear people saying, 'if only…….'. When you accept that you are responsible then you may start to make more appropriate choices and stop blaming people and circumstances for life's events.

Choices often rely on your knowledge base and indeed knowing that there are choices. Here you've seen that there are alternatives to the current medical paradigm. It is unfortunate that in the US and many Western countries insurance companies and health care systems only tend to pay for the conventional medical care. England has a slightly better choice in that homoeopathy is available on the health service but that's probably not widely known or generally available. In New Zealand traditional Māori healing is funded by the government but again that's not widely available because there are too few practitioners. Even within the conventional system we can choose to participate in a particular treatment or not if we have information to make that choice. Much of our current chronic disease is due on a physical level to diet and life style and exposure to toxic influences; we definitely have a choice in those departments. Other influences on our health status may be less tangible: purpose in life, sense of loneliness and disconnection, emotional garbage we carry around, lack of love; the list goes on.

When you realise that in order to be healthy and vibrant you have to avoid all the things which may have a negative influence, this includes things of a physical nature (toxins) and also non-physical influences. We all know people who drain our energy. The other side of the coin is to provide the body and mind with the building blocks of health. The following chapters will provide some more information to help along the way. We've already had an overview of the workings of the pharmaceutical world and how effective or not drugs are. Now we can delve more deeply into some of the more common concerns facing humanity at this juncture in our history.

References

1. http://en.wikipedia.org/wiki/Golden_ratio

2. http://en.wikipedia.org/wiki/Fractal

3. http://www.scenar.ru/en/

4. http://www.scenar-therapy.com/tutorials/komarova_ryazanov_scenar-therapy_035/clinical_examples_of_scenar-therapy_with_scenar_035-4.html

5. http://www.greenmedinfo.com/

6. http://www.neurolinkglobal.com/

7. http://www.tapping.com/

8. http://thebowentechnique.com/

Chapter 6 – THE BIG C

The war on cancer: Are we winning?

Of all the words in the English dictionary the word 'cancer' is probably the one word which instils fear and dread into most people; why is that? Waiting for that diagnosis, just to confirm what, in your heart of hearts, you already know. How long have I got doctor?

Most people know someone who has, or has had, cancer and the suffering they endured, both physical and emotional. Our medical doctors are doing the best they can within our current paradigm even though the very treatment protocols being used are responsible for some of the casualties.

We, the human race, have been battling cancer for centuries; it is only in the 20th century that its prevalence has escalated to epidemic proportions. We often describe someone undergoing cancer therapy as 'fighting for their life' and it is indeed truly a battle. When Nixon signed the National Cancer Act in 1971 the so called 'war on cancer' was supposedly advanced by allocating an ever increasing amount of public money to the cause; despite the huge amounts of money devoted to finding a cure, we are no nearer to that goal than we were in 1971. We are still using the same, although more refined, destructive methodologies. Radiation and chemotherapy which are central to most cancer treatments have not changed in essence since their discovery. These therapies are not selective in the tissues they destroy. The rationale behind using them is that they target rapidly dividing cells; cancer cells fall into that general category. If the treatments targeted only cancer cells that would be great as there would be few side effects, no collateral damage. Alas this is not the case; many tissues in the body divide rapidly: cells lining the gastro-intestinal tract (gut), bone marrow, immune cells and hair follicles are examples. These cells are damaged by the treatments and the resultant side effects ensue: nausea, vomiting, hair loss, infections to name some of them.

What does the word 'cure' mean in conventional cancer treatment? One might naively think it means you no longer have the disease, that however is not the case. Cure from cancer, like many aspects of modern medicine, is defined; the definition for statistical purposes, is surviving for 5 years after diagnosis. If you die after 5 years and 1 week then for the purposes of statistics you were cured! We are told more people are surviving for 5 years after diagnosis but what does that mean? It may give an indication that we are winning the war but are we?

The problem with statistics is that you can select certain data to make a particular argument to justify the use of resources in a particular way. We are now getting earlier diagnosis which is going to influence the 5 year survival and so we are not comparing like with like. If someone is diagnosed with stage 3 or 4 cancer which most likely was more common in 1971 then 5 year survival will more than likely not be as good as someone diagnosed with stage 1 or 2 cancer which is more likely to occur now. Don't forget it is 5 years from diagnosis. If you are diagnosing cancer several years earlier then this is going to affect the comparison isn't it? Many cancers progress slowly and so early diagnosis will have a large effect on 5 year survival figures; this doesn't mean you will necessarily live longer than you would have. Over recent years evidence is slowly surfacing that many social cancers are not really cancers at all and should never have been treated; if they weren't cancer then obviously that will skew the data also. This article gives more information on the subject.

http://www.greenmedinfo.com/blog/millions-wrongly-treated-cancer-national-cancer-institute-panel-confirms

An article published in the Journal of the American Medical Association in 2000 asks the question. 'Are increasing 5-year survival rates evidence of success against cancer?'

> *'......our analysis shows that changes in 5-year survival over time bear little relationship to changes in cancer mortality. Instead, they appear primarily related to changing patterns of diagnosis.* [1]

What the article is saying is that 5 year survival data can be misleading.

The absolute number of deaths is a more important focus i.e. what is my chance of dying rather than surviving 5 years. For a lay person (and indeed professionals) it is often difficult to understand the statistics; we have concepts such as:

- *5 year survival*
- *Relative benefit*
- *Absolute benefit*
- *Age adjusted rates*

We've looked at the difference between relative and absolute before. We now understand that 'cure' = 5 years survival after diagnosis. What is Age adjustment? Age adjustment is a technique to manipulate data to a standard population. A standard population is a list of the number of people in a particular age group and when you are comparing data from say 1971 and 2010 it removes any bias which may be due to age. Why would that be important? Surely it is the absolute number of people developing cancer and dying from cancer which is important not how old they are. As you age the probability of dying with cancer increases because you are subjected to carcinogenic influences for a longer period of time. The crude, non age adjusted, rates for 1971 and 2012 are shown below.

U.S. cancer rates

	1971[2]	2012[3]
Actual death rate /100,000 population	161	186
Total deaths from cancer	335,000	582,607
Actual incidence rate / 100,000 population	306	491
Population	207.6 million	312.8 million
Total number of cancer diagnoses	635,000	1,529,078

Despite all the rhetoric from the scientists and politicians who have their own vested interests in inflating the data, the absolute reality is that the number of cancer cases per 100,000 of population was 60% higher in 2012 than in 1971 and the death rate was 15% higher.

The sad reality is that the chance of developing cancer and dying of the disease is far greater now than in 1971. In all fairness there has been an improvement in death rates from the peak of 1990, most of this may be associated with a reduction in smoking.

Smoking is not only associated with lung cancer but many other cancers as well including cancers of the mouth, lips, nose and sinuses, larynx, pharynx, oesophagus , stomach, pancreas, kidney, bladder, uterus, cervix, colon/rectum, ovary, and acute myeloid leukaemia. You don't need to be a smoker to succumb to smoking related diseases; if you are breathing in second hand smoke, it's just as harmful.

It is understandable that if you reduce smoking then associated disease will decline and this of course applies to any negatively impacting lifestyle choice.

In a news article from CNN December 23rd 2011, Dr. Otis Brawley, chief medical and scientific officer of the American Cancer Society, made these comments with reference to the 1971 cancer act.

> **'Many thought its passage would lead to a cure for cancer within a few years.....**
>
> **'......Forty years later, the war is still being waged, and much of the optimism has faded.'**

No matter how good cancer statistics are made to look and despite the optimism of sensationalist headlines that appear in the media from time to time, more and more people are developing cancer and dying from cancer.

Why do governments of the western economies continue to pour vast amounts of your money into a strategy which is clearly not working very well? Cancer diagnostics and treatment is a vast industry, CAT scans, PET scans, x-rays, drugs, surgery, palliative care etc. During 2010 $125 billion dollars was spent on cancer 'care'; that's around $80,000 per incidence of cancer. *When you are diagnosed with cancer you become a financial asset to the industry.*

Why is it that treatment options sanctioned by the government as the *only* ones that can be used in law are themselves carcinogenic (i.e. cause cancer)? We don't even know what will happen if we have no treatment because mostly that is not an option which people choose or are even offered. People with cancer are desperate for a cure, they don't want to die and so they are in a vulnerable position and often do as they're directed as they don't see there's any other choice.

There are and always have been alternative treatment protocols for most diseases including cancer, these are neither funded nor recognised by the conventional system. In an interview with the British peer, Lord Saatchi, in The Telegraph newspaper (U.K.) May 2013[4] the following points were made:

He said he had been told by senior medical professionals that an estimated one in ten people are killed by their cancer treatment.

Cancer drugs and radiotherapy weaken the immune system, leaving patients vulnerable to potentially fatal infections.

Lord Howe (the health minister) said statistics were collected for when cancer was the cause of death but not when treatment of cancer was the cause of death.

Lord Saatchi was attempting to introduce legislation so that alternative treatment protocols could be legally offered.

Often doing nothing may be the best course of action. We are all going to die, that's inevitable, but to die due to a medical treatment seems a little perverse somehow. Cancer treatments violently suppress the immune system, the very cells you need to overcome cancer.

Chemotherapy, one of the main tools used in the conventional treatment cancer is not that effective.

> *A paper in Clinical Oncology Volume 16 Issue 8, discusses the contribution of cytotoxic chemotherapy to 5 years survival. The results showed that chemotherapy contributed only 2.1% to 5 year survival in the USA. The conclusion drawn was that the use of chemotherapy makes only a minor contribution to overall survival.[5]*

(Oncology = study and treatment of tumours)

Lord Saatchi clearly believes there are choices and these should be made available to everyone. If you have a heart attack there is a 50% chance you will die from it, no chance to do anything about it. With a diagnosis of cancer there is at least a window of opportunity to be able to reflect and to decide on a course of action.

Within the medical realm there is a phenomenon called diagnosis shock where a doctor gives the diagnosis and the prognosis; you are told you only have so long to live. Because the doctor is the authority figure his/her word is taken by many as totally factual and duly die at the appointed time. This can be likened to the witch doctor pointing the bone at you, very effective medicine. Do you recall the nocebo effect mentioned earlier? Some people are however less believing of the prognosis; they see this as an opportunity to change their lives and do things differently; there are many cases of people following alternative routes and curing their illness.

What is cancer?

Simplistically, cancer is the uncontrolled growth of cells. Every one of us 'does' cancer every day at the cellular level. Normal cells have a lifetime and then undergo programmed cell death or apoptosis as it's technically known. Cancerous cells do not die and in effect become 'immortal'; a cell line called HeLa is still being used in research today. The name HeLa is derived from its original donor, Henrietta Lacks, who died of cervical cancer in 1951.

Cancerous cells are normally recognised as abnormal by our immune system and removed. When this process is impaired cancerous cells are able to grow unchecked and produce a solid tumour mass which is diagnosed as cancer. A cancer mass doesn't suddenly appear; most cancers are slow growing and take several years to reach a size that can be detected. A cancer mass will be composed of different types of cells some of which are derived from what are called cancer stem cells. The cancer stem cells are particularly resistant to conventional treatments of chemotherapy and radiation, unlike the other cells within the cancer mass. Shrinking of the cancer mass by these treatments is seen as a positive outcome yet the reduction in the size only serves to concentrate the cancer stem cells which become more aggressive. For a more in depth article see:

http://www.greenmedinfo.com/blog/are-cancer-stem-cells-key-discovering-cure

Cancer cells are known to have a different type of metabolism from normal cells. Normal cells use oxygen and glucose (a sugar) to produce energy and this process is very efficient. Cancer cells lose the ability to utilise oxygen and revert to a more primitive anaerobic (without oxygen) metabolism. They basically use a fermentation process to produce energy which is very inefficient and requires large amounts of glucose. Cancer cells attract glucose preferentially because they have many more receptors for insulin which is needed to take glucose into the cells. This is probably why in the later stages of cancer you can get cachexia which is a wasting away of tissue and weight loss as the body starts converting fat and muscle into glucose[6].

Dr Otto Warburg received a Nobel Prize for his pioneering work on cell metabolic processes involving respiration and fermentation. He succinctly states that cancer has many secondary causes but only one primary cause and the primary cause is the change in the metabolism of the cell from respiration to fermentation. This change in metabolism leads to an increase in acid production in the cancerous tissue and since acidic tissues hold less oxygen they are more likely to favour cancer progression.

We think cancer is a disease because that is the current belief system. Cancer may be only a symptom of an underlying metabolic disorder. We do know what is driving this underlying aberration in our metabolism; mainly the foods we are eating (or not eating!) and the toxicity we are exposed to.

In the 1600s sailors were dying in large numbers from what was at that time a common 'disease'; scurvy. Scurvy was and still is a serious illness and is due to vitamin C deficiency. The cure was known in 1600, just eat some lemons! It was almost 200 years later that the cure was accepted by the medical profession and another 150 years before Albert Szent-Györgyi discovered vitamin C. Scurvy was and is a very serious condition, bleeding gums, teeth falling out, organ haemorrhage and death.

Scurvy is not a disease; it is a symptom of an underlying metabolic disorder due to vitamin C deficiency.

Beriberi, a condition which was rife in the 1800s to early 1900s is characterised by various symptoms associated with nerve dysfunction and ultimately leads to death. The incidence of Beriberi increased at this time due to the increasing consumption of polished rice and white bread; it is due to a lack of vitamin B1, thiamine.

Beriberi is not a disease; it is a symptom of a metabolic disorder due to B1 deficiency.

Pellagra was recognised around 1740 and is due to niacin, B3 deficiency. Pellagra affects the skin, digestive system and brain function and if not treated will cause death. In 1914 Joseph Goldberger concluded that pellagra was due to a dietary deficiency. This conclusion was politically unacceptable and was ignored. It wasn't until 1937 that Conrad Elvehjem discovered the cure.

Pellagra is not a disease; it is a symptom of a metabolic disorder due to B3 deficiency.

Rickets has been around a long time and it was particularly prevalent in the days of the work house where children were confined for long hours with no sun light. Lack of vitamin D is commonly known for the affect it has on bones (rickets). There are however a whole host of other problems that are only just coming to light in regard vitamin D deficiency.

Rickets is not a disease; it is a symptom of a metabolic disorder due to vitamin D deficiency.

I could go on 'ad nauseam' there are many cases of nutritional deficiencies which lead to disease; protein deficiency, mineral deficiency – iron, selenium, magnesium, zinc, cobalt, iodine etc., essential fatty acids, vitamins, oxygen.

Dr Joel Wallach is a guy whose original training was as a veterinarian. During his time working in this capacity he performed many autopsies on animals and he came to the conclusion that many of them were dying from nutritional deficiencies. Because of this he made the assumption humans must also be suffering from nutritional deficiencies. The doctors didn't think he could possibly be right! He went on to train as a naturopathic doctor and confirmed his suspicions as he started dealing with people. He wrote a book 'Dead doctors don't lie' ISBN 0974858102. And there's a you tube video if you're interested: http://www.youtube.com/watch?v=pCs9qMkPYzg

Deficiency of any essential nutrient will lead to its own set of symptoms and metabolic effects as the body's processes try to compensate, this is not a disease but merely a set of symptoms due to a metabolic malfunction which can be corrected with the appropriate nutrients. Do you get the picture?

The logical progression is to ask the question; might cancer be a metabolic disorder? This indeed may be part of the picture at least, as we will see.

There may be many deficiency diseases but there is no disease known to man that is due to a deficiency of a synthetic drug.

The reason the prevalence of cancer (and many other diseases) has increased must be associated with our dramatically changed diets and lifestyles and toxic overload that has occurred over the last century. Our basic biological functioning hasn't changed in that time frame, what has changed are the external parameters, the epigenetic factors as they're known.

We are exposed to more potential carcinogens (cancer causing agents) than ever before and our immune capacity is depleted for sure. We are seeing a dramatic increase in the prevalence of the many inflammatory diseases which are plaguing our western society, diseases of affluence, starvation in the midst of plenty. We are eating a calorie dense, nutrient poor diet. Our food and water supply is awash with toxins, mercury and other heavy metals, fluoride, aspartame, preservatives, msg and other flavour enhancers, nitrates, bromide, pesticides, drug residues etc. Our children are subjected to masses of vaccinations which have a profound over stimulating effect on the immune system which medical science cannot know the long term effects of. They are only interested in short term 'safety data'.

We are being told that certain foods like unsaturated vegetable oils are good for us and that saturated fat is bad. The opposite would appear to true, the evidence is mounting. Vegetable oils are high in omega 6 fatty acids which are the building blocks of substances in our body which in excess can cause inflammation. The majority of people in the western world have an omega 6 to omega 3 ratio of over 20:1. A healthy ratio should be much less between 1:1 and 5:1. We are eating much more meat than ever before particularly in the American diet. Meat is a source of arachidonic acid which is an omega 6 fatty acid and contributes towards this imbalance.

Saturated fats are chemically stable and therefore don't give rise to free radicals or reactive oxygen species (ROS) as they are currently termed. Poly-unsaturated fats easily produce free radicals and unless we have sufficient antioxidants to neutralise these free radicals they can cause havoc. This damage can manifest as inflammation, DNA damage, protein damage, premature aging, nerve cell damage etc. We can see how one aspect of our diet can lead to inflammation and DNA damage which in turn can lead to cancerous changes in the cell.

Free radicals are an important aspect of the equation. Because of the deficiencies in our diet we are unable to keep our antioxidant levels in the range needed to prevent cellular damage and this is the fundamental mechanism behind the majority of inflammatory conditions, DNA damage and its associated gene expression. We have been lead to believe that cancer and other conditions are genetic. Of course our genes are responsible for many things but it is only in the last century that we have had an epidemic (or dare I say pandemic!) of inflammatory diseases which include, asthma, eczema, arthritis in its various forms, cardio-vascular disease, Crohn's disease, MS, Alzheimer's and other neuro-degenerative disorders, macular degeneration, the list goes on. They are just names for different expressions of the inflammatory response.

To say these diseases are genetic is to say our genes have changed in the last 100 years which is highly unlikely. What has changed is our exposure to environmental influences and whether they are toxic or nutritional, they can have a profound influence on gene expression. It's the old story of nature or nurture, genes or environment; it has been shown that defective genes are responsible for only 1% of diseases[7].

We do know however is that cancer cells utilise much more glucose than normal cells and some of the latest research now shows that excessive sugar consumption can cause cancer[8]; sugar is 50% glucose. How many oncologists (cancer specialists) tell their patients to avoid sugar and simple carbohydrates (flour, pasta etc) which convert to glucose shortly after entering the body?

There are many things we can do to reduce our exposure to toxic influences and increase our antioxidant capacity. We will consider these things later as they are relevant to many of our chronic disease conditions, not only cancer. We have to become aware of these things because it is highly unlikely that your doctor will be able to advise you since this sort of information it is not covered in their under graduate or post graduate education.

Interestingly recent research has suggested that the generation of cancer within an organism is an ancient survival mechanism[9] which kicks into place when the organism is faced with dire survival conditions. The cancer cells revert to a more primitive metabolism in order to survive and these cells lose the property of apoptosis, normal cell death, and become immortal, well at least until the organism expires!

Conventional treatments used for cancer

As previously noted, there are only three types of treatment in medicine which have legal status: surgery, chemotherapy and radiation. So legally you can only cut it out, poison it or burn it with radiation. No one would deny the fact that these treatments are severe and the consequences for the body can be dire.

Conventional treatments tend to look at the tumour as being the problem yet the tumour is only the physical manifestation of an underlying issue. Chemotherapy and radiation may shrink the tumour initially which is seen by the doctors as positive progress, understandably.

As we know, tumours consist of a variety of cells including normal cells, most of which may be killed by the treatments. However the tumour stem cells are highly resistant to treatment and may remain despite the tumour shrinking. So although the tumour shrinks any small mass remaining will be composed of highly malignant stem cells. Chemotherapy and radiation are themselves carcinogenic and they also increase the chances of metastases, the shedding of cancerous cells which then relocate in the body and cause further tumours[10]. If you choose to have conventional treatment then choose positively and not because you've been give no other options and feel cornered. Positivity puts you in the correct mind set which will enhance any treatment; remember the placebo effect.

The minimum amount of information I personally would want to know is:

- *How sure are you that the diagnosis is correct?*
- *What does the treatment involve?*
- *What is the absolute success/survival rate?*
- *How long is my life likely to be extended by the treatment? Days, weeks, months, years?*
- *What are the side effects (including death) if any and my chances of experiencing them?*
- *What are my chances if I do nothing?*

- *What is the chance of the treatment causing metastasis? (metastatic cancer has poor prognosis)*
- *What is the chance of recurrence of the cancer?*
- *Will I need to continue with any type of medication after the treatment?*

<u>Cancer screening</u>

One of the main focuses in conventional therapy is screening for early detection, but how effective is this screening. Two of the most common screening procedures are for breast cancer and prostate cancer; two of the most common cancers.

> ***Mammograms are the main thrust of early detection of breast cancer. A report in the New England Journal of Medicine Nov 22nd 2012 concluded that even though breast cancer was being detected earlier due to screening, the number of women presenting with advanced cancer had only reduced by a small amount and suggested a 'substantial over diagnosis' and that screening has had little impact on breast cancer mortality [11].***

Many false positive results mean women are being treated when they don't need to be and many more women are suffering great anxiety because of incorrect diagnosis. The anxiety itself is a health issue because it has a suppressant effect on the immune system; cortisol, produced by the adrenal glands, has this effect. These women will suffer anxiety for a long time after such a diagnosis.

A Cochrane report from June 2013 stated this as one of its conclusions. It also confirmed the fact that screening did not reduce mortality from breast cancer and that over treatment was around 30%.

Many women present with 'lumps' which are diagnosed as cancer and they then undergo medical procedures. For many, these lumps would never develop into cancer. The article also shows that the NNT, or rather the NNS (number needed to screen), to prevent one person dying of breast cancer over a 10 year period is 2000. Read that again; if you subject yourself to breast screening then the chance of you living longer because of an early diagnosis is 1 in 2000. Further more you have a 1 in 200 chance of being over diagnosed and treated unnecessarily[12].

The screening method itself is carcinogenic and will be responsible for a number of breast tumours. The more X-rays you are exposed to the greater the risk. Here's what the National Cancer Institute says:

> ***'Mammograms require very small doses of radiation. The risk of harm from this radiation exposure is extremely low, but <u>repeated x-rays have the potential to cause cancer.</u>'[13]*** (Underline added)

The probability of regular x-rays causing cancer may be very low but why take that risk when the benefits are small? Of course the more x-rays you have the greater the risk.

Many instances of so called breast cancer are known as ductal carcinoma in situ, DCIS. In situ means in place, not migrating and left alone would often stay that way. For more information on the DCIS dilemma see 'The Sea of Uncertainty Surrounding Ductal Carcinoma In Situ—The Price of Screening Mammography' [14] also check out greenmedinfo[15].

Prostate cancer screening is another big area of contention. In a recent (2013) Cochrane review of 5 random controlled trials the following points were made:

> ***'...... Our meta-analysis of all five included studies demonstrated no statistically significant reduction in prostate cancer-specific mortality.....'[16]***

A meta-analysis is where data is drawn from several studies.

In one of the studies the NNS (number needed to screen) over a follow up period of 11 years to prevent one additional death was 1055. That may be an improvement over breast cancer screening but it's still a long shot; isn't it? Like breast cancer there are frequently false positives and over treatment.

It is also necessary to bear in mind that with any biopsy process, where a tissue sample is taken for analysis, if the tissue is malignant (cancerous) then there is a risk that cells are set free into the wider circulation and lead to metastatic growth elsewhere in the body. The prognosis for metastatic cancer is far worse than non metastatic cancer.

Since breast cancer and prostate cancer are two of the most common cancers and we have seen there is a problem of over diagnosis in these two areas. We might ask the question; how does over diagnosis affect the 5 year survival figures? Over diagnosis means it was never cancer in the first place so those people are more likely to 'survive' than someone who has cancer; this will skew the figures giving a more favourable picture.

What treatment alternatives are there ?

If you have cancer and are considering other options then it is important to have a qualified, knowledgeable and experienced practitioner to guide you. Any protocol has to be adhered to and given time. Cancer doesn't suddenly appear in your body, you may suddenly notice a lump but that will have been growing for sometime before it was big enough to be detected.

When we develop any serious condition it is easy to retreat into victim mentality; "what have I done to deserve this?" Taking responsibility for where 'you're at' is probably the most important task to take in hand. Just remember you will, ordinarily, have some time to decide what to do, you don't have to be bullied, no matter how gently, into making a decision about treatment. It's not the diagnosis that's important, it's what you do with it, how you process it. I know for most people this will be easier said than done.

Conventional chemotherapy and radiation treatments have a powerful immune suppressant effect; they knock out the very cells which your body needs to overcome the disorder.

There are many alternative treatments which are directed towards improving overall bodily health and the body's innate healing capacity will do the rest. There are no magic bullets; both effort and dedication are required; even so instances of dramatic recovery have been observed, as in the case of Anita Moorjani[17]. Anita had battled with cancer for several years and then reached crisis point, her story is amazingly interesting and an inspiration to us all, check it out, be inspired!

Dr Charles Majors was diagnosed with multiple brain tumours at age 39. He cured himself and wrote a book 'The Cancer Killers' which you can buy on Amazon.com, ISBN number is 978-1-933936-97-0. He thought he had a healthy lifestyle and was physically fit; he realised he needed to change some things in his life, he did so and his cancer was cured. You can read the protocols he used to cure himself in the book.

One of the first books I ever read on cancer was **'Cancer, why are we still dying to know the truth'** by Phillip Day, ISBN 0-9535012-4-8. In this book he discusses what is known as Metabolic Therapy.

Metabolic therapy

As far as I understand it, metabolic therapy uses a combination of vitamins, minerals, enzymes and healthy diet to bring the body's metabolism back into balance. One of the important ingredients is vitamin B17 (laetrile or amygdalin). Remember we discussed deficiency syndromes earlier on, well what if part of the cancer picture is a deficiency in this vitamin? We used to have much more of this vitamin in our diet in the past and this lack may be a contributing factor in the escalating prevalence of cancer. There was much controversy about this substance when it was first suggested as a cancer treatment, you can read all about it in the book and make up your own mind. I don't need to go into the details about how information from the most respected researcher of the time was distorted and ridiculed. An inexpensive treatment for cancer would cost the industry billions.

Vitamin B17 is an interesting molecule composed of glucose, benzaldehyde and cyanide bonded together. Because of the cyanide content is has been classified as dangerous by the authorities. Of course anything taken in excess can be poisonous and detrimental to health, conventional drugs are a classic example and yet they are not thought of as poisonous, are they? Even drinking too much water can have its problems. There is an enzyme (catalyst) called beta-glucosidase which splits the B17 into benzaldehyde and hydrogen cyanide, both toxic to cells, and glucose. There is an important difference between cancer cells and normal cells; cancer cells have

3000 times more beta-glucosidase than normal cells and are therefore more sensitive to the effects of B17. Interestingly normal cells have an abundance of another enzyme, rhodanese (or rhodanase), which converts the cyanide into thiocyanate which is metabolised through normal processes.

Remember we saw how cancer cells feed off glucose; the glucose part of B17 causes it to be drawn into the cell and acts almost like targeted therapy. There is plenty of information on B17 on the internet[18]; there is also much misinformation. As part of the process of empowerment you have to choose what your own world view and belief system is and also to have the courage to change your belief system if that is appropriate for you.

It is appropriate to repeat that if you choose metabolic therapy you need to find a suitably qualified doctor as the protocol involves much more than just B17. Proteolytic enzymes and other nutrients are an important part of the treatment. The 'Oasis of Hope' in Mexico is an alternative cancer clinic which incorporates metabolic therapy into their protocols, for more information see: http://www.oasisofhope.com/cancer_treatment.php

Many foods contain B17, a little research will reveal them. Apricot seeds and other stone fruit kernels are good sources of B17 and may be good to incorporate into your diet as a preventative[19]. Check the dose and don't overdo it; usually around 10-12 apricot kernels a day was thought by Ernst Krebs to be appropriate. As a word of caution take no more than 5 or 6 at one time/ in an hour.

<u>Gerson therapy</u>

Gerson therapy[20]was developed by Dr Max Gerson, a German born American doctor, in the 1920s. It is still going strong despite the negativity from the conventional system.

The therapy involves an organic plant based diet with lots of vegetable juices and coffee enemas. Vegetable juices have an alkalising effect on the body and also provide vital minerals which are needed for the body and its metabolic processes to function properly.

Coffee enemas have a powerful detoxification effect; substances in the coffee have a stimulating effect on the liver and cause the production of glutathione, one of the body's most powerful antioxidants. Glutathione can really only be made in the cells; if you take glutathione supplements they are broken down and not absorbed well into the cells where it is needed. Selenium is needed in the production of glutathione and many of us are deficient in this mineral. Remember Dr Joel Wallach mentioned earlier and his realisation that much disease is caused by deficiencies?

Check out the Gerson web site for more details: https://gerson.org/gerpress/ .

Homoeopathy

While there is much controversy about homoeopathy in general, there is even greater controversy regarding homoeopathic cancer treatments. As with any type of treatment the patient would like to be guaranteed a reasonable chance of success.

The level of success with homoeopathy is no different to other therapies in that it will depend on the skill and experience of the practitioner. There are many skilled practitioners in the field; it is always prudent to enquire of the practitioner's experience and results. One of my own personal experiences with homoeopathy is that of one of my lecturers who was cured of cancer. I think it was pancreatic cancer, which is particularly difficult to treat.

I attended a series of lectures given by Dr Ramakrishnan, a well known and respected homoeopath who has treated many cancer patients. If the cancer is diagnosed early, and this is the focus of modern diagnostics, then his success rate for some types of cancer is very good. Prostate and breast cancer are the two most common cancers and these respond very well to his treatment if presented early in the disease process. Dr Ramakrishnan's methodology is somewhat different from other homoeopathic protocols and may be the reason for his success rate. This is the opening paragraph from his website.

The treatment of Cancer can be quite successful with Homeopathy, often in conjunction with allopathic medicine in advanced cases. In early stages, particularly with breast and prostate, the success rate is close to 80% with compliance by the patient. Currently we have over 400 active Cancer cases and this number reflects the results we are seeing. Over the last 10 years there have been more than 3,000 Cancer cases that reflect long term follow up of those cured.

Check out his website[21], if you are not impressed with his credentials I would be surprised! He has offices in Chennai, New York, London, Dublin and Singapore. He also does SKYPE consultations.

Anthroposophical Medicine

This system of medicine was introduced by Rudolph Steiner, a philosopher and scientist who wrote books on many subjects related to the 'human experience'. He is responsible for the development of Steiner schools and bio-dynamic farming. Anthoposophy means wisdom of the human being. Anthroposophical medicines are made in a similar way to homoeopathic medicines. Anthroposophical treatment of cancer is offered in clinics throughout the world; it is particularly prevalent in Germany. One of the main medicines used is Iscador , made from mistletoe.

> *"Real medicine can only exist when it penetrates into knowledge which embraces the human being in respect to body, soul and spirit."*
>
> *–Rudolf Steiner*

Burzynski Clinic

Dr Stanislaw Burzynski founded his clinic[22] in 1977. His specialised treatment involves the use of biologically active peptides, which he calls antineoplastons. Treatment is targeted to the individual and up to date he has treated some 8000 people. He has received much persecution from the Texas Medical Board over the years; they have tried on several occasions to have his medical licence revoked. He has constantly fought them in court and was again successful in 2012 when the Board's case against him was dismissed[24].

Please watch this movie made about his work

http://www.youtube.com/watch?v=rBUGVkmmwbk#t=11

He has recently been before the TMB (2017) and again he won his case. One might ask why he is being so persecuted?

Ketogenic diet

If you recall we discussed the dependency of cancer cells on glucose and remember white table sugar is 50% glucose. The ketogenic diet involves the elimination of any food which converts to glucose in the body. The theory is that cancer cells will be starved and die as a result. Professor Thomas Seyfried of Boston College has recently published a book in which the ketogenic diet is investigated. Here is an extract from his academic profile as detailed on the Boston College web site.

> *'Our research program focuses on mechanisms by which metabolic therapy manages chronic diseases such as epilepsy, neurodegenerative lipid storage diseases, and cancer. The metabolic therapies include caloric restriction, fasting, and ketogenic diets......'*

> *'........ In the case of cancer, these therapies target and kill tumour cells while enhancing the physiological health of normal cells.....'*

> *'Experts in the cancer research field have praised this comprehensive study of one of science's hottest topics.'* [24]

<u>Other conventional approaches</u>

There are treatments that I consider are conventional yet for the most part they are generally outside the western medical protocols of surgery, standard chemotherapy and standard radiation therapy.

Photo-dynamic therapy (PDT) is a therapy where light sensitising substances are given and these are taken up by the cancer cells. Light of a particular wavelength is then applied and the reaction in the cancer cells causes cell death. Here is what the American Cancer Society (ACS) says about PDT.

Studies have shown that PDT can work as well as surgery or radiation therapy in treating certain kinds of cancers and pre-cancers. It has some advantages, such as:

- *It has no long-term side effects when used properly.*
- *It is less invasive than surgery.*

- *It usually takes only a short time and is most often done as an outpatient.*
- *It can be targeted very precisely.*
- *Unlike radiation, PDT can be repeated many times at the same site if needed.*
- *There is little or no scarring after the site heals.*
- *It often costs less than other cancer treatments[25]*

Here is what the Next Generation PDT site says:

> **'Next Generation PDT (NGPDT) has developed a uniquely effective Photodynamic Therapy (PDT) for the treatment of most cancers. By building on proven and existing medical research for PDT cancer treatments, Next Generation PDT is successfully treating a wide variety of cancers with minimal invasive procedures, and with greater effect than conventional therapies.'[26]**

Next Generation PDT is based in China.

Finally in this section there is a hospital in China which uses a selection of protocols often with a conventional slant but having far less of the side effect reactions. These are used along with Traditional Chinese Medicine (TCM)[27].

<u>Viral therapy</u>

Viral therapy has its origin in a place called Riga in Latvia and the treatment involves the injection of a virus which targets the cancer cells, it has been very successful.

Cancer cells are very 'clever'; they hide themselves from the immune system. The virus makes them visible to the immune system and once the immune cells can 'see' the cancer cells they can start to remove them; healthy immune system would be an advantage.

This therapy is also available at the Hope4Cancer Institute in Mexico.

★★★★★★★★★★★

Other modalities used in alternative clinics include: hyperbaric oxygen, hyperthermia, ozone therapy, enzyme therapy, sound and light therapy, use of electro-magnetic frequencies and others. Use an internet search to investigate these for yourself.

Cancer Prevention

Prevention of any disease is always a better option than trying to cure it. The body is a self regulating biological structure and is the vehicle of our more subtle energies. When you consider the way we abuse our bodies it is quite amazing that it is able to maintain homoeostasis (normal function). It can only do this up to a point at which time we start to develop symptoms and get sick. Of course there are examples of miraculous cures as in the case of Anita Moorjani mentioned earlier, for most of us however it doesn't happen that way and we have to put in some work. If we can do things in our everyday life to minimise our cancer risk then the work of cure can be largely avoided. Being aware of the potential dangers in our way of life and using an avoidance strategy is an important part of maintaining health.

So what can we do?

1. Eat an organic whole food diet, this implies no processed food. Why?

Organic = no chemicals, no GMO and more nutrients. Whole food = just that, nothing removed. One of the best whole foods is the humble egg! This natural whole food has been much maligned for many years due to the cholesterol misinformation. The tables seem to have reversed now and the egg is being seen as a healthy choice.

2. Remove potential toxic exposure in your personal and domestic environment, see the chapter on toxicity for further information. Why?

Toxins = potential carcinogens; toxins have to be metabolised or stored which increases the load on your homoeostatic (regulating) processes.

3. Make sure your diet has plenty of high quality fat. I don't mean vegetable oils as they are potentially harmful as you will see in the fat chapter. Make sure your omega 6 to omega 3 fat ratio is in balance. Why?

Fat is an essential source of energy which is much, much healthier than refined carbohydrate. See the chapter on sugar for more information.

Fat is needed to build cholesterol, nerve and brain tissue and cell membranes. You may think cholesterol is bad for you but that is just a belief that has been systematically drip fed to us over the last 4 decades. Cholesterol is needed for many things as we will see later. Omega 6 fats although essential are, in excess pro-inflammatory; inflammation is a precursor to many illnesses including cancer.

4. Make sure you have good levels of vitamin D. Why?

Vitamin D is a vital part of the immune system. See chapter on vitamin D and may be an independent factor involved with cancer risk.

5. Sort out your emotions. Why?

Negative emotions are progenitors (causes) of stress which is an immunosuppressant. Positive emotions lead to a sense of well being which is beneficial to health. Suppressed emotions are the worst, the energy is held deep within our energy field and will rise to bite us when we least expect it! If you have emotional 'stuff' from the past then resolving those issues will have a positive effect on your well being.

6. Minimise sugar and refined carbohydrates. Why?

Sugar feeds cancer cells; fructose in sugar (sucrose, table sugar is 50% fructose) has negative metabolic consequences (see later). Excess glucose (the other half of sucrose) leads to insulin resistance and diabetes and this increases cancer risk. Insulin like growth factor is a growth hormone linked to increased cancer risk. Controlling sugar in the blood will help normalise insulin and leptin, this will be discussed later.

7. Exercise your body in an appropriate fashion. Regular walking, swimming, cycling is good. Excessive exercise is not so good. Why?

Moderate exercise stimulates the circulation, strengthens muscles and more importantly reduces insulin resistance. Exercise helps the lymphatic circulation; this is profoundly involved with the removal of toxins from the tissues. Excessive exercise increases oxidative stress in the tissues, producing free radicals which can be tissue damaging. Also lactic acid production due to anaerobic (without oxygen) metabolism in the tissues is not so good.

8. Look after your microbiome. Why?

This is the trillions of bacteria which inhabit your gut and which we are slowly beginning to realise is of vital importance to health. The microbiome is intimately involved with immune function. The bacteria and other organisms have many beneficial roles including the production of certain vitamins e.g. B12

9. Maximise antioxidant intake. Why and how?

Free radicals (ROS = reactive oxygen species) are a natural part of metabolism but they do need to be dealt with as they can damage tissue and DNA. When high levels of antioxidants are available from the diet then there is no problem. Supplements are obviously an option but juicing of high antioxidant nutrients is probably a better and more nutritious way. You get the minerals too which are very important. Any vegetable and fruit that is highly coloured is high in antioxidants. Berries are particularly good. There is plenty of information about juicing for health. Check it out and be aware that excessive fruit juice = excessive sugar. There are many fruits with less than 5% sugar.

10. Eat plenty of organic cruciferous vegetables including broccoli, kale, cabbage and watercress. Why?

A substance in these vegetables, phenethyl isothiocyanate (PEITC), has been shown to be able to repair p53 gene. This gene normally regulates cell death (apoptosis) and if it becomes mutated by a toxin (carcinogen) for example then cells can grow uncontrollably leading to cancer. The good news is that even if cancer has developed then the mutated p53 can be returned to normal with these natural vegetables[28]). Did Gerson know this?

11. Take precautions to limit radio frequency exposures from electronic equipment such as cell phones, computers, Wi-Fi towers, etc. Why?

There is a growing body of information shedding light on the carcinogenic properties of excessive exposure. If it's not a problem then why are there limits of exposure in the small print and why are you told to keep a mobile phone a minimum distance from the body?

12. Incorporate more turmeric into your diet. Why?

Turmeric contains a substance called curcumin has been shown to target cancer stem cells. Turmeric is also a potent anti-oxidant and anti-inflammatory. Curry is also great to eat! [29]

13. Earth yourself by walking on the grass barefoot. Why?

Earthing draws electrons into the body and this has many health benefits. Just Google benefits of earthing for more information.

14. Don't use antiperspirants. Why?

They generally contain aluminium which can be absorbed into the lymphatic glands under the arm and spread to breast tissue and can have carcinogenic potential [30].

15. Ladies, ditch the bra or minimise wearing one. Why?

There is some evidence that there is a connection with wearing a bra and breast cancer. There are plenty of official references to say there is no evidence of this but who is funding the research? You decide[31 & 32]. A bra holds the breast in a restricted position. It is the natural movement which enhances the flow within the lymphatic vessels. This lymph flow is responsible for the removal of toxins from the tissues. Toxic build up = carcinogenic potential. Under wired bras with metal inserts can act as a radio antenna and may concentrate radio frequencies into the tissues of the breast, not good.

16. Avoid MSG (monosodium glutamate), Aspartame and other sources of glutamate. Why?

Glutamate promotes cancer cell proliferation[33].

17. Avoid xeno-oestrogens; these are foreign compounds which mimic oestrogen activity in the body. Why?

Estrogens can be proliferative i.e. they cause cells to multiply. We are exposed to many synthetic compounds which have oestrogen like activity. A full list of products is available at womeninbalance.org

This list is fairly comprehensive but I'm sure it's not exhaustive and as you do your own research you will no doubt come across other things you can incorporate into your life style or find to avoid!

If you are trying to adopt a preventative strategy then you are more likely to achieve success by changing things slowly one step at a time. If you over load the system with changes a strong resistance is likely to be felt! I am speaking from experience.

If you already have cancer then it is more urgent to adopt life style changes.

Endnotes

We have seen that current conventional cancer treatments have had little impact on cancer incidence and death rate over the last 40 years and millions of people have been treated unnecessarily over this time[34].There are alternatives which are systematically berated by the medical authorities even though people are benefitting from these therapies. These therapies tend to be gentle and obey the Hippocratic principle of 'first do no harm'; unlike chemotherapy and radiation.

Only conventional protocols are recognised by many western healthcare systems. We have seen how ineffective chemotherapy is and that is why 75% of doctors would refuse to use it on themselves[35]).

We know that radiation therapy can make tumours more resistant to treatment and hence more malignant[36]); cell survival is the basic driving force of all life.

Why are there are no choices for patients? The argument is that they are un-proven; the proof comes from talking to the patients as Dr Burzynski did when he called them to testify at his trial. The proof is the many patients successfully treated. Sure there are no double blind clinical trials for these alternatives but success of these alternatives cannot be denied. To me the proof of the treatment is that it still exists. Because it is illegal to advertise alternative treatments for cancer the availability is passed on by word of mouth from cured patients. The internet has only been accessible to the masses since the IT revolution of recent years. Some of these therapies have been around best part of a century. If there were no cured patients surely the treatments would have gone by the wayside much the same as bloodletting and leeches, although leeches are making a comeback[37]. Remember that conventional treatments just play the numbers game and as you've seen from previous chapters many people have to be treated to benefit a few. If chemotherapy and radiation treatments are statistically shown to be better that placebo then the result it is considered valid despite the small numbers that benefit. We do not know the result of doing nothing as that is not considered an option in cancer therapy trials; it is deemed to be unethical to deny a treatment.

The best 'treatment' for any life threatening disease is of course not to get it in the first place. Our diets, lifestyles and environments are of prime importance if we are to avoid becoming one of the ever increasing numbers of people succumbing to these conditions.

When searching for information on the internet you will often come across sites which try to smear alternative treatments. I am sure that there are professional smear practitioners paid for by the industry because of the potential threat to their profits. Propaganda has always had its place in swaying public opinion. By being aware of different approaches and coming into contact with people who have been cured by these methods you become empowered and can choose whether to believe the propaganda or not.

<u>Finally I will repeat that if you are considering an alternative approach to treatment it is imperative to do your research and find a suitably qualified, knowledgeable and experienced practitioner. None of the information given here is intended as a substitute for good medical advice, it is merely for educational purposes so that you can be better informed and question treatments before you agree to them or not.</u>

Most people only seek out alternative treatments when the conventional treatment has failed. This puts an inordinate burden on the alternative therapy since the patient will present in a weakened, demoralised and immune compromised state, none of which are conducive to recovery. Even so success is still possible; while there is breath in the body there is always hope.

References

1. https://www.ncbi.nlm.nih.gov/pubmed/10865276

2. http://onlinelibrary.wiley.com/doi/10.3322/canjclin.21.1.13/pdf

3. http://wonder.cdc.gov/cancer.html

4. http://www.telegraph.co.uk/news/health/10069585/15000-people-die-every-year-because-of-cancer-treatments-Lord-Saatchi-says.html

5. http://www.clinicaloncologyonline.net/article/S0936-6555%2804%2900222-5/abstract

6. http://www.ncbi.nlm.nih.gov/pubmed/1506607

7. http://www.greenmedinfo.com/blog/defective-genes-cause-less-1-all-disease

8. http://www.greenmedinfo.com/blog/research-reveals-how-sugar-causes-cancer

9. http://www.greenmedinfo.com/blog/cancer-ancient-survival-program-unmasked

10. http://www.greenmedinfo.com/blog/chemo-and-radiation-actually-make-cancer-more-malignant

11. http://www.nejm.org/doi/full/10.1056/NEJMoa1206809

12. http://www.cochrane.org/CD001877/BREASTCA_screening-for-breast-cancer-with-mammography

13. http://www.cancer.gov/cancertopics/factsheet/detection/mammograms

14. http://jnci.oxfordjournals.org/content/100/4/228.long

15. http://www.greenmedinfo.com/disease/breast-cancer-ductal-carcinoma-situ

16. http://onlinelibrary.wiley.com/doi/10.1002/14651858.CD004720.pub3/abstract;jsessionid=80DD9A666030D1204C5E8A2AB53EADB7.f01t02

17. http://anitamoorjani.com/

18. http://cancercure.ws/nitriloside.htm

19. http://www.livestrong.com/article/85705-foods-rich-vitamin-b17/

20. http://gerson.org/gerpress/the-gerson-therapy/

21. http://www.drramakrishnan.com/cancer.php

22. http://www.burzynskiclinic.com/

23. http://articles.mercola.com/sites/articles/archive/2013/01/19/cancer-doctor-burzynski.aspx

24. http://www.bc.edu/schools/cas/biology/facadmin/seyfried.html

25. http://www.cancer.org/treatment/treatmentsandsideeffects/treatmenttypes/photodynamic-therapy

26. http://www.nextgenerationpdt.com/

27. http://www.moderncancerhospital.com/cancer-treatments/

28. http://www.naturalnews.com/026138_cancer_p53_natural.html

29. http://www.greenmedinfo.com/blog/turmeric-extract-strikes-root-cause-cancer-malignancy?utm_source=www.GreenMedInfo.com&utm_campaign=c790852e24-Greenmedinfo&utm_medium=email&utm_term=0_193c8492fb-c790852e24-86805633

30. http://www.ncbi.nlm.nih.gov/pubmed/16045991

31. http://www.greenmedinfo.com/blog/ladies-ditch-bra-1

32. http://www.greenmedinfo.com/blog/cover-continues-new-study-claims-bra-cancer-link-myth

33. http://cancerdiscovery.aacrjournals.org/content/3/5/OF20.full

34. http://www.greenmedinfo.com/blog/millions-wrongly-treated-cancer-national-cancer-institute-panel-confirms

35. http://www.curenaturalicancro.com/en/75-percent-of-the-physicians-refuses-chemotherapy-themselves

36. http://onlinelibrary.wiley.com/doi/10.1002/cncr.27701/full

37. http://www.dailymail.co.uk/health/article-130983/Why-maggots-leeches-good-health.html

Chapter 7 – DIABETES, THE SWEET TRUTH

When I studied at university diabetes was classified into two distinct types, Type I was called juvenile onset as it occurred almost exclusively in the young. Type II was called maturity onset because it developed in older people, usually much older. Juvenile onset diabetes was usually insulin dependent as a result of damage to the insulin producing cells of the pancreas; the treatment was to give insulin injections which were life saving indeed.

The distinction between these two classifications is nowadays somewhat blurred since type II diabetes, what was maturity onset, is now occurring in young people, sometimes very young. Because of this blurring of what was generally a well demarcated classification two new descriptions have been introduced: Insulin Dependent Diabetes Mellitus (IDDM) for Type I diabetes and Non Insulin Dependent Diabetes Mellitus (NIDDM) for Type II diabetes. In Type II diabetes insulin is often given as well as medication; again the treatments for the two different scenarios is blurring. Recent research has proposed that Alzheimer's disease be called Type III diabetes because blood sugar issues are implicated in the aetiology.

Diabetes, NIDDM, has been occurring in younger and younger people for some years now. Information from the World Health Organisation shows that in 2013, 347 million people worldwide had diabetes. In 2004, 3.4 million people died from the consequences of high blood sugar[1]. According to the WHO 250,000 to 500,000 people die each year from the flu[2]. Whether we accept that figure as truthful may debatable if you care research the subject; many 'flu' deaths are due to pneumonia and other respiratory conditions but tend to be grouped together. However, if we take the WHO figures as factual, even at the higher level of half a million it is only about 15% of the deaths from diabetes.

The word pandemic is usually used in relation to infectious diseases but surely that aside we really have a pandemic on our hands and it's getting worse. The advertising which goes into "getting your flu shot' is huge compared with education on diabetes prevention and reversal yet the costs of diabetes far outweigh that of flu. The only people apparently benefitting from this situation are the drug companies, their shareholders and the medical professionals associated with the supply and distribution; diabetes, like all other major illnesses is big business. In 2014 total drug sales are expected to reach 1.1 trillion dollars[3]. By 2017 diabetes drugs alone will top $55 billion[4].

Why has diabetes become so common?

When the word diabetes is used it is generally referring to NIDDM, formerly Type II. In the early 1900s up to 1940 diabetes was very, very rare. After 1940 its prevalence began increase and by 1960 about 1% of the population of the U.S. had diabetes. Since then the numbers have been roughly doubling every 20 years. By 2000 it had reached 4% and by 2020 it will be around 8% if the trend continues[5]. What was happening post 1940 to result in this rapid rise in diabetes? One factor in the equation is that millions of chemicals have been manufactured since 1940 and of these around 80,000 are widely used. Our exposure to these chemicals is having a profound effect on our health and well being. Let's remember human biochemistry has developed over millions of years; it is highly complex and is indeed a miracle of nature. We are being continually exposed to these synthetic chemicals, chemicals that are not found in nature and which are foreign to our bodily biochemistry. Detoxification and removal of these compounds uses up our vitality and resources and indeed some can't be easily removed and so they are stored in our organs and tissues where they become problematical over many years; the effects are insidious and build up gradually. This exposure, together with the deterioration in our food quality, is likely to be a major contributor to ill health, including diabetes. Large numbers of people now suffer with diabetes and it is one of the most common causes of poor health and chronic disease; it is a precursor for the major diseases afflicting the western world, cardiovascular disease and cancer.

Children being born today, grow up to accept so many things as part of 'normal' everyday life. Generally speaking they are probably not aware of the hidden dangers in modern life and don't question their exposure to a toxic environment, their exposure to high levels of electromagnetic radiation, the poor quality of our water supplies, poor air quality, chemicals in processed foods, lack of nutrients in the food, toxic exposure, drug side effects and so on. How many adults even consider these issues?

If you take the time to sit back and ponder over the changes that have occurred in the last 70 years and the increase in chronic disease prevalence over that time, you may well conclude that there is an association.

So, what are we doing now that we didn't do in 1940?

1. We are eating:-

- *Far more sugar and refined carbohydrates, fruit juices and high fructose corn syrup.*
- *Less butter and animal fats (saturated fats) and more vegetable oils high in omega 6 fats (unsaturated fats). Excessive omega 6 causes inflammation.*
- *More processed foods, which are laden with chemicals to improve shelf life and palatability and which also may contain trans-fats.*
- *Fewer whole foods directly from our own gardens or locally grown.*
- *Foods which have high levels of insecticides, herbicides and other residues.*
- *Artificial sweeteners particularly Aspartame and its derivatives.*
- *More grains than before.*
- *Genetically modified foods with unknown long term effects in humans.*

2. We are:

- *Exercising less because we have more sedentary lifestyles.*

We use cars and other forms of transport even for short journeys (I used to walk several miles to and from school).

We sit in front of computers and TV screens for hours a day.

We are generally involved with less physical work generally.

- *Taking prescription drugs which have an effect on blood sugar and fats, for example*

Statins, Corticosteroids, Psychiatric medications, Blood pressure medications

For a comprehensive list see this link;
http://www.nps.org.au/conditions/hormones-metabolism-and-nutritional-problems/diabetes-type-2/for-individuals/medicines-and-treatments/medicines-that-affect-blood-glucose-levels .

- *Reducing our exposure to sunshine because of the fear instilled into us by the suntan/pharmaceutical industry that the sun causes cancer. See later on for more information about sun exposure and vitamin D.*

What exactly is diabetes?

Most people would probably be aware that diabetes is about too much sugar (glucose) in the blood and that they may need insulin or some other medication to control it.

This is essentially the situation; however in NIDDM (Type II diabetes) the reason the blood sugar (glucose) is not being controlled is multi-factorial and not just because we are not making enough insulin or that we have become insensitive to its actions. These effects are the end stage manifestation of the problem. The insulin model does serve the pharmaceutical companies since they can manufacture insulin very easily these days and also create drugs which will reduce blood sugar.

Generally, as mentioned previously, insulin used to be given only to Type I diabetics because indeed their pancreas was not producing insulin and of course this leads to a rise in blood sugar which is fatal if not corrected. By far the majority of diabetics are Type II and these are treated with diet and medication and often nowadays this is augmented with insulin injections because the drugs are not enough to balance blood sugar levels. Back in 1974 very little insulin was prescribed because Type I diabetes was rare. Now busy pharmacies need a large fridge to store the insulin which is being prescribed to Type II diabetics.

The way oral anti-diabetic drugs work is to stimulate insulin secretion from the pancreas, increase insulin sensitivity of the cells or affect glucose absorption or liver production of glucose.

The general perception is that the primary role of insulin is to control blood glucose. Not so, the control of blood glucose is secondary to insulin's main role as a storage hormone. Back in the days when food was scarce we needed to eat when food was available and store as much as we could (as fat) for when times were lean. Insulin's primary role is to change glucose into fat and in doing so the blood glucose levels fall. I repeat, the primary role of insulin is to change glucose into fat. This means that when glucose stores are full, and for most people that is an almost constant norm, any excess carbohydrate = glucose, is turned to fat and stored for a rainy day.

Just a point to note here is that glucose and what is normally termed sugar are not the same. Sugar is sucrose and is made of 50% glucose and 50% fructose. Many people, including medical professionals, use the word sugar when they actually mean glucose. The significance of this will be discussed later.

The more carbohydrate we eat, and all carbohydrate converts to glucose, the more insulin we produce, the more glucose is turned to fat and the more readily we put on weight ready for those lean times which of course never come because we have a continual supply of food from the supermarket. This continual stimulation of insulin secretion eventually leads to pancreatic exhaustion and/or a reduction in sensitivity of the cells to insulin and so more glucose remains in the blood. This rarely happened in earlier generations because refined foods were not available; we were eating whole foods, high in fibre and low glycaemic index. We also had more active lifestyles and burned more calories in our work. Exercise in whatever form improves insulin resistance and is why it is recommended; although some types of exercise are more effective than others and excessive exercise can be an issue for other reasons.

More recent research has uncovered the role of other hormones involved in the control of appetite. Appetite obviously affects food consumption and hence glucose levels. Leptin is known as the satiety hormone, the name is derived from the Greek word for thin (leptos). Leptin is mostly made by fat cells and travels in the blood stream to the brain where the signal is 'I've eaten enough' and so we stop eating. Leptin also increases energy expenditure.

Fructose is a major player in controlling appetite. Excessive fructose consumption eventually causes leptin resistance which is similar to insulin resistance and the cells in the brain which normally tell us we've eaten enough are switched off. So what happens? You got it! We eat more.

Remember that white table sugar, sucrose, is 50 % fructose.

Fructose and sucrose are in so many prepared foods and beverages and consuming these types of foods actually encourages us to eat more because we don't get the 'full' signal. This is great for the food industry profits but not so good for your waistline or blood sugar control.

Fructose is mostly metabolised by the liver and produces the very worst type of fat, very low density lipoprotein (VLDL). We'll discuss more about lipoproteins when we look at cardiovascular disease.

You may be asking yourself, why do we use sucrose and high fructose corn syrup (HFCS) in our food instead of glucose? The answer is because it is sweeter than glucose and the food industry exploits our desire for sweetness. Indeed sugar is highly addictive, even more than cocaine[6]!

Food science has become big business. One of the main goals is to fool us into thinking that certain foods taste good and that are healthy for us. We have had low fat paranoia for many years now. Fat makes food tasty so how does the food industry get around the problem of tasteless food? Answer – it increases the amount of sugar and salt, or should I say sodium chloride. Anybody familiar with cooking knows that sugar and salt complement each other. We will look at the difference between salt and sodium chloride later.

Appetite and control of eating is much more complex than the picture I've painted and anyone interested can read more about it here (7). Fructose however is one of the main players in our battle against obesity, diabetes, heart disease, hypertension etc.

Is fat an issue?
People are constantly bombarded with the idea that saturated fat is bad for them and poly-unsaturated oils are good. High fat is bad and low fat is good. Let's look at some of the information available and then you can make up your own mind and do your own risk / benefit analysis.

Firstly where did the idea that saturated fat was bad for us come from? In 1953 a guy called Ancel Keys, a professor at Minnesota University, published his 6 country study which clearly showed a correlation between heart disease and fat intake. It is to be noted however that he had data for 22 countries and could have easily shown the opposite correlation if he had picked 6 different countries!

It has been pointed out by Professor Robert Lustig of California University that Ancel Keys did not take into account the amount of sugar in the diet which as we have previously learned is metabolised in the body into the worst kind of fat. Ancel Keys' research is clearly flawed and yet it is the basis on which 60 years of dietary advice has been built. We will revisit the 'fat issue' when we look at heart disease which is the area in which low fat advice is heavily focused.

Can we lower our risk for developing diabetes?

Most definitely and the simple answer is a change in diet and lifestyle and elimination of toxicity from your life. This preventative strategy applies to many of the chronic illnesses we are dealing with as a culture. Like many things this is easier said than done but not impossible to achieve.

Food habits and addictions are difficult to overcome; be in no doubt we are addicted. If you start simply and do one change at a time you will be able to incorporate lasting changes into your food habits and life style. You will notice the benefits as your cravings decline and your health and vitality improve. The following are recommendation based on what I've read. Do your own research, become your own expert. Many people around the world are waking up and changing the way they live. See the film 'Fat, Sick and Nearly Dead' - http://www.fatsickandnearlydead.com/ .

If you are Type II diabetic and currently taking medication then it would be a great advantage to find a medical practitioner who is knowledgeable about food related issues and how diet and toxicity can influence your metabolic burden. If you are on medication then you do need guidance and support to monitor the changes in your blood sugar control as you alter your life style and hopefully get off the drugs.

The following is a list of ideas which may help you to achieve better health.

1. Simply eliminating all refined sugar (sucrose) and fructose (sodas etc) from your diet is likely to be immediately beneficial. Remember fruit juices are high in fructose and have the fibre removed. Whole fruit is better than fruit juice. Some fruits release sugars faster than others do your research.

2. If you remove refined and processed foods from your diet you will reduce the amount of hidden sugar and salt you are eating. These foods also contain preservatives, flavour enhancers and many other chemicals which may be a burden to your metabolism. Any food which comes in a box is likely to fall into this category.

3. Artificial sweeteners are definitely not a healthy choice and consuming these can lead to weight gain and other toxic reactions[8 & 9]. If you need to use a sweetener then stevia is a natural option. You may not like the flavour initially but stick with it you will get used to it. I used to have two spoons of sugar in my tea/coffee and when I stopped it was awful for a couple of weeks, then I got used to it and now I don't like any sugar in my tea or coffee as the sweetness tastes awful. This just goes to show how your preferences can change with a little perseverance.

4. Investing in a good quality juicer and making green juices will have powerful health benefits. Green juices are predominantly made from vegetables; you can put a lot of nutrients into your body this way and achieve better health. Watch the movie 'Fat, sick and nearly dead'[10].

5. Eat organic food if you can afford it. It is becoming much more sort after now and often prices of organic vegetables are not dissimilar to supermarket prices. The next best thing is to buy an ozonator which can be use to decontaminate your food and water and as an air freshener. Ozone combines with highly toxic pesticide and herbicide residues and neutralises them[11 & 12]. As a word of caution if you do get an ozone generator do not use it in a confined space ,open the windows; the ozone is not intended to be inhaled in large quantities.

6. Exercise is important for reducing insulin resistance and obviously improving general health and well being. It is important not to overdo it. Excessive strenuous exercise can create an excess of free radicals. These are tissue destroying, highly reactive molecules. Simple regular walking and swimming are both excellent forms of regular exercise. In the days when most of us were thin and diabetes free, there were no gyms or exercise programs to join. We maintained our health with good nutrition and work/school related exercise.

7. A good immune system health is vital to overall health. Ask yourself, where is my immune system? You may come up with maybe, in my blood or certain organs or even if you're knowledgeable, in my lymphatic system. All of these are partially correct. The biggest area and concentration of immune functioning cells is actually in your gut[13]. You can deduce from this that the health of your intestinal system is highly significant. This subject will be addressed later in the book.

8. Vitamin D status is implicated in many disease conditions including diabetes so it is important to make sure your levels are adequate. Again this will be elaborated on later.

9. If you are taking prescription medicines then get them checked out for potential side effects, weigh up the pros and cons and make an informed choice about the benefits or risks. If you decide to reduce you medications then do it with guidance from an appropriately qualified person.

End notes

The high incidence of diabetes is most definitely a modern diet and lifestyle related phenomenon; 100 years ago death from diabetes was rare, in 1998 in America it was the 7th leading cause of death. This may well be under reported and is therefore a conservative figure. Higher ranked death risks such as cancer and heart disease can, in many cases, be attributable to diabetic aetiology[14 & 15].

In the U.S. in 2012 around 29 million people had diabetes and 86 million had what is called pre-diabetes, which means that unless they change their lifestyle they will more than likely develop diabetes and need medication. In the western world the probability of developing a diabetic state is roughly around 1 in 3.

Diabetes has many associated complications [16].

- High blood pressure (hypertension).
- Imbalance in fat metabolism (dyslipideamia).
- Low and high blood sugar crises (hypo/hyperglycaemia).
- Increased risk of heart attack and cardiovascular disease/death.
- Increase risk of stroke.
- Problems with blood microcirculation leading to kidney and eye problems.
- Amputations due to poor circulation causing gangrene.
- Increased risk of cancer.

If this list is not enough to make you want to avoid this situation then I don't know what will. Medications will only ever address the symptoms of the disease which may delay progression it will not address the cause of Type II diabetes which is related to the things we've discussed. The ball is squarely in your court when it comes to diet and lifestyle changes. Diabetes has massive economic consequences both for governments and individuals. Why spend your money on doctor's fees and drugs when you can spend it on improving your lifestyle and quality of food.

References

1. http://www.who.int/mediacentre/factsheets/fs312/en/

2. http://www.who.int/mediacentre/factsheets/fs211/en/

3. http://www.reuters.com/article/2010/04/20/us-pharmaceuticals-forecast-idUSTRE63J35O20100420

4. https://www.visiongain.com/Press_Release/405/Diabetes-drugs-market-will-reach-55-3bn-in-2017-with-further-growth-to-2023-predicts-visiongain-in-new-report

5. http://www.ncbi.nlm.nih.gov/pubmed/21709279

6. http://www.nydailynews.com/life-style/health/white-poison-danger-sugar-beat-article-1.1605232

7. http://themedicalbiochemistrypage.org/gut-brain.php

8. http://articles.mercola.com/sites/articles/archive/2012/08/09/artificial-sweeteners-worse-than-sugar.aspx

9. http://www.holisticmed.com/aspartame/

10. http://www.fatsickandnearlydead.com/

11. http://www.oocities.org/wasim166/ozone.htm

12. https://www.air-zone.com/water-ozone-generators/

13. http://www.ncbi.nlm.nih.gov/pmc/articles/PMC2515351/

14. https://webappa.cdc.gov/sasweb/ncipc/leadcaus9.html

15. http://www.heart.org/HEARTORG/Conditions/Diabetes/WhyDiabetesMatters/Cardiovascular-Disease-Diabetes_UCM_313865_Article.jsp

16. http://www.diabetes.co.uk/diabetes-complications/diabetes-and-cancer.html

Chapter 8 - TOXIC SHOCK - ENVIRONMENTAL DISASTER?

A toxic substance is essentially a poison. A poison as we all know may make you ill or cause your death. Most toxic exposure is a little more subtle in that the effects are often slow and insidious, they build up over time and we don't generally notice a reaction until we start experiencing unexplained symptoms.

When I use the word environment in the title, I am referring to the environment within which we live and the environment within our bodies. Both are equally vulnerable to toxic exposure. We have more synthetic chemical exposure than at any other time in our history. We are subjected to ever increasing levels of ionising and non-ionising radiation. Our food, water supply and the air we breathe is polluted with industrial waste, agrochemicals, pharmaceuticals, radio isotopes and heavy metals.

Nowadays children are rarely born in a pristine state; devoid of toxic compounds in their bodies[1]. So their immature detoxification systems are already challenged at birth. As they go through life they are subjected to an almost daily barrage of substances which will ultimately have an impact on health, they start to show disease symptoms and of course these symptoms are somewhat of a nuisance and so drugs are prescribed to suppress those symptoms. The cause is rarely addressed or even acknowledged. So what are these toxins we are exposed to throughout life?

Vaccines

Vaccines are probably the first toxins we are exposed to when we come into this world. The following is a list of vaccines given to children in the United States. A similar list of vaccines is evident in most western cultures, U.K., Europe, Australia and New Zealand; the recommended schedules may be different. Vaccination starts at birth and continues through 18 to old age; a customer for life!

If Only You Knew

<u>Age in MONTHS</u>

	0	2	4	6	12	15	18
Hep B	*	*			*		
RV		*	*	*			
DTaP		***	***	***			***
Hib		*	*	*		*	
PCV		*	*	*		*	
IPV		*	*			*	
Influenza					*		
MMR					***		
Varicella					*		
Hep A					*		
Men							
HPV							
	1	8	7	6	7	3	3

<u>Age in YEARS</u>

	2-3	4-6	7-10	11-12	13-15	16	17-18
Hep B							
RV							
DTaP		***		***			
Hib							
PCV							
IPV		*					
Influenza	**	***	****	**	***	*	**
MMR		***					
Varicella		*					
Hep A							
Men				*		*	
HPV				**			
	2	11	4	7	3	2	2

Key : **Hep B** = hepatitis B; **RV** = rotavirus; **DTaP** = diphtheria, tetanus and Pertussis; **Hib** = Haemophilus influenza B; **PCV** = pneumococcal conjugate vaccine; **IPV** = inactivated polio vaccine; **MMR** = measles, mumps and rubella; **Hep A** = hepatitis A; **Men** = meningococcal; **HPV** = human papilloma virus. (* = number of vaccines)

Total number of individual vaccine doses given by age 6 years = 48[2].

(You might be interested to note that the Centre for Disease Control (CDC) holds 20 or so vaccine patents; is that a conflict of interest?)

So 48 doses of 14 types of vaccine will be given to the average child by the time they are 6 years of age. That's a massive amount of immunogenic material (i.e. causes the body to produce antibodies) not to mention all the other ingredients in vaccines.

Other vaccine ingredients

- *Formaldehyde – this is a preservative used in embalming fluid.*
- *Monkey cell cultures – vaccine will be contaminated with monkey tissue*
- *Cow cell culture - vaccine will be contaminated with bovine tissue.*
- *Human cell cultures. (Is this cannibalism?)*
- *Egg proteins – Inclusion of these can result in food allergies.*
- *Aluminum (Aluminium) – an adjuvant which is included to stimulate an enhanced antibody response. Unfortunately Aluminum is a potent neurotoxin and can cause nerve and brain damage.*
- *MSG – an exitoxin.*
- *Mercury - thimerosal (thiomersal) (meningococcal and influenza multi-dose vials); Mercury is a known neurotoxin.*
- *Antibiotics.*
- *Polysorbate 80 (Tween 80) Detergent; Aluminum binds to this and the detergent aluminum complex can pass the blood brain barrier and enter the brain leading to adverse effects.*

These are some of the more disagreeable vaccine additives, for a full list see reference[3].

At the age when all these vaccines are given the immune system has not yet matured, it is still developing in response to natural challenges which is how it has been since man has been on the planet. The immune system probably does not reach maturity until puberty; it may be earlier but certainly not by 6 years old.

We may think we know an awful lot about how the immune system functions but there is much more that we don't know. We are only just beginning to realise the complex interactions between the immune system and the nervous system. A branch of research known as psycho-neuro-immunology is in its infancy.

When research is done into the safety of vaccines then it is short term, looking for acute effects. We do not know the long term effects of over-stimulating an immature immune system. We do know that there has been a massive increase in immune related pathologies over the last few decades.

In the US figures for 2012 show 9.3% of children have asthma[4] and around 10% of children have eczema[5]. Brain disorders in children are on the increase, we have ADHD (attention deficit hyperactive disorder), ADD (attention deficit disorder) and autism. All these conditions were relatively rare a few decades ago. There may well be other factors involved as vaccines are only one of many toxic, immune altering assaults being endured by the current world population.

Do vaccines cause damage? Most definitely they do, otherwise why is there a vaccine damage compensation fund[6]? From 1989 - 2013, $2,500,000,000 ($2.5 billion) had been paid out to victims of vaccine damage[7]. Each vaccine that is bought has a levy which goes into the vaccine damage fund.

Whether vaccines work or not is another story and references have been given in earlier chapters for the keen reader to pursue. The relevance here is that a massive amount of immunogenic material (something that promotes a reaction from the immune system) is injected under the skin and thence directly into the blood stream along with all the other ingredients listed above. Under normal circumstances disease causing entities only enter the body through the mouth or lungs and more rarely through a breach of the skin

When a person is exposed to a naturally occurring disease the antigenic response occurs to that disease alone and the immune system has time to react and develop immunity and this is true lifelong immunity. I personally had experienced many of the so called childhood diseases: measles, rubella, scarlet fever, chicken pox. I now have natural immunity. Vaccination does not confer lifelong immunity, this is the reason why so many doses are needed and probably why older people are now getting childhood diseases as the vaccine effects wear off. The answer from the medical perspective is to give more doses over longer periods of time. Where will it end?

In summary, vaccines contain many potentially toxic components and although these ingredients may be within accepted safety limits for an individual vaccine (and you have to think to yourself, 'is any level of toxic material safe?'), the combined level of toxins from all these vaccines must represent a substantial risk to the individual.

There is mounting evidence that when the immune system goes into overdrive, due to hyper-stimulation from all these vaccines, circulating immune complexes produced can attach to normal tissue and then our immune system identifies this as 'non-self' and starts to attack and destroy it[8].

Whether you agree or disagree with the philosophy of vaccination, it cannot be denied that multiple antigen exposure is not usual in nature. This presents a gross over stimulation of an immature immune system. Multiple vaccinations expose an individual to high levels of chemical toxins and other antigenic material of animal origin injected directly into the body bypassing the normal defence mechanisms. There are no long term safety studies which categorically show that vaccines are indeed safe.

In the modern western medical systems the average child, by age 6, has had all this material injected into them and then there are other vaccines throughout life depending on circumstances, HPV, tetanus, small pox, yellow fever, typhoid, anthrax, Lyme disease, polio, rabies, TB, shingles, and others in the pipeline. Is it any wonder our immune system is confused? The scientists say it is O.K. to inject all this material; what does your common sense say? How many times has science given the all clear only to retract it later on? Is this scientific experimentation with our children any different to what happened in the concentration camps of WWII?

Heavy metals

Aluminium is one of the first heavy metal exposures in childhood in the form of vaccine adjuvants mentioned above. Later on the use of cosmetic products is very common, certainly in Western society, and one of the most widely used products is an antiperspirant. Many of these produced by the big manufacturers contain aluminium; aluminium blocks the sweat ducts through which normal perspiration takes place. Around the armpit there are lymph nodes (part of the immune system) into which some of this aluminium is absorbed and this can then enter the tissues of the area, the most notable of which is breast tissue[9].

Another source of aluminium exposure is cookware. When used over many years there is a slow leeching of aluminium into your food and especially if you use sodium bicarbonate in your greens. This used to be common when I was young. Sodium bicarbonate is alkaline and will enhance aluminium extraction from the cookware.

Aluminium exposure is linked to Alzheimer's disease[10] and possibly other brain disorders such as autism[11].

The build up and effects of aluminium are slow and insidious. A wise person would probably go out of their way to minimise exposure.

Mercury exposure for most people is from some vaccines and dental amalgam in your mouth. More and more countries are banning the use of mercury in fillings yet there are still many dentists out there who think it is safe. The U.N. has recently ratified a treaty that requires the reduction and phasing out of mercury amalgam due to the toxic effect on the environment. What about the toxic effect on your brain and other organs. Dental amalgams are around 50% mercury mixed with mainly silver, hence silver fillings. Once in place they leak mercury which can be readily shown[12].

This is an extract from the CDC (centre for disease control-US) website:

"Inhalational exposure is the most typical route of elemental mercury toxicity. Acute toxicity might result in fever, fatigue, and clinical signs of pneumonitis. Chronic exposure results in neurologic (nerve, brain), dermatologic (skin), and renal (kidney) manifestations. Signs and symptoms might include neuropsychiatric disturbances (e.g., memory loss, irritability, or depression), tremor, paresthaesias (disturbance in sensation such as tingling), gingivostomatitis (inflammation of gums and mouth area, flushing, discolouration and desquamation (peeling of skin) of the hands and feet, and hypertension (high blood pressure)[13]."

(I have added the bracketed information for clarification.)

It is unlikely you will get acute exposure to mercury unless you are involved in an industry which uses mercury, remember the mad hatters of the 17th century. The chance of chronic exposure is however a real possibility if you have amalgam fillings.

If you are considering having amalgam removed from your mouth it is important to find a biological dentist who will use the correct protocols for removal. They should be removed in order of highest electrical current first to lowest last and a rubber dam used to stop any mercury being swallowed. For more information on safe removal of mercury amalgams check the reference[14].

Another source of mercury exposure is in our diet, believe it or not; a major source is seafood, particularly oily fish like tuna. The Natural Resource Defence Council has a very comprehensive list of mercury levels in fish[15]. Be careful with fluorescent light fittings and some low energy bulbs as they contain mercury and if broken may cause un-necessary exposure.

There is little doubt that mercury is most definitely toxic; minimising exposure would be a prudent choice in order to avoid associated health issues. If you want to read more about how mercury exerts its toxicity then check the reference[16].

Lead poisoning is not common but something to be aware of[17]. Lead is found in old paint and so decorating in older houses might be an issue if you're burning off paint. Also older toys may have lead paint on them, particularly important for young children who are more vulnerable to lead poisoning. Old pipe work can be made of lead and so could be a source of potential contamination to your water supply. Art supplies may contain lead in the pigments and other potentially harmful metals like cadmium.

Lead is highly toxic with effects generally building up over time; continual exposure to low levels, of which you might not be aware, may be an issue. For more information refer to the reference previously given.

Cadmium[18] **and Arsenic**[19] are two other elements which may pose an occupational hazard although we all probably get some unnecessary exposure.

Sources of Cadmium exposure include:

- Food sources
  - Rice and wheat grown in contaminated soil
  - Large ocean fish concentrate cadmium
  - Refined foods which have protective zinc removed and retain cadmium
  - Canned foods – solder contains cadmium
- Batteries, semiconductors
- Cigarette smoke
- Motor oil and exhaust
- Phosphate fertiliser production

Some common sources of Arsenic exposure

- Agrochemicals – pesticides, herbicides, fungicides
- Drinking water contaminated with the above
- Wood preservatives
- Clay ceramic enamels
- Paints
- Tobacco
- Occupational exposure
  - Smelting industry
  - Electronics industry
  - Coal power plants
  - Glass manufacture
  - Fireworks
  - Agrochemical spraying
  - Wood treatment

These lists are not exhaustive but if you have any of the exposures listed and have unexplained symptoms then check out the references as they give detailed symptoms of toxicity. You may ask yourself: "how do I know if heavy metals are an issue?" If you have known exposure then the situation is somewhat self evident. Hair mineral analysis can give some indication of toxicity[20]. There is some controversy about this methodology but it is non invasive and if any sign of heavy metal does show up then you can have confirmatory blood tests.

It is possible to remove heavy metals from the body by chelation therapy; vitamin C in high doses is particularly important for mercury removal. Check this out for more information on heavy metal detoxification; http://customers.hbci.com/~wenonah/new/9steps.htm

Fluoride and Bromide

The arguments for and against fluoride in our water continue. Whether you are for or against, the idea of mass medication without individual consent is surely a gross infringement of our human rights; is it not?

It is argued that fluoride prevents tooth decay in children and there may be some evidence to support this but why is no one in government making noises about the poor diets and level of nutrition these kids are receiving. The amount of sugar and refined carbohydrates in their diets, the amount of phosphoric acid they consume in cola drinks. Many soda/cola drinks have a pH of around 2.5[21].The pH scale goes from 1 to 14 where 1 = very acid and 14 = very alkaline. Stomach acid is between 1 and 3 this is strong enough to dissolve bone.

Is it possible that soda drinks might be involved with dissolving teeth? What about the sugar in these drinks? The sugar feeds the bacteria which produce acid which dissolves the teeth.

For more interesting facts about phosphoric acid check the reference[22].

Fluoride is a by-product of industrial processes which also contribute to direct contamination of the environment with fluoride[23]. The idea that fluoride might be beneficial arose in the 1940's yet it seems to be ignored that sugar has a huge detrimental impact on tooth health[24]. Rather than giving a toxic substance to supposedly make teeth 'stronger', we should be addressing the cause; sugar and phosphoric acid.

The sugar industry has huge power and political sway and the mountain of industrial chemical fluoride waste has to be disposed of somewhere. Does this have something to do with the situation?

Fluoride was once prescribed as an anti-thyroid drug[25] because fluoride will displace iodide which is important for making thyroid hormone. This may be fine for those few people who have an over active thyroid but for the majority of folks suppression of the thyroid is not a great idea.

Another issue with thyroid under function is bromide which like fluoride displaces iodide. Bromide exposure is becoming more and more prolific, in home furnishings and even in our bread. Iodide used to be added to bread as an improver nowadays potassium bromate (KBrO3) is used. As you can see this molecule has bromine (Br) in it. Bromide like fluoride is an endocrine disruptor and also a known carcinogen[26].

Hypothyroidism (low thyroid function) is now occurring in epidemic proportions. The conventional treatment is to give l-thyroxine which is the synthetic purified form of the thyroid hormone.

Here is a quick rundown on *thyroid hormone*. The thyroid gland produces thyroxine which has 4 atoms of iodine in the molecule (hence the abbreviation T4). This is the least active form of the hormone. T4 is converted to T3 (3 atoms of iodine) which is the most active form of the hormone. This conversion requires selenium (Se). If you are selenium deficient then this reaction will not go well.

I never really understood why T4 is prescribed when T3 is the most active form? I suppose the assumption is that everyone has enough selenium.

When I was first in practice as a pharmacist hypothyroidism was relatively rare and it was usually women who had it. Nowadays it is common for men to have the problem and the numbers have increased significantly. I couldn't find a reference to confirm this it is however my personal experience being in the industry so to speak.

Before thyroxine came on the scene patients were given whole thyroid extract which contained both T3 and T4, which makes sense doesn't it? A growing number of people are now asking for this after doing some research on the subject. In practice it is quite common to have quite high doses of thyroxine because the symptoms are not resolving, if the individual is not converting T4 to T3 this is understandable.

The point is that for optimal thyroid function we need to limit exposure to bromide and fluoride as much as possible and ensure iodine intake is optimal.

We will look at this more in a later chapter.

Agrochemicals

Agrochemicals are chemicals used in agriculture to increase food yields, fertilisers, insecticides, weed killers (herbicides), fungicides, synthetic plant hormones and other growth factors.

The top six companies in 2013 had a turnover of around $42 Billion. That's a large amount of money and I suggest the reason why these companies have so much power and influence over government policies.

Are these substances toxic to the environment and humans? Let's investigate.

Chemical fertilisers are in common use in non-organic agriculture. One of the main ingredients is nitrate and this can be washed out of the soil and into our water supply. If you live in an agricultural area it is always worth getting your water tested. Nitrates are used to condition the meat you see at the butchers or supermarket, they give the meat a nice red colour which presumably makes you think it is good quality.

Nitrates can convert into carcinogenic nitrites and nitrosamines[27] in the gut; they are particularly dangerous to new born infants. If you have high levels of nitrate in your water then a reverse osmosis filter or water distiller will remove it, an ordinary water filter will not. Like most things occasional exposure is not likely to be an issue but if you are constantly bombarding your body with a potentially toxic substance then it may become an issue over time.

Rapid release calcium phosphate (superphosphate) is yet another issue. Excess phosphate in the body can have health consequences[28]. Excess phosphate in the body can be due to metabolic processes but why expose yourself to a potential problem if you can avoid it? Calcium phosphate may have implications in colorectal cancer[29]. Various phosphates are also used in the food industry as food additives, e338, e339, e340, e341, check your labels!

Herbicides and insecticides pose a much greater danger to our health. Glyphosate (roundup) is one of the most ubiquitous substances used in agriculture. The half life of glyphosate in soil is given as 1 to 174 days[30]. So after this time there will be 50% of the amount of glyphosate left in the soil and after double this time there will be 25% left. This may be O.K. if you are just using it as a weed killer but glyphosate is sprayed onto genetically modified crops to control weeds; the crops are resistant to glyphosate. The question we must ask is; do the crops contain any glyphosate residue? The answer is yes, crops do contain glyphosate residue and in 2013 the Environment Protection Agency massively raised the accepted limits[31]. Why were the limits raised? The reason is that the farmers have to use more glyphosate because weeds are becoming resistant, much like bacteria have become resistant to antibiotics[32].

The next question to ask is; **is glyphosate toxic to humans**? The answer, not surprisingly, is also yes[33].

In 2007 around 180 million pounds of glyphosate (double the 2001 figure) along with 350 million pounds of other herbicides were sprayed onto American crops. Obviously a whole lot more was used worldwide on crops and also we have to add non commercial use in our gardens. Most weed killers you buy in the shops are glyphosate based. Years ago, sodium chlorate was the universal weed killer for use on areas where you wanted nothing to grow; it was very effective and cheap, it was then removed from the market because you can make explosives out of it. I wonder if that was the real reason.

Glyphosate in combination with other ingredients such as wetting agents has recently been shown to be much, much more toxic to humans[34]. Glyphosate is found in many waterways[35], it is present in human tissue (if you eat GMOs) and animals fed GMO foods[36]. It accumulates in the body and is present in breast milk being fed to the next generation[37].

I hope you're getting the picture that herbicides are a big problem in relation to human health. We do not know the long term consequences of exposure to these substances. We're told it is safe, by the authorities, those very authorities who accept safety studies from the industries manufacturing the products, *is it corruption*? You decide.

Insecticides come in various guises; the two common categories are organophosphate and carbamate. These substances disrupt nerve transmission in the insects and they die. Unfortunately the very same nerve transmission system, which involves acetylcholine, is present in humans. Sarin gas used in chemical warfare is a similar type of chemical to those used in insecticides.

In 2013 an article in National Geographic tells of an episode where pesticides were blamed for the deaths of 25 children[38].

If you work with insecticides then you will no doubt wear protective clothing, but how many of us use these substances in our gardens and on our vegetables without being fully aware of the potential dangers? If you are exposed to small doses over long periods of time what effects are these substance having on your health without you knowing?

From the EPA:

'The health effects of pesticides depend on the type of pesticide. Some, such as the organophosphates and carbamates, affect the nervous system. Others may irritate the skin or eyes. Some pesticides may be carcinogens. Others may affect the hormone or endocrine system in the body[39]. '

Without labouring the point too much, chemicals used in agriculture, whether commercially or at home, have an element of toxicity which may be detrimental to your health. There are many more chemicals of the ....cide variety, a list is available on the EPA web site, check them out[40].

Is our food toxic?
There are many potentially toxic issues with our food and we will investigate the subject in a later chapter. For now we can answer the question with a profound yes. Some of the food choices people are making are directly related to the level of health or sickness they are experiencing, no doubt.

Is our medical system toxic?
Isn't it interesting that we use the word pharmaceuticals and not medicines. Pharmaceuticals are just synthetic chemicals which we use in our bodies supposedly to make us healthy.

 As we've seen from a previous chapter drugs don't really work that well for most people, even though the adverts we see are very convincing. They don't actually restore health either but merely suppress the symptoms of disease.

The side effects of drugs can be sometimes irritating, sometimes dangerous and sometimes lethal yet most people don't even consider that the little blue, red or green pill they've been given to improve their health status could be potentially deadly.

Various researchers have looked at the number of deaths due to medicine and by medicine I mean all medical interventions not just drugs. Death by medicine is termed iatrogenic and estimates vary depending on whose figures you take but lie somewhere between

780,000 and 1,000,000 per year in the USA[41]. These figures are now well out of date and come from around 1998-2001.

To put that into context, deaths from heart disease in 2010 were 597,689 and from cancer 574,743 so by that reckoning medicine is <u>the</u> leading cause of death[42]. Does that piece of information ever make the news headlines? I wonder why? Who's controlling the media?

These figures don't take into account the number of people harmed by the medical system and who survive only to live their lives in a compromised fashion with a reduced quality of life.

I don't need to say any more, plenty of people before me have said it all. Check out some of the references, be informed and choose wisely before you subject yourself to any medical procedure.

<u>Toxic emotions</u>

Do not underestimate the role of your emotions; negative emotions are a big drain on our vitality. Reduced vitality leads eventually to ill health.

We live in a world where there is constant fear smouldering within our being. We have constant war and strife throughout the planet, natural and some not so natural disasters, financial and family pressures, health concerns, the list goes on....... These all add to our fears about survival, the most basic of our fears.

We often have anger within us: the way we are treated by our friends, family, the government, the justice system, the medical system, again the list goes on......... Occasionally this anger wells up within us and is usually vented on our loved ones or some unsuspecting person who happens to be around, we then feel guilt and remorse.

Many people have a basic lack of self worth. The expression of their individuality is suppressed at school, at home, in the work place. Just conform to how everyone else wants you to be then you'll be happy. Toe the line and do as you're told; how many people are in a job they hate? How many times a day do you have to 'bite your lip'? Suppression of the feelings you experience during these times can exact a harsh toll on your health.

There are more rules and regulations in society now than ever before. There is little privacy, with surveillance technology and internet snooping on our every action.

How does all this make people feel? Most may not be consciously aware that these things affect the subconscious mind and wreak havoc within the immune system.

Instead of being free expressions of our human individuality the majority of us are cajoled into conformity, mediocrity and subservience.

What effect does all this have?

Pent up emotions are expressed through bodily discomfort and disease[44]. Many alternative health modalities recognise this fact but conventional medicine has still to wise up. If negative emotions have a somatic effect (an effect in the body) which leads to health deterioration then they are definitely toxic; don't you agree?

Weather modification programs

You may or may not have heard the word chemtrail, if you haven't then you may be surprised or even shocked to find out that weather modification programs employ aircraft (private and commercial) to spray metal particles at a high altitude which are supposed to have a positive effect on climate dynamics by reflecting solar radiation.

There has been seeding technology using silver nitrate to cause rain for many years. The current spraying programs, termed 'geo-engineering', have been ongoing for some time now and use fine particles of aluminium, barium and other metals along with other substances[44]. These materials will eventually, under the force of gravity, fall to earth where they will contaminate our crops, soil and water and also the very air that we breathe.

Toxicity lurking in our homes

How often do you consider that the products you use in your home could be potentially toxic?

Remember toxicity manifests in two ways. Acute toxicity is hard to miss, you are exposed to something and the body reacts almost immediately. Hair dyes are a good example; they often contain phenylenediamines which can be a problem for some people. Reactions range from localised skin rashes to more generalised allergic reactions and even anaphylactic shock and rarely death[45].

The second, more common type of toxicity is chronic toxicity due to repeated exposure over time. This type of toxicity is insidious and you will be, for the most part, unaware of it. Most household products contain manufactured chemicals.

There are detergents, bleaches, disinfectants, air fresheners, carpet cleaners, fabric cleaners, mould and mildew cleaners, antibacterials, toilet cleaners and fresheners, insect sprays, spider treatments and so on.

These products are an everyday part of the modern way of life; what people don't realise is that by being constantly exposed to these products absorption and assimilation into the body is likely to occur. Many of these molecules are fat soluble and are concentrated in our fat deposits. This is also the case with the fat in animal meats we consume; they may be laden with toxins to which the animals have been exposed. You must also remember that when you use these products, not only are you exposing yourself to toxicity but also the environment as well; they end up in the air, in the water and in the soil.

Fortunately there are natural substitutes for most things. Often simple things which may be 'old fashioned' are still highly effective at doing the job. Check out the items listed below.

- Vinegar[46]
- Sodium Bicarbonate (Baking Soda)[47]
- Sodium Carbonate (Washing Soda)[48]
- Borax[49]

These four lowly substances can replace most of your toxic chemical products. You lose nothing by trying them and your supermarket bill will certainly fall. A good book on this subject is 'Wendyl's recipes for a cleaner life' ISBN 978-0-473-30020-3.

You may ask, why have these products gone out of use?

Is it because it is beneficial to humanity and the Planet to use chemicals instead of these cheap alternatives? Have you been brainwashed by seductive advertising to think that these synthetic chemicals are better? Are company profits and big business the driving force?

Personal care products

Why are they called personal care products? Do they care for us really? If you take the time to look at the ingredient list on some of the skin care products you will be amazed at the number of chemicals in them, they're the ones with the big long names you can't understand.

You may think that it's not a problem, yes? It may not be if these compounds stayed on your skin and didn't compromise the skin's natural activities like perspiring and vitamin D production for example. Generally speaking, people probably don't think of the skin as an organ yet it is the largest organ in the body[50]. Anything you apply to the skin will, more than likely, be absorbed through the skin into the blood stream and spread around the body, just like if you eat something it is digested and absorbed into the body. The pharmaceutical world uses this in drug delivery systems; you've all heard of nicotine patches for example in smoking cessation treatments.

Sun screens are one of the most widely used personal care products in this age of sun phobia. Is the sun really as dangerous as it is made out to be? Is part of this sun phobia created by an industry with profit motivation? Does this industry have your health as their motivation?

Sun burn, like any burn, is not to be recommended. That's fairly obvious to most people and tissue damage of any kind is to be avoided. What you may not be aware of is that sun exposure is vitally important to your health and well being and we will look at this further when we investigate vitamin D.

Melanoma is considered the most serious form of skin cancer and is responsible for two thirds of skin cancer deaths. We have been promoting the heavy use of sunscreens for many years. The slip, slop, slap campaign was started in 1981 yet since that time the incidence of melanoma has increased on a worldwide basis. In the USA melanoma rates have been steadily rising since 1992[51], in Europe the incidence doubled between 1993 and 2011[52] and in Australia where the slip, slop, slap campaign started, there has been a doubling in incidence between the years 1986 – 2006[53]. It would appear that the campaign is having little effect despite the aggressive advertising, maybe there some other factors involved.

It is a fact that the UV falling on earth is increasing, presumably because of the destruction of the ozone layer. Most people are familiar with this but why are the high factor sun screens not protecting us? Another question to consider is; can sun screens be absorbed into the body and cause health issues?

Oxybenzone, octinoxate and homosalate are commonly used chemicals which are known to penetrate the skin and even appear in breast milk. They have been shown to be hormone disrupters and can affect reproductive hormones and/or thyroid function. Octocrylene penetrates the skin and appears in breast milk and is responsible has high rates of skin allergies as is avobenzone[54]. Other ingredients found in many skin care products including sun screens are phthalates, another hormone disrupter, and parabens an oestrogen mimic that may be implicated in breast cancer[55].

Good old zinc oxide cream is a reasonable alternative choice; it is effective and least toxic. Unfortunately zinc oxide tends to be the least cosmetically accepted unless you're on the ski slope. Be cautious with the use of zinc oxide and titanium dioxide in nano-particle form. Nano particles are extremely small and can penetrate the skin and enter the blood stream. These are relatively new formulations and we do not yet know the long term consequences of applying them to the skin. At the moment they appear to be a safer option but who knows what the future will reveal? There is some evidence that nano particles increase levels of free radicals which cause tissue damage and cancer[56]. This research is in its infancy, being forewarned about the potential dangers allows you, the consumer, to make a choice. Many times in human history things have been promoted as safe only to discover at some later time that the reverse is true. Remember doctors used to advertise cigarettes as both enjoyable and safe[57].

One factor which I'm sure is involved with skin cancer and indeed any cancer is the deterioration in our nutrition, particularly antioxidants which are vitally important to skin protection. High anti-oxidant levels in the blood are vitally important for mopping up those free radicals (reactive oxygen species, ROS) which are produced by the action of UV radiation in the skin. We will revisit this subject in the food chapter.

Genetically Modified Organisms (GMOs)

There is much controversy around the world regarding GMOs: Are they healthy? Are they safe? Do they provide good nutrition? Almost everyone must surely be aware of the GMO debate. The GMO producers and government bodies tell us that they are equivalent to non GMO crops and they use the term 'generally regarded as safe' or GRAS.

Governments generally accept the statements made and the research presented by the producers of these products as being valid. But is it? Like most things developed for human consumption animal testing is the model which is used to determine safety, GMOs are no exception. When rats were fed GMO corn in company trials they seemed to be O.K. but the trials were only short term, typically 90 days, not over the lifetime of the animal.

Professor Gilles-Eric Séralini has pioneered some independent research where GMO food was given over the lifetime of the test animals. This research showed unequivocally that the rats developed tumours and organ damage of various types[58].If you really want to understand the evidence then study the information on Professor Séralini's web site given in the reference.

Be aware that the development of GMO's is not really about feeding the world it is about controlling the food supply to humanity. All the GMO seeds are patented by the companies who developed them, this means that the farmers have to buy seed from the manufacturers and are not allowed to collect their own seed as they have traditionally done. Monsanto, Du Pont, and Syngenta own around 50% of the world's seeds. And 10 companies own 67% of the world's seeds[59]. These figures are increasing as more and more GMO plant varieties are being developed. Even if GMOs were safe, which Professor Séralini's experiments clearly show they are not; how can it be morally and ethically acceptable in our society for these few companies to control our food supply?

Why is there a resistance to the labelling of GMO foods by the food industry in America? If the foods are safe as they say they are then what's the problem? The big companies must be aware that a growing body of people instinctively know that GMO foods are not good and would like to avoid them if they have a choice. This is what they don't want, for consumers to have a choice.

Another facet of the GMO debate is that these crops are Round Up ready. Round Up is Monsanto's glyphosate product. This is an herbicide to which the plants are resistant. Unfortunately, as you've seen previously, more and more is being used because of the growing tolerance to its effects by the weeds. When will the mad scientists accept that man cannot better nature; we have to work with nature to solve our problems otherwise we are just creating a new set of problems. To paraphrase Einstein; *we cannot solve the problems we create with the same level of thinking that created them.*

Nutrient levels in GMOs are supposed to be equivalent at least to non GMO food. Is this true? Maybe not[60].

Just a note on labelling; in those countries which label GMO ingredients if a GMO ingredient is below a certain level it may not be on the label. Know your GMO species and use prudent caution. Some of the top GM crops are:

- Corn
- Soy
- Cottonseed
- Alfalfa (used to feed dairy cows)
- Canola
- Sugar beets

GMO products may often be disguised in animal feed which is not for human consumption; we will consume GMOs indirectly by eating animal products.

Bacillus Thuringiensis (bt) is a micro-organism which kills caterpillars, it is a natural insecticide. Plants have been genetically modified to contain the bt gene which is responsible for this effect. This gene is in the plant so every time you eat one of the plants you eat this gene. Although this gene cannot be incorporated into human cells research shows that it can be transmitted to bacteria that inhabit your gut, the micro-biome, a vital part of your immune system[61]. The question is; how might this transfer of genetic material impact your micro-biome and ultimately your health?

So what's the bottom line with GMOs?

- *They are potentially carcinogenic and organ damaging.*
- *They may have reduced nutrient levels compared to non GMO foods.*
- *They are likely to contain herbicide residues.*
- *They are transgenic, containing genes from other species never encountered before in our food.*
- *We do not have sufficient data to prove long term safety information.*
- *Seed companies are controlling the world's food supply.*

I advise you to become knowledgeable on this subject; it is not going to go away. Enough people need to express their will if politicians are to be persuaded to act on our behalf, the exact reason they were elected. By adding your voice to the growing numbers of concerned citizens the tipping point will be reached and the government will then have to follow the lead of the people. It would be wise to do your homework before you eat these aberrations of nature. Make an informed choice and demand proper labelling. Ask why is there such resistance to labelling GMOs if they are safe, what's the problem?

We surely have a right to freedom of information, the choice to decide what we put into our bodies. Ask yourself; are our democratic rights and basic human rights being violated?

Toxic information

You live in a world where you are constantly bombarded with sensory input; visual, audio, smell, taste and touch. These things are almost taken for granted as being part of everyday life, so much so that for the most part you block it out. Constant background information is being fed into your subconscious mind. Do you know that your subconscious mind remembers everything? That fact may surprise you because generally speaking you may have, on occasion, difficulty in consciously recalling a piece of information: somebody's name, a telephone number, an appointment somewhere? Even so it has been shown that any experience or sensory input you have had can be recalled in the most vivid terms under hypnosis. What most people have is difficulty in dragging the information out of the subconscious into the conscious mind, our everyday mind.

This ability to absorb absolutely everything is used by advertising companies, government agencies and the medical system. For example during the build up to winter we are constantly bombarded with images of people getting colds, the message to get a flu shot, how medicines can make you better. All this information may go over your head at the time but your subconscious is taking it all in and almost programming you to develop the symptoms, it's the time of year to get a cold or flu and dutifully under subconscious direction your body obeys. This is an example of what is called predictive programming. You can see when you think about it how such information can be toxic to your system.

Do you remember we talked about the nocebo effect earlier on; this is another example of toxic information which can be lethal. When the doctor says you have 3 months to live the nocebo effect kicks in and the words are empowered to become true.

In everyday life you are bombarded with images and news stories which you see or hear in your conscious mind. The emotions generated by this news unfortunately for the most part will sink into your subconscious mind and affect your behaviour and also things like your voting habit. Why is there so much anger, fear and antisocial behaviour? Is it anything to do with the images people are subjected to, the video games the kids are playing and the TV programs everyone is influenced by?

Edward Bernays was the father of public manipulation. Check out these links[62 & 63].

Ionising radiation
Most people will know that ionising radiation, the radiation that atomic bombs and nuclear power stations give out, is highly dangerous and often lethal. Of course the military uses atomic bombs because they create rather a large explosion and shock wave which decimates large areas and kills lots of people almost in an instant. The fact that the material is highly radioactive and leaves a legacy of health carnage for a long time may or may not be part of the strategy. Who wants to live in a radioactive world? Of course with the nuclear disasters the world has been exposed to, (Chernobyl, Fukishima) the levels of exposure are on the increase; the tons of depleted uranium shells used in the Middle Eastern wars of recent years have contributed to this.

We know that radiation can damage our DNA, the code within our cells which controls life, and this can then lead to cancer.

How many of you consider this fact when you have your routine X-rays?

X-rays, including CAT scans which are whole body x-rays, are ionising radiation with the potential to cause tissue damage and cancer.

Sometimes there may be a compelling reason to have an x-ray and the benefit may be worth the risk. The justification for routine x-rays may not be quite as clear cut and most definitely increases the chance of harm, yet they have become an ever increasing part of medical and dental diagnostics.

Mammography is a routine procedure that millions of women are undergoing with great regularity because of the highly emotive advertising campaigns, the inherent fear of cancer and the desire to avoid it. The question is; how safe is mammography and does it have any real benefits?

> *'Recent radiobiological studies have provided compelling evidence that the low energy X-rays as used in mammography are approximately four times – but possibly as much as six times - more effective in causing mutational damage than higher energy X-rays. Since current radiation risk estimates are based on the effects of high energy gamma radiation, this implies that the risks of radiation induced breast cancers for mammography X-rays are underestimated by the same factor[64].'*
>
> *The risk may be low but '........<u>repeated x-rays have the potential to cause cancer[65]</u>.'*

There are many official sites which clearly state that there is a risk. They see it as acceptable, you may also; it's your choice.

The amount of radiation you get in one routine mammogram is approximately equivalent to the annual amount of background radiation you receive to your whole body[66]. If I understand that correctly, when you have a mammogram the dose to your breast tissue alone over say a 10 minute time interval is equivalent to the dose your whole body gets in a year from background radiation.

Here are a couple of excerpts from a patient leaflet produced by the Danish Cochrane site; the Cochrane database being the gold standard for independent research.

"If 2000 women are screened regularly for 10 years, one will benefit from the screening, as she will avoid dying from breast cancer. At the same time, 10 healthy women will, as a consequence, become cancer patients and will be treated unnecessarily.'

'Screening produces patients with breast cancer from among healthy women who would never have developed symptoms of breast cancer. Treatment of these healthy women increases their risk of dying, e.g. from heart disease and cancer[67].'

The information here is quite staggering and clearly states that the risk far outweighs any benefit of mammography.

There is a much safer alternative; thermography. This method will detect any unusual heat signature in the breast tissue. Tumours develop their own blood supply (angiogenesis) which increases the heat signature at the site of the tumour.

Dental x-rays are another routine procedure to which patients subjected themselves to on a regular basis. This never used to be the case but seems now to be a modern trend. Why are routine x-rays needed if there is no problem at the time of the appointment? The argument is that early problems may be detected, but at what cost? As we've seen from the previous information on mammography, if you're having regular x-rays then this will most definitely increase the chance of ionising radiation tissue damage.

'Regular X-rays have long been a feature of routine dental checks and few of us gave them a second thought - until last week when a new study warned that these scans could double the risk of developing thyroid cancer. '

Daily Mail UK 2010[68].

'Radiation exposure to the thyroid among both children and adults is currently the strongest known risk factor for thyroid cancer.'

American thyroid association 2012[69].

In the April 10, 2012 edition of American Cancer Association journal 'Cancer', a study came to the conclusion that frequent dental x-rays increase the risk of meningioma, a common type of brain tumour[70]. **Clearly dental x-rays like mammograms have the potential to cause cancer.**

CAT (CT) scans are whole body or part of body x-ray. For those of you who like big words CAT is an acronym for Computed Axial Tomography. The following information is taken from radiologyinfo.org[71].

Procedure	Approx. Radiation dose	Background Radiation equivalent
CT Abdomen & Pelvis	10mSv	3 years
X-ray Spine	1.5mSv	6 months
CT Spine	6mSv	2 years
CT Chest	7mSv	2 years
CT Heart	12mSv	4 years

The chart shows the amount of radiation you will receive for a particular procedure compared with the time to receive the same amount of radiation from background sources. A CT scan of the abdomen for example gives you 3 years of background radiation in a single dose and is equivalent to 100 chest x-rays at 0.1mSv per dose mSv = millisieverts).

For the complete chart and further information check out the reference.

An article in the New England Journal of Medicine[72] clearly states that what is considered low dose radiation exposure from CT scans has carcinogenic potential, particularly in children and should only be used when absolutely necessary and not as a routine diagnostic tool.

Electro-Magnetic Field exposure

EMFs as they are more commonly referred to belong to the class of radiation termed 'non-ionising'. Even though they are less energetic than ionising radiation, in the modern world our exposure is constant.

These frequencies have always been around because of background radio waves from outer space. Since the discovery of radio and wireless telegraphy the density of radio frequency waves in our environment has been steadily increasing. We are only just beginning to realise the potential harms that chronic exposure to this type of radiation can cause.

High tension power lines are ubiquitous in our environment; they carry high voltage current in the order of 275,000 to 400,000 volts. For those of you who are unfamiliar with electrical circuits you need to be aware that any circuit has an associated electric and a magnetic field which are pretty strong if you are directly underneath the cables. Fortunately these fields are greatly reduced as you move away from them, typically 1-2% of the maximum field strength at 25 metres away.

There is much controversy about whether power lines present a health hazard. If you live directly under a power line or less than 25 metres away then that could pose a health hazard. Increased risk of childhood leukaemia and other issues have been associated with living near power lines[73]. Whether a health risk has been proven or not; if you are aware of potential dangers then you can make a choice, can't you?

By far the commonest source of EMFs the majority of people come into close proximity with is communication technology. Cell phones, cordless (DECT) phones, internet routers, cell phone towers and more recently smart meters. We do not know the long term consequences of exposure to these EMFs. We do know that humans have only been exposed to them at the current levels for a relatively short period of time. There is a growing body of information which suggest something isn't quite right and there is plenty of anecdotal evidence; which of course science rejects.

On 31st May 2012 the WHO/international agency for research on cancer (IARC) classified radio frequency electromagnetic fields as possibly carcinogenic to humans[74].The research continues. In the meantime it would be prudent to limit exposure by using hands free and texting. Children are particularly susceptible because they have thinner skull bones and therefore there is increased penetration of the EMFs and also an increased heating effect. Cell phone radiation is similar to microwave radiation used in cooking!

Smart meters are being introduced throughout the world and many people are experiencing health problems. If you have one or likely to have one then it is in your own interest to check it out, particularly if you have experienced health issue since installation. Here is one person's story[75].

Interestingly Lloyds of London have recently excluded injury from EMF exposure from their policies[76]. What do you make of that?

Endnotes

We have investigated many areas of potential toxicity in our lives. Some are obvious if you sit back and think about it, some are not so obvious. Many have a slow and insidious detrimental impact on our health. If you compare yourself at birth to an empty vessel, devoid of toxic substances; in a pristine state so to speak; as you make your journey through life you are exposed to the toxic influences described and the vessel begins to fill up. Depending on your innate vitality, your body may or may not compensate. Your ability to detoxify and remove the offending materials will depend on many things. If you are not able to remove them, your vessel will eventually become full and start to overflow as the homoeostatic mechanism within the body begin to falter, this overflow will manifest as disease symptoms. Reducing toxic exposure is only one aspect of maintaining health but it is one which you can, more or less, have an influence on if you so choose.

You can avoid most of the things we've discussed. You can adopt protocols to detoxify your system. Conventional medicine has nothing to offer in terms of removing toxic build up, it is not considered important; there are no drugs which can do the job, only drugs to treat the symptoms of a body in disarray.

As a society, enormous amounts of money are spent on superficial cosmetic products and yet little attention is given to the functioning of the most vital organs which are responsible for elimination of all the rubbish in the system, the colon, liver and kidneys in particular, are organs which deserve special attention.

Conventional medical wisdom says that cleaning out your colon is a waste of time if you'll excuse the pun. They have nothing to offer you even if they did consider it valid. Most people have a concept of regular bowel movement which is far from ideal. 'Regular' can be anything from once a day to once a week! There is a reflex called the gastro colic reflex which causes the colon to contract in response to the stomach being stretched. When you eat, the stomach is stretched and so the colon should contract and cause the urge to defecate. If you eat three times a day you should in theory defecate three times a day. Most people would probably consult a doctor and say they have symptoms of excessive bowel activity! So you see true regularity in the bowels is far away from the norm most people experience. The colon lining is a highly absorptive structure which is one of the reasons drugs can be given rectally. If you have waste matter stagnant in your colon then any toxins therein, can be and will be reabsorbed into the circulation instead of being eliminated.

Consider that a sluggish bowel can retain pounds of old toxic and poisonous faecal matter (10-20 pounds is not unusual, and up to 65 pounds has actually been reported). It should be noted that doctors rarely see this accumulated matter during colonoscopies because patients are given purgatives to clean out their intestinal tracts before the colonoscopies, thus removing the evidence -- but they do see the effects, the herniations of the colon aka diverticuli[77].

The time between eating and elimination should be in the region of 12 to 24 hours, anything more means a potentially toxic situation is in process. The liver and kidneys are the organs most affected by toxic molecules, including pharmaceutical drugs. These organs metabolise and eliminate the blood borne toxins. The ageing process along with a life time of toxic exposure leads to a deterioration in function of these vital organs. The liver is probably the most important organ of blood detoxification. It is the organ which converts those nasty chemicals into molecules that can be eliminated from the body. The liver has a remarkable regenerative capacity, even so, it will have its limits. Non-alcoholic fatty liver disease (NAFLD) is becoming much more common. Fatty liver disease used to be related almost exclusively to alcohol consumption, this is no longer the case.

Non-alcoholic fatty liver disease (NAFLD) is rapidly becoming the most common liver disease worldwide. The prevalence of NAFLD in the general population of Western countries is 20-30%[78].

How many doctors consider in earnest the impact of toxic exposure and multiple drug therapy on our liver and kidneys? There are no studies done on multiple drug therapy. We literally do not know the impact on our system yet many people, particularly the elderly take their drugs on trust. Sometimes 15 to 20 different drugs each day, believe me I've seen it many times. By paying attention to your toxic load you can improve your health status and reduce the potential for disease manifestation. Certain nutrients like high dose vitamin C can help the body eliminate heavy metals (mercury, lead etc.). If you have mercury fillings it is almost a daily necessity to take a good dose of vitamin C; liposomal C is the best as it is almost completely absorbed and avoids the bowels tolerance issues. For those who think high dose vitamin C is dangerous, Alan Smith, the New Zealand dairy farmer who recovered from swine flu after his family insisted he be given intravenous vitamin C, was given 600 to 700 grams (<u>grams not milligrams</u>) over a week by IV injection[79].

Homotoxicology is a branch of homoeopathy which assists the body to detoxify. Let me tell you a story to illustrate this.

When we lived in England we had a dog named Ben. Ben was a rescue dog and had been in and out of kennels a number of times and had had multiple vaccine exposures. Being naturopathically minded we thought he had been over exposed and decided to give him some homoeopathic medicine to help him overcome any potential future health issues. We gave him a series of remedies which included Thuja and the canine vaccines in homoeopathic dose.

Within 24 hours Ben started discharging a green 'gunk' from his eyes and he developed lumps all over his skin. Over a week these lumps, together with the attached fur started to drop off, his skin became clear and his eyes recovered. That was a great detox reaction!

Ordinarily homoeopathic detoxification for humans would aim for a more gentle approach to avoid too much discomfort but sometimes the body just 'does its thing'. People forget that the skin is the biggest organ in the body. You may look upon those spots and blemishes a little differently from now on!

Naturally conventional medicine, for its own reasons, is highly sceptical about such methodology because it chooses to ignore the energetic reality in which we exist. We all function within the paradigm we choose; the important thing is to have that choice and the courage to create our own belief structure based on the best available information.

References

1. http://articles.mercola.com/sites/articles/archive/2009/12/31/232-toxic-chemicals-found-in-10-babies.aspx

2. http://www.cdc.gov/vaccines/parents/downloads/parent-ver-sch-0-6yrs.pdf

3. http://www.vaccinesafety.edu/components-Excipients.htm

4. http://www.cdc.gov/nchs/fastats/asthma.htm

5. http://nationaleczema.org/research/eczema-prevalence/

6. http://www.hrsa.gov/vaccinecompensation/index.html

7. http://www.vacfacts.info/national-vaccine-injury-compensation-program---payout-data.html

8. https://www.scribd.com/document/326207834/Basic-Immunology-4Ed-Chapter-11-Abbas

9. http://www.healthline.com/human-body-maps/axillary-lymph-nodes

10. http://www.ncbi.nlm.nih.gov/pubmed/21157018

11. http://www.ncbi.nlm.nih.gov/pubmed/22099159

12. http://www.youtube.com/watch?v=9ylnQ-T7oiA

13. https://emergency.cdc.gov/agent/mercury/mercelementalcasedef.asp

14. http://dentalwellness4u.com/freeservices/amalremov2.html

15. http://www.nrdc.org/health/effects/mercury/guide.asp

16. http://articles.mercola.com/sites/articles/archive/2013/01/06/dr-shade-on-mercury-exposure.aspx

17. http://www.healthline.com/health/lead-poisoning#Risk%20Factors3

18. http://www.arltma.com/Articles/CadmiumToxDoc.htm

19. http://www.patient.co.uk/doctor/Arsenic-Poisoning.htm

20. http://www.arltma.com/HairAnalysis.htm

21. http://www.livescience.com/7198-acids-popular-sodas-erode-tooth-enamel.html

22. http://blog.fooducate.com/2009/06/30/11-quick-facts-about-phosphoric-acid-yes-that-chemical-in-coca-cola/

23. http://www.nofluoride.com/food_and_water.cfm

24. https://www.ncbi.nlm.nih.gov/pmc/articles/PMC4168053/

25. http://fluoridealert.org/issues/health/thyroid/

26. http://www.ncbi.nlm.nih.gov/pmc/articles/PMC1567851/

27. http://www.livestrong.com/article/509298-how-nitrates-nitrites-affect-our-bodies/

28. http://www.ncbi.nlm.nih.gov/pmc/articles/PMC3120105/

29. http://www.greenmedinfo.com/article/calcium-phosphate-has-been-shown-increase-preneoplastic-lesions-colons-mice

30. http://pmep.cce.cornell.edu/profiles/extoxnet/dienochlor-glyphosate/glyphosate-ext.html

31. https://www.organicconsumers.org/news/monsantos-minions-us-epa-hikes-glyphosate-limits-food-and-feed-once-again

32. http://farmindustrynews.com/ag-technology-solution-center/glyphosate-resistant-weed-problem-extends-more-species-more-farms

33. http://www.ecowatch.com/california-glyphosate-kennedy-2225578913.html

34. http://www.greenmedinfo.com/blog/research-roundup-herbicide-toxicity-vastly-underestimated

35. http://toxics.usgs.gov/highlights/glyphosate02.html

36. http://omicsonline.org/open-access/detection-of-glyphosate-residues-in-animals-and-humans-2161-0525.1000210.pdf

37. http://www.organicconsumers.org/articles/article_29697.cfm

38. http://news.nationalgeographic.com/news/2013/07/130718-organophosphates-pesticides-indian-food-poisoning/

39. https://www.epa.gov/pesticide-science-and-assessing-pesticide-risks/human-health-issues-related-pesticides

40. http://www.npic.orst.edu/ingred/ptype/index.html

41. http://www.wnho.net/deathbymedicine.htm

42. http://www.cdc.gov/nchs/fastats/deaths.htm

43. http://www.gilead.net/health/mindsick.html

44. http://www.globalresearch.ca/chemtrails-the-consequences-of-toxic-metals-and-chemical-aerosols-on-human-health/19047

45. http://www.theguardian.com/lifeandstyle/2001/may/17/healthandwellbeing.health5

46. http://www.rd.com/home/150-household-uses-for-vinegar/

47. http://www.care2.com/greenliving/51-fantastic-uses-for-baking-soda.html

48. http://www.care2.com/greenliving/the-wonders-of-washing-soda.html

49. http://www.onegoodthingbyjillee.com/2013/10/30-little-known-uses-for-household-borax.html

50. http://www.aad.org/dermatology-a-to-z/for-kids/about-skin

51. https://seer.cancer.gov/statfacts/html/melan.html

52. http://www.cancerresearchuk.org/cancer-info/cancerstats/types/skin/incidence/#trends

53. http://www.smasa.asn.au/Portals/3/Melanoma%20factsheet.pdf

54. http://www.ewg.org/2014sunscreen/the-trouble-with-sunscreen-chemicals/

55. http://thegoodhuman.com/?s=parabens

56. http://www.sciencedaily.com/releases/2012/05/120507131951.htm

57. http://www.ncbi.nlm.nih.gov/pmc/articles/PMC1470496/

58. http://www.gmoseralini.org/about-us/

59. http://www.gmwatch.org/gm-firms/10558-the-worlds-top-ten-seed-companies-who-owns-nature

60. http://articles.mercola.com/sites/articles/archive/2013/04/30/monsanto-gmo-corn.aspx

61. http://earthopensource.org/gmomythsandtruths/sample-page/5-gm-crops-impacts-farm-environment/5-11-myth-horizontal-gene-transfer-gm-crops-bacteria-higher-organisms-unlikely-consequence/

62. http://www.youtube.com/watch?v=qiKMmrG1ZKU

63. http://www.historyisaweapon.com/defcon1/bernprop.html

64. http://www.ncbi.nlm.nih.gov/pubmed/16498030

65. http://www.cancer.gov/cancertopics/factsheet/detection/mammograms

66. https://www.aapm.org/publicgeneral/mammography.asp

67. http://nordic.cochrane.org/screening-breast-cancer-mammography

68. http://www.dailymail.co.uk/health/article-1284843/Just-safe-X-rays-dentist.html

69. http://www.thyroid.org/american-thyroid-association-ata-issues-policy-statement-on-minimizing-radiation-exposure-from-medical-dental-diagnostics/

70. http://www.webmd.com/brain/news/20120410/dental-x-rays-linked-brain-tumors

71. http://www.radiologyinfo.org/en/info.cfm?pg=safety-xray

72. http://www.nejm.org/doi/full/10.1056/NEJMra072149

73. https://www.safespaceprotection.com/emf-health-risks/emf-health-effects/power-lines/

74. http://electromagnetichealth.org/electromagnetic-health-blog/iarc-rf-carc/

75. http://www.electricsense.com/7769/smart-meter-radiation-refugee-emf-lawsuit/

76. http://thebridgenewsservice.com/2015/02/26/school-boards-left-on-the-hook-for-wi-fi-injuries/

77. http://jonbarron.org/colon-detoxification-vs-colonics

78. http://www.ncbi.nlm.nih.gov/pubmed/20460905

79. http://articles.mercola.com/sites/articles/archive/2010/10/29/high-dose-iv-vitamin-c-found-useful-for-near-terminal-swine-flu.aspx

Chapter 9 – FOOD GLORIOUS FOOD

What is food? The answer may appear to be reasonably obvious; everyone knows what food is; don't they? If you answer the question at the basic level then food is what you eat when you are hungry, right? Let's go one step further. Food is what you eat to supply you with energy, that's why you're hungry, you need a refill. Is food's only function to give us energy?

Well, I think most people, or I would hope most people, realise the food they eat becomes the body they inhabit. You are what you eat or more accurately what you absorb, this has been said many times by many people and I claim no originality.

In our modern western world food has become a focus of entertainment; 'let's go out to eat' is almost a mantra in modern society. The food and drinks industry has grown immensely over the last century. What used to be the privilege of the rich and famous is now available big time to the average person. This trend has advanced at a steady pace ever since Edward Bernays started the trend of enticing people to spend their money on things of desire rather than need[1].

As more and more families required two incomes to buy all these things they wanted, the restaurant culture and particularly the 'fast food' element expanded rapidly. With the increasing influence of television advertising it wasn't long before children were pressurising their parents for a 'big Mac' or some other quick food fix. The advance of the supermarket culture and packaged foods created a whole new industry of so called 'convenience' foods, another marketing coup for the fast food industry. Straight out of the packet, into the microwave and into your stomach, gone in 60 seconds!

Food processing has become a scientific discipline in which vast amounts of money are spent researching how to make food taste so good that people become addicted and want more regardless of the consequences. Be under no illusion, the foods are addictive and the consequences of that addiction are dire.

If we look at how our food quality has deteriorated over the last 100 years and particularly in the last 50 years we can get an understanding of how health has equally deteriorated. O.K. let's consider some of the things that have affected our foods.

Chemicals in Our Food

The first and second world wars were a great driving force for the research and production of new chemical entities with the petroleum industry as a major player. There are literally thousands and thousands of manufactured chemical compounds used in industry today. Inevitably some of these will find their way into our food supply and some of these chemicals are applied directly to our food: pesticides, herbicides, artificial fertilisers, etc; the potential toxicity of these has been discussed previously. We are needing to use more and more of these chemicals on the crops due to development of resistance to their effects, because of this, the allowable levels of these substances in our food is being raised to accommodate this. One such recent example is Monsanto's glyphosate (Roundup)[2]. Our body chemistry is the same now as it was before the introduction of all these chemicals into our food supply and we have not developed the biochemical pathways to adequately deal with this chemical onslaught. The result is an increased burden for our detoxifying and elimination mechanisms; many of these chemicals are fat soluble and if they can't be processed for elimination they are stored away in our fat deposits, this is not a good situation as you can imagine.

Specific food additives are actively introduced directly into processed foods to improve appearance, flavour and shelf life. These additives are given E numbers and are usually listed on the packaging although you wouldn't know what they are unless you memorised the list. There are around 300 food additive chemicals categorised as colouring agents, preservatives, antioxidants, emulsifiers, thickeners, stabilisers, gelling agents and others; some of these are natural substances and some are artificial.

Aspartame (canderel, nutrasweet, equal) is an artificial sweetener which has been promoted as a healthy alternative to sugar: but is it? Aspartame is a compound composed of methanol (wood alcohol), aspartic acid and phenylalanine and is broken down to these components in the body. This may not be a problem if you only use it occasionally however if you are consuming large quantities of diet sodas and some artificially sweetened foods and pharmaceuticals there could be big health issues for you.

In the body methanol converts to formaldehyde and then to formic acid both of which are toxic. Formaldehyde is the chemical used in embalming fluid! Aspartic acid is an amino acid naturally occurring in protein. When it is consumed as an isolated compound it behaves differently in the body; it is now categorised as an excitotoxin. An excitotoxin is a substance that stimulates nerve and brain cells to fire off indiscriminately which can result in all sorts of neurological problems; much the same with MSG (mono sodium glutamate) another flavour enhancer. Phenylalanine can easily penetrate the blood brain barrier, enter the brain and disrupt certain neurotransmitter functions[3].

Aspartame has over 90 known side effects[4]. Check out the reference; you may be suffering from some of the affects of aspartame if you are a regular user.

Artificial sweeteners are used by people because they think it is a healthier option than sugar and helps with blood glucose control. This is a fallacy[5]; I remember once talking to a work colleague whose husband had recently been diagnosed with type II diabetes. He had switched to using artificial sweetener and had noticed that after drinking a diet soda his blood sugar went up!

Genetically Modified Organisms (GMO)

It seems that there is a great momentum from the giant agrochemical companies, like Bayer, Syngenta, Monsanto and Dupont, to control the world's food supply. In the first instance this has been through the use of chemicals but since 1994 the emphasis has been moving toward GMOs[6]. The goal of these companies is to patent GM seeds for all the major food crops so that they own the seeds. Farmers will no longer be able to save seeds for replanting as this will be a breach of the patent. Now this might be bad luck for the farmer's profits but what are the consequences for you, the consumer?

The FDA has deemed that GMO foods are 'Generally Regarded As Safe' - GRAS. What is this acceptance based on? It is based on the industry's own trial data which follows the health of GMO fed animals (usually rats) for around 90 days. During this time period there were apparently no problems and hence the GRAS status.

Gilles-Éric Séralini, a French professor of molecular biology at the University of Caen, did experiments where he gave GMO feed to rats over their whole lifetime. This is a more appropriate investigation as it is intended for humans to eat these products over their whole lifetime. I hope you agree with this logic.

What did professor Séralini find?

Rats fed GMOs over their whole life developed abnormalities in internal organ function, particularly the liver and kidney which are the main organs of detoxification and elimination, and more importantly they developed multiple tumours[7].

Why do the agro companies not want GMO containing foods to be labelled? Maybe they know that if the consumer has a choice GMOs will not be popular. You are not being allowed to vote with your dollar. The choice in how you spend your money has a big influence on product development.

Many, many countries are banning GMOs[8], why is that? Presumably the reason is because they do not regard them as safe for human consumption or there are other health issues and concerns. In India the farmers have invested their whole livelihoods in GM cotton. Many of these farmers have, over time, developed serious health problems; animals that were grazed on the left over plant material have died[9] and there has also been large scale crop failure. The whole GM cotton fiasco while not being wholly responsible has had its part to play in over 270,000 farmer suicides since 1995[10].

Ask yourself these questions:

- *Why would you want to eat something for which there is no long term safety data?*
- *Can you believe the assurances from the voice of authority when there have been so many lies?*
- *Why are the agro companies spending millions of dollars on blocking the attempts to label GMO foods?*
- *Why are you not being given a choice?*

The only way to avoid gross exposure to GMOs is to buy certified organic food. This applies all over the world not just in America. If a processed food has less than a certain amount of a substance then it doesn't have to be included on the label, this includes GMOs[11]. Animal feeds may contain GM residues and in this way the GMOs enter the human food chain. So although growing GMOs might be prohibited in a particular place they may be arriving through the side door so to speak. Buying meat only produced from grass fed animals becomes a necessity if you are concerned about GMOs. Grass is the natural food for the ruminant animals that humans raise as a food source.

You may think you cannot afford to buy organic after all it most definitely is more expensive. Ask yourself; how much do I value my health and that of my family? Surely it is better to eat less of a more wholesome food than more of one that is potentially toxic. Almost everyone in the western world eats more food than they need and so cutting back a little may add years to your life.

We all spend our money on things we do not need to thrive: cigarettes, alcohol, junk food, entertainment, mobile phones, the latest gadget, going to the cinema, designer labels, vacations etc. Now I'm not suggesting that you should live the life of an ascetic (holy man) however there are choices and you can choose to give up some of the luxuries in life in order to afford good quality food that *will give* you a more healthy life. If you put good materials into your body you will spend less on health care.

For an in depth look at GMO facts see this reference:

https://www.amazon.com/gp/product/0993436706/ref=as_li_tl?ie=UTF8&camp=1789&creative=390957&creativeASIN=0993436706&linkCode=as2&tag=gmwatchorg-20&linkId=47YUPEAHJ2CWWCZP

More on Food additives

As mentioned previously there are over 300 listed food additives or E numbers[12]. Not all E numbers are potentially harmful but you have to know what's what. Aspartame (E951) and other artificial sweeteners are not a healthy option as we've seen. The healthiest option is to down regulate your need for sweet food. Flavour enhancers which contain glutamate (E620 – E625) are also, like aspartame, neurotoxins and when consumed regularly may present a health issue. If you want to know the effect of a substance avoid it for three months then re-introduce it and see how you feel. My wife is particularly sensitive to MSG (E621). We once had a meal in a Chinese restaurant and within minutes of starting the meal she broke out in a hot sweat with severe palpitations. We always ask now if the food contains MSG. Many places are now advertising 'no MSG'.

Fast food is an interesting source of food additives. The following additives may be used in fast food products[13]:

- *L-cysteine (E920) – an amino acid (part of a protein) used to increase dough pliability. It is sourced from duck feathers and human hair.*
- *Sand (Silicon dioxide – E551) – used as an anti-caking agent in processed beef and chicken.*
- *Wood (Cellulose – E460) – used as a thickener and stabiliser and to reduce the reliance on more expensive ingredients. The cellulose is obtained by chemical processing of wood pulp*
- *Plastic putty (dimethylpolysiloxane – E900) – used to stop fryer oil from foaming.*
- *Preservatives made from petroleum (Tertiary butylhydroxyquinine- TBHQ – E319) – used as a preservative. Maximum permitted level is 0.02%. There is a limit because too much is lethal. You would however need to eat an awful lot of product to consume this amount.*
- *Fertiliser (ammonium sulphate – E517)) – used as yeast nutrient.*
- *Cochineal beetle (carminic acid – E120) – red food colouring*
- *Mechanically separated meat – bone with meat attached is passed through a sieve under high pressure to separate the meat and producing a paste like product. This is then 'flavoured' to make it palatable. Watch out for it in your next hotdog!*

These additives and many others are regarded as safe (GRAS) by the regulatory authorities such as the FDA. Like everything else it depends on your exposure. *Caveat emptor-* let the buyer beware! The best way to avoid food additives is to buy fresh organic produce. All processed foods and packaged foods have additives. Start to make you own food instead of giving the responsibility to others less interested in your health. There are enough cooking shows and books around; be inspired. Demand proper labelling so you have a choice as to what you and your loved ones consume.

Grain fed animals

Are cows meant to eat grass or grains? Of course the answer is grass, just plain old grass. What is the difference between grass fed and grain fed? The difference is the composition of fatty acids in the meat and milk.

There are certain essential fatty acids that we have to eat because we can't make them ourselves. These fatty acids are needed to make substances called eicosanoids. That's a big word, let's move on quickly! These substances act as powerful cell messengers and direct certain processes within the body; they have an important role in the immune system and any imbalance can have health consequences.

O.K. so there are two main types of these essential fatty acids (EFAs), omega 6 and omega 3. Most people these days have heard of omega 3 because we're encouraged to eat oily fish. Omega 3 is thought of as 'good'. I don't know why we have to delineate nutrients as good or bad, any essential nutrient is just that, essential. The problems arise when they are out of balance and this is exactly the situation most people find themselves in today. Excess omega 6 fatty acids over omega 3 will produce a tendency for inflammation in the body. Inflammation can manifest as eczema, asthma, arthritis, heart disease, degenerative brain disorders, cancer and so on.

Back to the original question grass or grain; the fact is that the meat from grain fed animals has a lower level of omega 3 fatty acids. So if you are eating a lot of fast food you get a double whammy. The animals from which the meat is produced are more than likely grain fed and the food is, more than likely, cooked in vegetable oil which is a source of omega 6 fatty acids. The normal healthy ratio of omega 3 to omega 6 should be between 1:1 and 1:5; for most of you the ratio is between 1:25 and 1:50. That is a huge difference and is a major contributing factor to all the inflammation that is evident in western societies[14]. So grass fed is best, insist on it.

While we are on the subject of grains, farmed salmon are often fed a diet of grains which again affects the levels of omega 3 fatty acids in the fish. Farmed salmon contains only 50% of the omega 3 of wild caught salmon and it also has a host of other toxic stuff in it[15].

Hydrogenated fats are vegetable oils through which hydrogen has been passed and are used in many processed foods because they don't go rancid as quickly and therefore give the product longer shelf life. One of the problems with the hydrogenation process is the production of Trans fats; these trans fats are highly detrimental to our health. We will be looking in depth at the 'fat' controversy and how we have been following what now appears to be an incorrect dietary protocol for the last 50-60 years.

<u>Pollution</u>

Ever since the start of the industrial revolution and the burning of coal and oil the atmosphere in which we live has been a source of exposure to ever increasing level of pollution. The pollution falls to the ground and is incorporated into the soil and water and then our food. Industrial processes may have limits on the amount of pollution they are allowed to discharge into the atmosphere but many of these pollutants will accumulate over time in the soil and water supplies. Some pollutants are discharged directly into the water (fresh and sea) and air, some are applied directly to the land and some are released accidentally (e.g. Chernobyl).

What are pollutants that I am referring to?

- *Heavy metals – mercury is particularly significant and is found in appreciable levels in oily fish, especially larger fish like tuna. Weather modification programs are a significant source of other heavy metals.*
- *Organic compounds – agro chemicals, pharmaceuticals, household and industrial wastes, poly-chloro biphenyls (PCBs), phthalates the list is endless.*
- *Radioactive materials – from nuclear power plants, detonation of bombs, depleted uranium weapons used extensively in recent wars.*
- *Gases such as sulphur dioxide which cause acid rain.*
- *Exhaust from motor vehicles; the lead may have been removed from the fuel but there are many other noxious compounds being ejected from the exhaust pipes of around a billion cars worldwide.*
- *Industrial pollution expelled from the chimneys of processing plants, gases, heavy metals, volatile organic compounds and particulate matter.*
- *Household pollution from the many chemicals that are now used and which generally end up down the drain.*

All these exposures add to our toxic load and contribute towards the decline in health seen around the world.

What can we do? If you are aware of a source of toxic exposure you can take measures to avoid it or minimise exposure, what I would call damage limitation. Some things are impossible to avoid, we all have to breath and so anything in the air likely to be inhaled. The water you drink can be filtered to remove most toxic substances. High dose vitamin C is useful for helping the body to remove heavy metals[16]. Many foods can help with radiation detoxification[17] and since many radioactive materials are heavy metals vitamin C is important. Also zeolite (from volcanic ash) binds radioactive materials[18]. Was it a coincidence there was a large volcanic eruption in Chile after the Fukoshima disaster?

Nutrient deficiencies

For many years now we have been employing highly intensive farming practices using large amounts of artificial fertiliser which only supply the basic materials needed to promote plant growth, namely phosphorus, potassium and nitrogen (P,K,N). We have not been replacing the micro-nutrients, the trace minerals, which are vitally important to our health. So even if you are eating what appears to be a wholesome, healthy diet, it may not contain the minerals that you need. Again organic food is likely to be better because natural fertilisers, properly prepared compost and crop rotation should be used. Crop rotation is the time honoured way to maintain a healthy soil.

We may ask the question; how important are these trace minerals? They are so important that our farmed animals will die very quickly without them and this is why they are given mineral licks. Humans will also get sick and die if we don't get these essential minerals. We seem to have a greater capacity to adapt and stave off death from these deficiencies but if they continue the inevitable is likely to be unavoidable.

Magnesium is not a trace mineral it is present in the body in relatively large amounts around 35g for an average person. It is important and essential for over 300 chemical reactions in our body to occur efficiently. Despite this importance many people are deficient and this is an important contributing factor to many disease conditions[19].

Selenium is an example of a trace mineral which is deficient in many places of which New Zealand is a good example. Selenium is known to be important for protection against cancer[20] yet selenium supplementation is not generally recommended.

Boron, another mineral which is important in bone and joint health particularly[21], is often deficient.

Additional to the problem with reduced nutrients in food many people have to contend with the problem of drug induced nutrient depletion. Yes, drugs can cause nutrient losses! We will look more in depth at essential nutrients and the consequences of deficiencies later on.

Many of the essential vitamins and phyto nutrients (=plant based) are likely to be reduced during processing and transportation of our foods around the globe.

Sugar and Salt

These two items could well go in the food additives section as indeed that's exactly what they are. The addition of sugar and salt to so many of the foods people are eating has become routine practice in our fast, convenient food era. As we've discussed before, sugar and salt are used to disguise the poor flavour of fat free foods.

The word salt needs a little clarification. The salt that is added to foods generally is refined salt, aka sodium chloride. Sodium chloride bears as much relation to salt as refined sugar does to beetroot. Salt in its natural form comes in two forms, rock salt and sea salt. Both of these natural forms contain many trace minerals and remember these are the essential minerals we need for optimum functioning. So when you read a food label and it says salt, then understand that it means refined salt unless otherwise stated. Why would you want to use refined salt when the natural form is so much more beneficial to health?

Salt is necessary for health, it is the major component of your body fluids, the fluids that surround all your cells. Sodium is a necessary part of nerve cell transmission. The key to wise use is to avoid refined salt and processed foods that contain it and use natural salt with all those trace minerals. Drink plenty of water throughout the day. Eat foods flavoured with fat thereby avoiding added sugar and sodium chloride.

Milk

I started the chapter by asking the question; what is food? I might ask the same question regarding milk; what is milk?

Actually milk is, and only ever has been, the white stuff that comes mainly out of cows and goats. The white stuff that most people buy as milk from the supermarket is in fact <u>processed </u>milk. Several things happen during milk processing which denatures the product. The first process is pasteurisation in which the milk is kept at around 145 to 150

OF for 30 minutes; this is to kill any potentially harmful bacteria. Unfortunately the process also kills any useful bacteria, like lactobacilli, which help populate your micro biome. Pasteurisation might be justified for people with a compromised immune system but for the majority of healthy people it is not necessary. If the cows are treated well and are themselves healthy then so is the milk; otherwise their calves would be getting sick wouldn't they? Cow reared in intensive farming sheds where they are not fed with their natural diet, grass, are often far from healthy and mastitis is common. These animals have a high exposure to antibiotics; this situation is more likely to be the source of harmful bacteria and why the milk needs pasteurisation.

When pasteurised milk 'goes off' it goes bad and is unusable. When raw milk sours it can be used in other ways as it is still full of good health promoting bacteria. Pasteurisation also has an effect on the milk protein and this may result in promoting allergic sensitisation[22].

Enzymes contained within the milk are mostly destroyed by the pasteurisation process. These enzymes help to digest the milk solids, the proteins and sugars; this is why many people who have issues with processed milk are OK with whole raw milk. Lactose intolerance is quite common and occurs when an individual loses the ability to digest lactose; raw milk contains lactase which digests lactose and so raw milk may not be a problem in these individuals.

Milk is often promoted as a good source of calcium and certainly there is controversy around this as you will see if you look into it. One thing for sure is that the assimilation of calcium is helped by an enzyme called phosphatase, pasteurisation destroys this enzyme.

Another problem with processed milk is the removal of fat to make so called low fat milk. This is quite ridiculous since whole milk is a low fat product at around 3 to 3.5%; in comparison meat may contain between 5 and 11% fat.

The problem with milk fat is homogenisation; homogenisation breaks the fat globules into very, very small droplets which can be absorbed directly into the lymphatic system without undergoing digestion. If the fat is taken out of milk then the absorption of vital nutrients such as vitamins A and D will be hindered. These vitamins are fat soluble and require fat to be taken into the body.

Farmers are continually looking for methods to increase yield; more milk, more profit. In the U.S. Bovine Growth Hormone (BGH) has been approved by the FDA for use in dairy farming to increases the milk yield. BGH increases the level of Insulin-Like Growth Factor (IGF) which appears in the end product and is not destroyed by pasteurisation. IGF promotes cell proliferation and is implicated in some cancers; best avoided.

Any drugs given to the animals will have residues in the milk. On the whole you can see that low fat processed milk has many negative qualities and yet it is being promoted as a healthy option; you look at the information and decided for yourself.

http://www.raw-milk-facts.com/enzymes_T3.html

Endnotes

Why are people eating so much food? The reason maybe, is that because our foods are laced with toxins and low in trace nutrients, vitamins and minerals, we need to eat more to supply the body with those micro nutrients which are deficient and which are necessary for the functioning of our metabolic pathways including detoxification. We are also being exposed to very high levels of sugar and refined carbohydrates which are addictive and encourage us to eat more; is it any wonder we have the epidemic of obesity and metabolic syndrome?

Convenience foods may be just that but the long term inconvenience of being sick is not so attractive. If you choose to spend your money on empty calories full of potential toxins then you are much more likely to notch up some hefty medical bills later on in life and have time out from the things you enjoy doing.

The governments which we elect to look after our interests are not going to change the outlook in the short term, the food industry lobbyists are far too powerful and the political motivation is lacking. Only you can be the change, by voting with your dollars, by demanding transparent labelling and even starting your own backyard veggie garden.

<u>References</u>

1. http://en.wikipedia.org/wiki/Edward_Bernays

2. http://www.organicconsumers.org/articles/article_27491.cfm

3. http://www.wnho.net/aspartame_brain_damage.htm

4. http://www.sweetpoison.com/aspartame-side-effects.html

5. http://articles.mercola.com/sites/articles/archive/2014/10/01/artificial-sweeteners-raise-diabetes-risk.aspx?e_cid=20141001Z3_DNL_art_1&utm_source=dnl&utm_medium=email&utm_content=art1&utm_campaign=20141001Z3&et_cid=DM56956&et_rid=676436806

6. http://gmoinside.org/gmo-timeline-a-history-genetically-modified-foods/

7. http://www.gmoseralini.org/research-papers/

8. http://www.organicconsumers.org/gefood/countrieswithbans.cfm

9. http://www.i-sis.org.uk/MDSGBTC.php

10. http://articles.mercola.com/sites/articles/archive/2012/04/03/gmo-crops-affect-farmers.aspx

11. http://www.gmo-compass.org/eng/regulation/labelling/89.gmo_labelling_guidelines_threshold.html

12. http://www.food.gov.uk/science/additives/enumberlist

13. http://www.mnn.com/food/healthy-eating/stories/8-creepy-mystery-ingredients-in-fast-food

14. http://articles.mercola.com/sites/articles/archive/2012/01/12/aha-position-on-omega-6-fats.aspx

15. http://articles.mercola.com/sites/articles/archive/2013/07/09/farmed-salmon-dangers.aspx

16. http://articles.mercola.com/sites/articles/archive/2013/01/13/mercury-detoxification-protocol.aspx

17. http://www.hungryforchange.tv/article/19-foods-to-naturally-detox-radiation

18. http://www.naturalnews.com/032265_zeolites_radiation.html

19. http://www.naturalnews.com/023511_magnesium_body_deficiency.html

20. http://www.lef.org/magazine/2012/ss/selenium-protect-against-cancer/page-01

21. http://www.regenerativenutrition.com/boron-osteoporosis-arthritis-allergies-menopause-hormones.asp

22. http://www.ncbi.nlm.nih.gov/pubmed/18588554

Chapter 10 – NUTRIENT DEFICIENCY

How many times has your doctor told you that as long as you get a balanced diet you will get the nutrients that you need? That may have been true once upon a time; unfortunately it may not be the case now with the crops produced by intensive farming methods using chemical fertilisers. Let's have a brief look at some of the nutrients we may be missing in our diets and lifestyle choices. I say brief because it is not intended to go into depth regarding each nutrient, there is plenty of information available for those of you who want more. The purpose here is just to give a level of understanding which can help with choices you make.

The vitamin D connection

When is a vitamin not a vitamin? Answer; when it's called vitamin D. Are you surprised to hear that vitamin D is not a vitamin? According to the Oxford English dictionary this is the definition of a vitamin:

> *'Any of a group of organic compounds which are essential for normal growth and nutrition and are required in small quantities in the diet because they cannot be synthesized by the body'*

Vitamin D is synthesised in the skin from cholesterol under the action of sunlight, that's why it's called the sunshine vitamin.

Vitamin D therefore does not comply with the definition of a vitamin does it? So if vitamin D is not a vitamin what is it? The answer surprisingly is that it is a hormone, and what is the definition of a hormone according to the Oxford English dictionary?

'A regulatory substance produced in an organism and transported in tissue fluids such as blood to stimulate specific cells or tissues into action.'

Clearly we have been misinformed about this stuff called vitamin D. We do get it in our food supply from things like eggs, dairy, meat and oily fish but it only becomes essential if we do not get enough sunlight exposure. This was the situation back in the work houses of the 1800's where children in particular developed rickets due to lack of sun light and hence vitamin D.

What has been happening over the last few decades regarding sun exposure? We have been told that the sun is dangerous and we must cover up, apply high factor sunscreen and avoid the sun. People generally tend to ignore the avoidance bit since we all like to be in the sun, it's our natural way of being. Since they ignore the avoidance advice they tend to use large amounts of sunscreen. Sunscreens and allied products are big business, the products are promoted heavily and scare tactics employed to encourage you to comply.

Now don't get me wrong, over exposure to the sun can certainly be dangerous and damaging to the skin. Like all things in life moderation is the key. Too little is not helpful, too much may be harmful, be sensible, if you were meant to be brown you would have been born that colour. Just because the glossy magazines give a false image of beauty and health, you don't have to comply, do you?

O.K. vitamin D is probably called that because its other name, colecalciferol, is a bit of a mouthful!

We now know, as previously stated, that vitamin D is a hormone and as such it is a signalling molecule which influences many aspects of our metabolism and hence our health status. For long enough it was accepted that the role of vitamin D was in bone health and that's where the story ended and indeed that's what I was taught. That was a long time ago and things move on, except in the world of medical science where it takes a long time for something new to catch on. Remember it takes 50-100 years to change an entrenched belief system.

I said earlier that vitamin D is made from cholesterol; it would appear therefore that there is a double whammy at work here, lack of exposure to the sun and cholesterol lowering medication. Does this strike of conspiracy theory or just medical ignorance? I'll leave you to ponder.

Most nutrients often have officially recommended blood levels and for vitamin D if it is over 30ng/ml that's considered O.K. (1ng = 1,000,000,000th of a gram). Is that enough? Many people have low levels of vitamin D. A CDC report from 2011 showed that a third of Americans are deficient[1]. Vitamin D is only made in the skin between the hours of 10am and 3pm due to the angle of the sun in the sky and the way UV-B rays penetrate the atmosphere and if you live above around 40° north or below 40° south then you won't be making any during late autumn to early spring. This is the time when it can be truly called a vitamin because you need to get it from your food or if you've had adequate sun exposure during the summer you will hopefully have stored enough to last you through the winter. Of course if you live on the equator or in the tropics you make it all year round providing you get adequate sun exposure.

What is adequate sun exposure? Approximately 5–30 minutes of sun exposure between 10 AM and 3 PM at least twice a week to the face, arms, legs, or back without sunscreen usually lead to sufficient vitamin D synthesis[2]. You can produce 10,000 to 20,000 units of vitamin D in 30 minutes, it is fat soluble and you store it for a rainy day. If you do not get that level of sun exposure then it is more important to get it from your food or a supplement. When I was a child it was common practice to take daily cod liver oil which supplies around 2000 units in a teaspoon (adult dose). Unfortunately there may be issues with heavy metals in our present polluted seas. Please keep in mind that: <u>**Sensible sun exposure is necessary; burning yourself to a crisp is not only unnecessary but highly undesirable.**</u>

As a matter of interest the skin cancer rate has increased dramatically over the last 35 years in spite of the hard hitting messages from the medical and sunscreen industries. In the UK (which doesn't get that much sun!) the rate has gone up 7 fold for males and 4 fold for women during the period 1975-2011[3]. Clearly there's something else going on, it's not just about avoiding the sun. This quote from The National Library of Medicine gives an indication of other factors.

> *'We therefore conclude that the large increase in reported incidence is likely to be due to diagnostic drift which classifies benign lesions as stage 1 melanoma. This conclusion could be confirmed by direct histological comparison of contemporary and past histological samples. The distribution of the lesions reported did not correspond to the sites of lesions caused by solar exposure. These findings should lead to a reconsideration of the treatment of 'early' lesions, a search for better diagnostic methods to distinguish them from truly malignant melanomas, re-evaluation of the role of ultraviolet radiation and recommendations for protection*

from it, as well as the need for a new direction in the search for the cause of melanoma.'[4]

<u>***National Library of Medicine***</u>

What is this saying? Melanoma occurs on areas of skin other than those exposed to solar damage; diagnostic methods need to be improved (remember diagnosis accuracy spoken of earlier) and the cause of melanoma is not known.

As I said previously vitamin D has traditionally been known for its role in bone health. As time goes by the importance of vitamin D in many other health conditions is being realised as this quote indicates.

> ***'......vitamin D is connected to a variety of other diseases that include different cancer types, muscular weakness, hypertension, autoimmune diseases, multiple sclerosis, type 1 diabetes, schizophrenia and depression.....'[5]***

<u>***National Library of Medicine***</u>

Note that vitamin D is important in the prevention of cancer, including skin cancer. It is also vitally important for mental health. If you are deficient then you are much more likely to suffer from depression. It is also becoming clear how important vitamin D is in relation to the immune system[6]. If the immune system is compromised then all sorts of disease states can develop as indicated above. Is it any wonder there is this epidemic of diseases, when people en masse are being steered away from this vitally important nutrient? Knowledge is power; get to know the implications of low vitamin D and get your level checked. If your doctor won't do it you can send away for a test kit and do your own[7]. You may find conflicting advice as to the correct levels of vitamin D[8]. The vitamin D council gives the highest levels and that's the level I personally choose to accept. They say that a blood level of 60-80ng/ml is the right amount and up to 100ng/ml is still within normal parameters. When I tested mine it was 99ng/ml, I do spend a lot of time outdoors in the sun!

It is not the purpose here to go into the detail of how vitamin D is essential to much of our cellular function and hence our overall health and vitality. Others have already done this; Dr Michael Holick is a good source of information[9]. The sole purpose here is to make you aware of the importance of vitamin D and to prompt you into making sure you have sufficiency. The best source of vitamin D is sunlight exposure as we've seen and you cannot produce too much from sunlight exposure; your body will convert any excess to other compounds which we're only just beginning to understand. Keeping out of the sun and taking a standard vitamin D supplement 400-600IU per day may prevent rickets and osteomalacia but it may not prevent the host of other diseases previously mentioned.

What was the treatment for tuberculosis pre-antibiotics? Convalescence in the sunshine!

Vitamin K

If you take a vitamin D supplement then it is important to take vitamin K2 as well. This will ensure that calcium is mobilised into the bones and not elsewhere; vitamin D without K2 can be associated with arterial calcification which you don't want[10]. Vitamin K is also important in other areas of health; it is best known for its role in blood clotting but is also needed for bone health, brain function, healthy teeth and immune function. These are things that we know of; there are most likely other functions that we don't know of. Most people get enough vitamin K for blood clotting but may be not enough to protect them from the other health issues[11].

Magnesium

What make plants green? Answer; chlorophyll, the green coloured pigment which captures photons of sunlight and uses that light energy to manufacture chemical bond energy in the form of glucose. Glucose is made from carbon dioxide and water; magic! Plants take carbon dioxide out of the air and what are humans doing? Cutting down the rain forests; great!

The chlorophyll molecule has at its centre an atom of magnesium and it is this magnesium which is vitally important in many of life's processes. Magnesium is an essential nutrient that plants need to make chlorophyll.

Magnesium is essential to all life, without it there would be no life as we know it.

Now we don't have this ability to make glucose by capturing sunlight (although as we've seen we do make vitamin D) nevertheless magnesium is equally important to us and is an essential nutrient. At least 300 enzyme reactions involve magnesium. An enzyme reaction can be likened to the catalytic converter in your car; it makes a reaction proceed more quickly and efficiently. Biological reactions tend to be rather slow if left to their own devices and so enzymes are needed to speed them up. If there is insufficient magnesium then we won't have efficient cellular activity and this will impact on our health at the physical and mental level.

Only about 1% of the magnesium in your body is found in the fluid outside of the cells and therefore a blood test is a poor indicator of magnesium status. 99% of the magnesium is inside the cells and so it is the intracellular status that needs to be determined. Magnesium deficiency is often not considered and yet it is so prevalent and is associated with many symptoms, here are some of them:

- *Muscle weakness and spasms*
- *Muscle cramps and twitching, twitches around the eyes*
- *Tremors*
- *Nausea*
- *Anxiety, depression, nervousness, irritability*
- *High blood pressure*
- *Irregular heart beat*
- *Type II diabetes*
- *Respiratory issues*
- *Dizziness*
- *Fatigue*
- *Potassium deficiency*
- *Difficulty swallowing*
- *Poor memory, confusion*
- *PMS*
- *Digestive problems*
- *Bone and teeth disorders*

We know cellular energy production relies on magnesium being present; magnesium is necessary for the relaxation of muscles after contraction. The heart is a muscle, and blood vessels have muscle within the vessel walls. Magnesium is essential for proper nerve function and bone health. The symptom list is easily related to these areas of activity which is by no means exhaustive. For an in depth look at magnesium see reference[12 & 13].

According to the US government:

> **'An analysis of data from the National Health and Nutrition Examination Survey (NHANES) of 2005–2006 found that a majority of Americans of all ages ingest less magnesium from food than their respective EARs.'** [14]
>
> **EAR = estimated average requirement**

If you're not getting enough magnesium in your diet then the conclusion must be that you are deficient, yes?

Only 30-40% of dietary magnesium is absorbed[15] and absorption from supplements will vary depending on the form of magnesium. Many cheap supplements have magnesium oxide in them which is poorly absorbed, maybe as low as 4%, magnesium aspartate has up to 70% absorption however the aspartate part is an excitatory neurotoxin when floating freely in the blood stream.

What's the best form of magnesium supplementation? Transdermal magnesium, a solution made from ancient sea minerals, applied to the skin, it is absorbed through the skin into the blood stream[16].

<u>Iodine</u>

Hands up all those of you who loved chemistry at school; I don't see many hands! Well before I talk about iodine I want to just have a quick review of the halogens, I'll keep it simple.

The word halogen means 'salt former'; the halogens are a group of elements which all have similar chemical properties and include fluorine, chlorine, bromine, iodine and for completion astatine which is radioactive and doesn't hang around for long.

Fluorine is the smallest atom and iodine the largest which in practice means that the fluorine has a greater pulling force on electrons and is more reactive than iodine. Fluorine reactions are violent and often explosive because of this electronic affinity. Iodine reactions are much more sedate and more suited to biological reactions which tend to be slow without enzyme (catalyst) involvement.

O.K. that's enough chemistry for one day, just bear in mind this relative reactivity.

The generally recognised role of iodine is in the production of thyroid hormone, tetra-iodothyronine, thyroxine or T4 for short. Tetra means four; there are four iodine atoms in the molecule. The other component of thyroid hormone is the amino acid tyrosine. In the body tissues T4 is converted to tri-iodothyronine, T3, which is biologically more active. This conversion requires selenium and so you can see if you are deficient in iodine or selenium then you are not going to get an optimum thyroid response.

The thyroid has been described as the master gland in terms of its influence on cell energy.

Thyroid hormones regulate energy and metabolism, they influence the autonomic nervous system; this controls among other things, heart rate and blood pressure, digestion and bladder function. They regulate feeding, glucose metabolism and heat production by an effect in a part of the brain called the hypothalamus[17].

In summary thyroid hormones are involved with:

- *Cell energy regulation*
- *Correct nerve function*
- *Regulation of food intake*
- *Regulation of heat production*
- *Regulation of glucose metabolism*
- *Probably numerous other functions*

Here is a list of symptoms, caused by under functioning of the thyroid, from the Mayo clinic[18].

- *Fatigue*
- *Increased sensitivity to cold*
- *Constipation*
- *Dry skin*
- *Unexplained weight gain*
- *Puffy face*
- *Hoarseness*
- *Muscle weakness*

- *Elevated blood cholesterol level*
- *Muscle aches, tenderness and stiffness*
- *Pain, stiffness or swelling in your joints*
- *Thinning hair*
- *Slowed heart rate*
- *Depression*
- *Heavier than normal or irregular menstrual periods*
- *Impaired memory*

How much iodine is enough? The RDA (recommended daily allowance) is set at between 110 and 290 micrograms depending on age and pregnancy and lactation status[19]. The average intake of iodine in Japan, where they consume a lot of iodine rich foods, is much higher than this RDA value. Some sources say that Japanese iodine intake is up to 13-14mg a day[20], other 'more official' sources put it at 1- 3mg a day[21]. Even at 1-3mg this is 6 to 20 times the RDA for an adult.

How do you know if you need more iodine? Standard urine testing does not give an accurate picture of iodine status; an iodine loading test is more accurate. This test involves taking a loading dose of iodine (50mg) and collecting urine over 24 hours which is then sample tested. If you have sufficient iodine in your system then you will excrete 90% of this dose i.e. 45mg.

Only 3% of the iodine in your body is found in the thyroid gland. Where is the rest? It is in the rest of your cells and its role is only just being recognised. Many systems need iodine to function optimally. Breast tissue is particularly susceptible to iodine deficiency and fibrocystic disease is associated with that[22]. Iodine is important in prostate health and the incidence of prostate cancer in Japan is much lower than elsewhere.

One of the big issues with iodine is its displacement by other members of the halide group. Fluorine in the form of fluoride, and bromine in the form of bromide will displace iodine and therefore increase the demand for iodine. Iodine in the form of potassium iodate was used as a bread improver until the 1960's when it was replaced by potassium bromate.

Bromine compounds come in many forms and are ubiquitous in the modern age. They are found in fire retardant chemicals, pesticides, cleaners, some medicines. We are generally exposed to much higher levels of bromine than we used to be and this has a negative effect in iodine biochemistry and a disrupting effect on our endocrine system. You can read more about bromide and the theory of bromide dominance at:

http://www.breastcancerchoices.org/bromidedominancetheory.html

Fluoride has a similar disruptive effect on thyroid function. The fluoride added to your drinking water is a waste product of the fertilizer industry. For more information on fluoride check out Thyroid UK:

http://www.thyroiduk.org.uk/tuk/treatment/fluoride.html

Dr David Brownstein is well versed on the subject of iodine and his book 'Iodine why you need it, why you can't live without it' is an informative book and it is easy to read and understand[23].

Selenium
The importance of selenium in the conversion of T4 to the more active T3 was mentioned in the last section. The RDA for selenium is 55 micrograms. China, New Zealand and parts of Europe have a problem with deficiency and people with HIV can become depleted since the virus gobbles up selenium.

What else is selenium involved with?

'Because of its effects on DNA repair, apoptosis, and the endocrine and immune systems as well as other mechanisms, including its antioxidant properties, selenium might play a role in the prevention of cancer'[24]

Apoptosis is the term given for programmed cell death, something that doesn't occur in cancer cells and why they grow out of control.

Selenium is necessary for the synthesis of glutathione peroxidase, an important anti-oxidant enzyme which protects against cell damage.

Zinc
'Zinc is involved in numerous aspects of cellular metabolism. It is required for the catalytic activity of approximately 100 enzymes and it plays a role in immune function, protein synthesis, wound healing, DNA synthesis, and cell division. Zinc also supports normal growth and development during pregnancy, childhood,

and adolescence and is required for proper sense of taste and smell.'[25]

As can be seen from this extract, zinc is another important mineral for which the adult RDA is around 10mg. You can easily take a zinc taste test to determine your status[26]; this is available at many pharmacies.

Boron

I include boron because it is a trace mineral that people wouldn't ordinarily consider and ask themselves; am I getting enough? Boron seems to be intimately involved with calcium and magnesium metabolism which makes it particularly important for bone and joint health. Like most nutrients boron has many functions in our body; read here for further information[27].

An interesting article on the use of boron in the treatment of arthritis is called the Borax Conspiracy[28]. Borax is a household chemical that was used widely until the advent of modern chemical cleaners; it is still a good source of boron. If you choose this option you need to make sure you are confident of making up the correct strength. You can also buy boron supplements.

Chromium

Chromium exists in two forms known as trivalent and hexavalent which simply means one can form three bonds with other compounds and the other six. The trivalent form is the form of the trace mineral which humans need; the hexavalent form is highly toxic and was brought to public awareness in the film 'Erin Brokovich'.

We don't know too much about chromium but what we do know is that it is important in the regulation of insulin activity and hence blood sugar.

Glucose Tolerance Factor (GTF) is synthesized in vivo from absorbed dietary chromium, and acts as a physiological enhancer of insulin activity, binding to insulin and potentiating its action about three-fold.

So GTF enhances insulin activity, why in 40 years of pharmacy practice have I never once seen GTF (found in brewer's yeast) or chromium prescribed?

> ***A review of the numerous physiological actions of insulin suggests a number of therapeutic applications for GTF, in such diverse ailments as diabetes mellitus, hyperlipidemia, reactive hypoglycaemia, obesity, cancer, protein malnutrition or malabsorption, endogenous depression, Parkinsonism, hypertension and cardiac arrhythmias. GTF supplementation may also have value in preventive medicine[29].***

Vanadium

Vanadium compounds are highly colourful; it was named after the Norse goddess of beauty Vanadis. Vanadium has been shown to have insulin like activity.

Vanadium is used for treating diabetes, low blood sugar, high cholesterol, heart disease, tuberculosis, syphilis, a form of "tired blood" (anaemia), and water retention (oedema); for improving athletic performance in weight training; and for preventing cancer[30].

I've never seen this prescribed either.

Cobalt

Cobalt is an essential trace mineral and component of vitamin B12, cyanocobalamin. Vitamin B12 is essential for production of red blood cells and has important function in the central nervous system and DNA synthesis.

B12 along with other 'methyl donors', is important in the conversion of the amino acid homocysteine to methionine[31]. Homocysteine may be an independent risk factor for cardiovascular disease (see later). B12 may help protect the brain in Alzheimer's disease. It is important in preventing and treating pernicious anaemia, this is caused by a lack of intrinsic factor in the gastro–intestinal tract. Intrinsic factor is needed to facilitate B12 absorption.

Manganese and Copper

These two trace elements are also important in bone formation and deficiency is implicated in the development of osteoporosis. No doubt there are other areas of importance we haven't discovered yet.

Iron

Iron, as most people are aware is important for the production of red blood cells as it is the central component of haemoglobin, the red blood pigment which carries oxygen to the tissues and carbon dioxide from the tissues for elimination. Iron has many other roles in the body; it is involved in many enzyme systems.

When people take an iron supplement it is commonly in the form of inorganic iron such as ferrous sulphate. Inorganic iron is poorly absorbed; the RDA for iron is around 14 mg for an adult; iron supplements of ferrous sulphate contain 65mg of iron per 200mg of ferrous sulphate. Because of the poor absorption you need to take a large dose to get your 14mg; a typical one a day iron tablet contains 325mg of ferrous sulphate which is equivalent to 105mg of elemental iron. What is the iron that remains in your gut doing? The large proportion of the dose that is unabsorbed is responsible for the gastro-intestinal side effects of nausea, vomiting, constipation and diarrhoea. What is generally not considered and maybe somewhat controversial is that iron in the form of 'ferrous' $Fe2+$ is an electron donor, i.e. it loses an electron to become $Fe3+$. This is an oxidation reduction reaction. The iron is oxidised and 'something else' is reduced. This is the reason vitamin C is often given with ferrous sulphate, to prevent this. This can have consequences.

> *Co-supplementation of ferrous salts with vitamin C exacerbates oxidative stress in the gastrointestinal tract leading to ulceration in healthy individuals, exacerbation of chronic gastrointestinal inflammatory diseases and can lead to cancer. Reactive oxygen and nitrogen species (RONS) have been ascribed an important role in oxidative stress. Redox-active metal ions such as Fe(II) and Cu(I) further activate RONS and thus perpetuate their damaging effects[32].*

> **_National Library of Medicine_**

Naturally like most nutrients the best form of iron is the iron from food; organic liver is great if you're not a vegetarian.

<u>Oxygen</u>

You may be puzzled by this one. How can we be lacking oxygen when we breathe it in all the time? In actual fact most people only breathe very shallowly using the upper part of their chest and only partially filling the lungs. Deep breathing using the diaphragm to completely fill the lungs will get much more oxygen into the circulation. Cancer hates oxygen, cancer cells grow in the absence of oxygen and is why they employ a fermentation process using sugars instead of oxidative phophorylation found in non cancerous cells. Anything which encourages deep breathing is beneficial, yoga, tai chi or chi gung are examples.

<u>Endnotes</u>

People take supplements for many reasons and it is important to choose wisely. The body is an orchestra and when it is in harmony the same tune is sounding throughout the structure. Nutrient deficiencies will cause the body to go out of tune and disease symptoms will manifest.

What is the best source of nutrients? Our food of course, unfortunately much of our food may be deficient in the very nutrients we need. We can increase the value of our food by avoiding junk food and processed food; by choosing organic whole foods and by using juicing as a way to extract more nutrients in a smaller volume.

During illness it may be necessary to increase our intake of certain nutrients like vitamin C for example. The body's demand for nutrients is not static but dynamic; this variability will depend on many factors and stressors we encounter in everyday life. Supplements should not be necessary if our food was wholesome and complete and we have a good balanced diet. If you choose to take supplements remember that they vary in quality and while the label may state a certain quantity it does not mean you will absorb that amount. Magnesium oxide is a classic example where absorption is around 5-10%. Vitamin C is only absorbed at around 20% and this is why liposomal vitamin C is so much better at around 90%. The point is to ask questions about the products you consume; blind ignorance can be an expensive waste of your resources.

If you are taking medications from your doctor it is important to realise that certain foods and nutrient supplements can interfere in the therapeutic response of the drug. This may be additive or subtractive and is why you need accurate advice. Many doctors might say to avoid nutrients that might interfere because they don't know the potential dangers or benefits but to my mind if a nutrient enhances a drug effect so that you can take less of a drug then that has to be beneficial. If on the other hand if a nutrient reduces a drug effect so you need to take more then that is maybe not so good. Drugs are well known for causing nutrient depletion such that it may become life threatening. The potassium loss caused by certain diuretics is one such example. The bottom line is that you need good information to make good choices and that information may not always be forthcoming from the sources you expect it to come from.

References

1. http://www.cdc.gov/nchs/data/databriefs/db59.htm

2. http://ods.od.nih.gov/factsheets/VitaminD-HealthProfessional/

3. http://www.cancerresearchuk.org/cancer-info/cancerstats/types/skin/incidence/uk-skin-cancer-incidence-statistics

4. http://www.ncbi.nlm.nih.gov/pubmed/19519827

5. http://www.ncbi.nlm.nih.gov/pubmed/18767337

6. http://www.ncbi.nlm.nih.gov/pmc/articles/PMC3166406/

7. https://betteryou.com/vitamin-d-testing-service

8. https://www.vitamindcouncil.org/further-topics/i-tested-my-vitamin-d-level-what-do-my-results-mean/#

9. http://drholick.com/

10. http://articles.mercola.com/sites/articles/archive/2013/10/19/vitamin-d-vitamin-k2.aspx

11. http://www.ncbi.nlm.nih.gov/pmc/articles/PMC3321262/

12. http://www.magnesiumeducation.com/how-magnesium-works-why-it-is-important

13. http://www.greenmedinfo.com/blog/magnesium-deficiency-symptoms-and-diagnosis

14. http://ods.od.nih.gov/factsheets/Magnesium-HealthProfessional/

15. http://ods.od.nih.gov/factsheets/Magnesium-HealthProfessional/

16. http://www.ancient-minerals.com/magnesium-supplements/

17. http://www.cell.com/trends/molecular-medicine/abstract/S1471-4914%2813%2900072-5

18. http://www.mayoclinic.org/diseases-conditions/hypothyroidism/basics/symptoms/con-20021179

19. http://ods.od.nih.gov/factsheets/Iodine-HealthProfessional/

20. http://www.lef.org/magazine/2009/10/Halt-on-Salt-Sparks-Iodine-Deficiency/Page-01

21. http://www.thyroidresearchjournal.com/content/4/1/14

22. http://www.globalhealingcenter.com/natural-health/iodine-and-breast-health-6-things-you-need-to-know/

23. http://www.drbrownstein.com/

24. http://ods.od.nih.gov/factsheets/Selenium-HealthProfessional/#h6

25. http://ods.od.nih.gov/factsheets/Zinc-HealthProfessional/

26. http://www.clinicians.co.nz/zinc-taste-testing/

27. https://www.organicfacts.net/health-benefits/minerals/boron.html

28. http://www.health-science-spirit.com/borax.htm

29. http://www.ncbi.nlm.nih.gov/pubmed/7005627

30. http://www.webmd.com/vitamins-supplements/ingredientmono-749-vanadium.aspx?activeingredientid=749&activeingredientname=vanadium

31. http://advances.nutrition.org/content/3/1/54.short

32. http://www.ncbi.nlm.nih.gov/pubmed/14728718

Chapter 11 - VITAMIN C

This vitamin has a long and controversial history. It is a relatively simple molecule and is made from glucose in most animals except primates (including humans) and guinea pigs. Goats produce around 13,000 mg of vitamin C daily and under stress produce much more, up to 13 times normal levels; so why is the recommended allowance for humans so low[1]? Let's face it, most humans are under stress of some sort; stress markedly increases our requirement for vitamin C.

The official recommended daily allowance (RDA) for vitamin C in humans is around 100mg, this is three orders of magnitude less than the stressed goat's requirement. Goats and humans are mammals and get equally stressed depending on the environment and stressors they are subjected to. It would seem that the RDA is not sufficient to support us during stressful periods; it's most likely not enough to support us during non-stressful periods either!

The RDA for humans is set at a level to prevent acute deficiency which leads to clinical scurvy, the source of many a sailor's death in the early years of seafaring.

Why is vitamin C so important?

Vitamin C is important in the production of collagen. Collagen is the basic structural material that holds you together and without sufficient vitamin C your tissue integrity will be severely compromised. This is what Linus Pauling a two times Nobel Laureate says about collagen:

'A person who is dying of scurvy stops making this substance, and his body falls apart, his joints fail, because he can no longer keep the cartilage and tendons strong, his blood vessels break open, his gums ulcerate and his teeth fall out, his immune system deteriorates, and he dies.'[2]

I hope you get the idea that it is very important to get enough of this vitamin.

Scurvy due to acute vitamin C deficiency may be rare nowadays but heart disease is not, it is in fact the number one killer in western society. In 2010 almost 600,000 people in the U.S. died of heart disease. There is a body of evidence that would suggest that a chronic underlying deficiency of this vital nutrient is at least in part responsible for this pandemic of cardiovascular disease[3].

If you're not able to repair connective tissue (collagen) properly then the body in its infinite wisdom will substitute inferior molecules to make a 'patch'. If you have damage to your blood vessels and it is not 'patched' then you will bleed to death. Unfortunately these patches are the start of the inflammation and atherosclerosis which leads to heart disease.

The initial damage to blood vessels is an inflammatory process which is the root cause of many of our chronic disease states.

In what other areas is vitamin C important?

- *Vitamin C has a natural antihistamine effect not by blocking histamine receptors like conventional antihistamines but by reducing the amount of circulating histamine in the body[4].*

- *Healthy collagen is vital to a healthy body as it is the substance which holds us together as previously stated. People think that for healthy bones they need calcium, which they do, but do not consider that the bone matrix into which the calcium and other minerals, particularly magnesium, are deposited is composed of collagen. Collagen is a protein and requires vitamin C for its manufacture as we've seen. The bottom line is that osteoporosis, and I mean true osteoporosis and not something defined by the WHO as we've discussed before, may be the result of deficiency in vitamin C and poor collagen synthesis, as well as mineral deficiencies. Remember that the body has an inbuilt intelligence which directs the vital functions within thus maintain the viability of the organism; this functionality has evolved over eons of time. The homoeostatic mechanisms will direct resources to the most important parts of our physical structure. Bones are less important than say blood vessels. If a bone breaks you do not generally die, at least not immediately. If a blood vessel breaks in your heart or brain then you may well die.*

- *Vitamin C is anti-viral because it increases the production of Interferon[5] an important part of the immune defence against viruses. There are other postulated mechanisms for anti viral activity including enhanced antibody response[6]. At the first sign of any viral infection, flu for example, taking therapeutic doses of vitamin C may be highly beneficial. Vitamin C given intravenously can be life saving as was the case with a New Zealand farmer who was saved by high dose vitamin C[7], up to 100 grams daily over a week or so. Read that again, 100 grams intravenously (I.V.), that's 100,000 milligrams! His total dosage over the time he was very sick was around 700,000 mg. If you have serious disease then taking inadequate doses is not likely to help. Using liposomal vitamin C might be a good initial response until you can get I.V. vitamin C. Liposomal vitamin C is extremely well absorbed into the blood stream via the oral route, around 90% compared with only 20% from a standard preparation.*

- *Vitamin C is a water soluble antioxidant which means it has important activity inside the cells, reducing the levels of free radicals which are destructive to cell structures. This antioxidant activity is important in relation to toxins in our diet. Nitrites appear in certain food products like smoked meats. Nitrites can form nitrosamines in the gut and nitrosamines are carcinogenic. Vitamin C reduces this effect.*

- *Heavy metals are an ever increasing toxic problem in our environment. Vitamin C has the important ability to combine with heavy metals and allow them to be excreted from the body via the kidneys. This is particularly important with mercury exposure which is ubiquitous in our environment as outlined previously.*

- *Vitamin C can regenerate other important anti-oxidants like vitamin E*

- *Vitamin C is involved with the conversion of cholesterol into bile acids in the liver. This is how cholesterol is eliminated from the body. So low C can lead to high cholesterol[8]).*

More and more pathways which involve this vitamin are being discovered; there are no drugs which can replace its wide spread actions.

This section on vitamin C could have been included in the missing nutrients chapter. Although this chapter is short I felt that the importance of vitamin C warranted a separate chapter. Much has been discovered and written on this nutrient and the purpose here, in line with the intention of the book as a whole, is just to bring certain points to your attention and awareness; the bones of the matter so to speak.

References

1. http://blog.livonlabs.com/goat-vitamin-c-production/

2. http://www.vitamincfoundation.org/collagen.html

3. http://vitamincfoundation.org/suppress.htm

4. http://www.ncbi.nlm.nih.gov/pubmed/1578094

5. http://www.ncbi.nlm.nih.gov/pmc/articles/PMC3659258/

6. http://orthomolecular.org/resources/omns/v05n09.shtml

7. http://articles.mercola.com/sites/articles/archive/2009/09/24/IV-Vitamin-C-Used-to-Recover-Terminal-Swine-Flu-Case.aspx

8. http://orthomolecular.org/resources/omns/v05n09.shtml

9. http://www.ncbi.nlm.nih.gov/pubmed/4685043

Chapter 12 - WATER – THE FLUID OF LIFE

Water is something we all take for granted. That is until there is a shortage and then our attention is more focused in preserving our supplies. How many of us think or even realise how important good quality water is to our health and vitality?

You may live for several weeks without food but only a few days without water.

In countries where water borne diseases are endemic you only have to clean up the water supply for the health of the population to be vastly improved.

Do you know what's in your water? You can be assured it is not pure H_2O. Water naturally contains minerals dissolved out of the rocks as the water passes through them, these are generally good for us.

Many of our modern practices contribute to poor water quality:

- *Intensive farming practices using artificial fertilisers, pesticides, herbicides and insecticides. Animal excreta which may contaminate the water course.*
- *Industrial processes which release contaminants directly into the water or into the air where they are brought to earth in rainfall.*
- *Water additives which are supposed to confer health benefits e.g. fluoride.*
- *Chlorine needed to reduce bacterial growth.*

Many of these toxic contaminants have been highlighted in a previous chapter and will not be detailed further. The purpose here is to bring to your awareness that the water you are drinking may not be quite what it seems. If in doubt have a water quality analysis performed, good water filters are available which can remove most 'rubbish'. A reverse osmosis filter will even take out fluoride.

Water constitutes around 70% of our body weight; this value will vary depending on the information source but is a good average. If you consider the water which is combined within the chemical structure of your body then this figure will be much higher, fats and carbohydrates are water and carbon dioxide.

So how important is it to have adequate hydration? Severe dehydration is a medical emergency but how many of you are functioning at a sub-optimal level of hydration? The body's intelligence is directed towards self preservation. If water intake is inadequate then the available water will be channelled to the most important areas, your organs and the least important areas such as skin and joints will become dehydrated leading to symptoms of dysfunction. People spend large amounts of money on skin moisturisers; how do you think they work? They prevent water loss and also draw water from the deeper skin layers; try drinking more water to maintain skin health, hydration comes from within. Joints have a lubricating fluid, synovial fluid, which helps to reduced the friction and wear in the joints. Chronic low level dehydration can be an issue and be a contributing factor in joint pain[1].

Mild dehydration which is a reduction of around 1.5% of bodily water can have a marked effect on mood, energy levels and ability to think[2]. This is not surprising as the brain contains almost 75% water and water loss will impair function.

In a book by Dr F Batmanghelidh 'The body's many cries for water'[3], he details his experiences in treating chronic disease by getting his patients just to drink more water. The book is a fascinating read and gives many insights into one of the contributing factors to the chronic ill health seen in our modern societies.

I'm sure you get the point, drinking enough unadulterated pure water is vitally important to health. When I say pure please be aware that the stuff that comes out of most people's taps is not likely to be pure.

Water, H_2O, is an amazing molecule; it has what is called a dipole which means it has positive and negative parts due to the oxygen having a stronger attraction to the electrons which form the bond between the hydrogen and oxygen. The dipole allows adjacent water molecules to attract each other and form hydrogen bonds, in this way a lattice structure can build up and this is the reason water is liquid between 0°C and 100°C unlike the heavier hydrogen sulphide, H_2S, which is a gas; there are no hydrogen bonds in hydrogen sulphide. Without the hydrogen bonding water would be a gas. Did this happen by chance?

The medical system of homoeopathy has had a long history of ridicule by conventional science because of the lack of 'active ingredient' in the homoeopathic remedy. We are now beginning to understand the structure of water more clearly and that it may have a liquid crystal structure; the idea that the water structure can hold information from another substance is not as silly as once imagined. Various researchers have shown that water can hold the memory of other substances. One of the first was Jacques Benveniste[4]a French immunologist and more recently French virologist, Luc Montagnier[5], a Nobel prize winner.

Another pioneer in the field of water structure is Dr Masuru Emoto who has done a great deal of research into how emotions and other energy fields can affect the structure of water crystals in the frozen state[6]. When a negative emotion such as anger is directed to a water sample and then the water frozen, the crystal structure is amorphous and not well formed. When a more positive emotion or thought such as peace is directed to a water sample the crystal structure is beautiful. Also tap water samples fail to give a good crystal structure unlike pristine mountain water.

The number of scientists prepared to step out of the box is growing; Gerald Pollack is working on what he calls the 4th phase of water[7] which has novel implications. The point I'm trying to make is that we should be treating our water and the water we put into our bodies with maybe a little more respect and knowledge of the importance it has to our health. It may be that the water in our bodies is influenced by what it contains when we drink it and also what emotions we experience. It is clearly being shown that water carries information.

As with most new areas of science there will be the sceptics and professional debunkers, they abound. We just have to recall the words of Arthur Schopenhauer:

All truth passes through three stages

- *Firstly it is ridiculed*
- *Secondly it is violently opposed*
- *Finally it is accepted as being self evident*

Many people have vested interests in the current paradigm, if water has memory and this is proven absolutely then it will totally change our view of biology and medicine, this could be a big problem for those entrenched in the current world view and the concept will meet strong resistance?

Before finishing this chapter I'd like to say a few words about salt. Salt and water balance are intimately linked. If you lose salt you also lose water, this is how diuretic drugs work; they cause the kidney to eliminate salt and the water tags along with it.

What actually is salt? A simple question, and so is the answer. Real salt comes mainly from two sources, sea salt and rock salt; the rock salt was in fact sea salt at some distant point in history and so all salt is really from the sea. In this form it is a healthy product. Himalayan mountain salt contains around 80 other minerals and elements other than sodium and chloride.

The white condiment that most people call salt is in fact refined salt which consists of purified sodium chloride and anti-caking agents, no trace minerals. Of course salt is needed to maintain life; it is not the 'criminal' it is made out to be. We used to preserve our food in salt and hypertension and heart disease was not an issue back then. Adequate salt is needed for correct water balance in the body, it is vital for nerve and muscle function and for producing your stomach acid.

A recent Cochrane review[8] has indicated that there is scant evidence to back up the idea that salt restriction = extended life. This has to be the outcome of any intervention otherwise it is pointless, isn't it? Salt restriction may have a very slight blood pressure reducing effect but it appears that this doesn't translate to more years of life. We see the same story as for other interventions which only alter biological markers and don't have the outcome of life extension. This quote from the Scientific American says it all.

> *This week a meta-analysis of seven studies involving a total of 6,250 subjects in the American Journal of Hypertension found no strong evidence that cutting salt intake reduces the risk for heart attacks, strokes or death in people with normal or high blood pressure.* [9]

Salt is important in our diets for many reasons. For more information on the beneficial role of salt see 'Salt your way to health' by Dr Brownstein [10].

References

1. http://www.livestrong.com/article/448421-does-drinking-more-water-help-with-joint-pain/
2. http://today.uconn.edu/blog/2012/02/even-mild-dehydration-can-alter-mood/
3. http://www.watercure.com/
4. http://www.tcm.phy.cam.ac.uk/~bdj10/lectures/benveniste99.html
5. http://homeopathyplus.com/french-nobel-prize-winner-supports-memory-of-water/
6. http://www.masaru-emoto.net/english/water-crystal.html
7. http://articles.mercola.com/sites/articles/archive/2013/08/18/exclusion-zone-water.aspx
8. http://www.cochrane.org/CD009217/VASC_reduced-dietary-salt-for-the-prevention-of-cardiovascular-disease
9. http://www.scientificamerican.com/article/its-time-to-end-the-war-on-salt/
10. http://www.drbrownstein.com/Salt-Your-Way-to-Health-p/salt.htm

Chapter 13 - GOOD FATS, BAD FATS, WHO'S CONFUSED?

Over the years, actually several decades, the public has been indoctrinated with the idea at a conscious and sub-conscious level to truly believe deep within our being that animal fat is bad for us and vegetable oils are good. This brainwashing has no class boundaries, professionals and lay people alike have the same view on this subject and there is no doubt in the minds of many health care professionals that animal fat causes heart disease.

Cigarettes come with a health warning because we absolutely know that there are health issues associated with smoking, heart disease being one of them. The reduction in heart disease over the last few decades is most likely due, in part, to the reduction in smoking prevalence and not to reduction of animal fat consumption.

Back in the 'good old days' prior to the 1920's most fat consumed was of animal origin. Even margarine, invented by the French as a cheap butter substitute was made from animal fat before hydrogenation of vegetable oils was more common. As improved hydrogenation capabilities were developed margarine became made more exclusively from vegetable oils.

Hydrogenation (addition of hydrogen to the oil molecules) turns the oil into a solid, higher melting point, fat. During the hydrogenation process, TRANS fats are produced which are now known to be very unhealthy. Earlier on you saw how Ancel Keys, the progenitor of the fat hypothesis for heart disease, cherry picked the data which gave a biased result. He also didn't take into account the amount of sugar in the diet or consider other risk factors such as smoking, lack of exercise and alcohol consumption. A rule in statistics is that correlation does not imply causation; Ancel Keys must have overlooked this! All in all the research was a little simplistic and yet dieticians, food scientists and the medical community have been blindly following his conclusion for far too long now.

We have been following the low fat, high carbohydrate diet advice for over 50 years now. Carbohydrates are good to eat without any issues because we've been told that it's OK, they are good and healthy; the food pyramid that has been expounded during this time period clear displays carbohydrates in the form of grain based foods at its base: bread, pasta, cereals, rice, biscuits, cakes and so on. It may show sugar and confectionary at the top of the pyramid which implies use sparingly but what it doesn't tell you is that all carbohydrates, particularly highly refined carbohydrates, like the ones listed, rapidly release glucose sugar into the blood stream shortly after they've been eaten. The body doesn't care what the source is, glucose is glucose, and excess glucose in the body has to be removed so it is converted into fat and stored, as you've previously learned. The following charts shows some interesting data (<< means much less than, < means less than).

Year	Heart disease deaths /100,000[1]	Cigarettes consumed per person[2]	Butter consumed Lbs per person[3]	Cheese consumed lbs per person[3]
1700	?	<<54		
1800	?	<54		
1900	137	54		
1910	159	151		
1920	159	665		
1930	214	1485	18	
1940	292	1976	17	
1950	355	3522	10.5	
1960	369	4171	8	
1970	362	3985	5.5	16.4
1980	336	3851	4.5	21.9
1990	289	2827	4.3	28
2000	258	2092	4.5	32.2
2010	193	1278	4.9	35

Year	Frozen dairy products consumed per person[3]	Eggs consumed per person[4]	Margarine consumed per person[5]	Sugar consumed lbs per person[6]
1700				4
1800				6
1900				48
1910			1.3	
1920			2.5	72
1930			2	
1940			2	78
1950		379	6.5	
1960		323	9	78
1970	25.8	302	10.5	
1980	25.4	266	11	86
1990	23	230	10.5	
2000	24	247	7.5	106
2010	21.6	243(2008)	2.5	

Looking back over the last 100 years, if we exclude the deaths from influenza associated diseases in 1918, heart disease has been the No 1 cause of death. The incidence of heart disease is still higher now than it was when we were consuming a high saturated fat diet in the early 1900's. Heart disease accounted for 1 death in 10 back then and now it is 1 death out of every 4. Granted, people were dying of other things in the early 1900's but it wasn't heart disease from high dietary fat consumption. Let's look at some U.S. data comparing products consumed over the last century and the death rate from heart disease. Some of the data points in this chart are missing because I couldn't find suitable data and some data point are approximate because they were taken from graphs; the accuracy is sufficient to see the trends.

> **Prior to 1900 heart disease was quite rare, I could find no data for this time period however reverse extrapolation of the data set might indicate this. The death rate from heart disease climbed steadily from the early 1900s to its peak in1960s to 1970s; during that time butter consumption and egg consumption declined. Interestingly cheese consumption has steadily increased since the 70s as heart disease mortality has declined. Strikingly the heart disease death rate mirrors the cigarette smoking and margarine consumption data. Sugar consumption has increased markedly over the century and as you know excess sugar = fat production in the body.**

The idea that consuming butter and cheese and eggs causes heart disease is not very convincing; is it? Heart disease was peaking in the 70s when margarine consumption was at its highest while butter consumption had reached what was an all time low at that time. Whole milk consumption was on its way down (data not shown) and cheese consumption on its way up, quite dramatically. Cheese obviously didn't get the same bad press as butter, but then it is difficult to produce low fat cheese. When I was at school in the late 50's early 60's we used to get free school milk and also had milk delivered to the door at home. The milk generally had cream floating on top and we used to have to shake it to mix it. This showed that the milk had not been homogenised which is the common practice now.

Homogenisation reduces the fat droplet size so that it doesn't separate out. When you drink homogenised milk the fat particles are so small that they can be absorbed directly into the lymphatic vessels which join with the thoracic duct which empties directly into the heart. You get undigested fat being deposited into the heart! Homogenisation also increases the absorption of xanthine oxidase from the milk. This can have a twofold effect; firstly xanthine oxidase can increase levels of uric acid which is implicated in raised blood pressure and secondly xanthine oxidase can increase the level of reactive oxygen species (ROS) which are implicated in endothelial dysfunction and may therefore damage the lining of the arteries contributing to heart disease[8].

Are butter and cheese and whole unprocessed milk implicated in heart disease? You decide.

Margarine has no vitamin D in it; unlike butter which is a good source of vitamin D. Vitamin D is very important in cardiovascular health[9] and in maintaining correct blood pressure[10]. One thing margarine does contain is TRANS fat. This may be less so now than the early days but at the peak of the heart disease deaths it was very evident. TRANS fats are produced during the industrial hydrogenation of vegetable oils and they have been shown to increase levels of LDL cholesterol, the so called 'bad' cholesterol. Without going into technical details of what a TRANS fat is, it is sufficient to know that <u>industrially created</u> TRANS fats are structurally incompatible with biological systems. The defenders of the 'vegetable oil is best' paradigm may say that there are TRANS fats occurring naturally in our diet. True, there are some TRANS fats in animal fat and we also make some in our bodies from certain components of animal fat; these TRANS fats are not a problem as their chemical structure is recognised by the body. Conjugated Linoleic Acid (CLA) is one such TRANS fat and is very healthy for the body[11]. The industrial processed TRANS fats are different and we cannot process them. This is an example how a piece of information can be used to justify putting toxins in the food supply.

Willet et al reported findings from the Nurses Health Study, a prospective study involving more than 85,000 women, showing that intake of trans fatty acids was significantly and independently associated with incidence of CHD. The association was only seen for trans fatty isomers from hydrogenated vegetable oils. The mainly different trans isomers from ruminant fats did not show such an association. A case-control study in 239 people suffering an acute myocardial infarction found that after adjustment for age, sex and energy intake, intake of trans fatty acids was directly related to risk of myocardial infarction. Those with the highest intake of trans fatty acids had twice the risk of myocardial infarction as those with the lowest intakes after adjusting for other cardiovascular risk factors. As with the Nurses Health Study, the association was only seen for trans isomers from partially hydrogenated vegetable oils." (From: Department of Health (1994) Nutritional Aspects of Cardiovascular Disease, Report of the Cardiovascular Review Group of the Committee of Medical Aspects of Food Policy (COMA). Report No. 46. London: HMSO.)

Because vegetable oils are mostly unsaturated they are chemically more reactive and are more easily oxidized to form free radicals which are tissue damaging. This is the process by which oils develop rancidity and is why your local fast food restaurant is constantly changing the fryer oil. In the days when lard was used it was only infrequently changed. I remember my mother had a deep frying pan with lard in and it was *never* changed, only topped up and her fries were always great!

If you consume rancid oils you are eating free radicals; I think most people are aware of the danger from free radicals. For those who aren't, they can cause cell and DNA damage by ripping electrons away from important molecules. DNA damage can be a precursor to cancer. Heating vegetable oils also accelerates free radical production.

In the oil industry they used something called the 'iodine value' and this represents the amount of iodine a fat can absorb and is indicative of the unsaturated bonds within the oil and the stability of the oil. The higher the iodine value the more unstable the oil. I'm sure you've seen when you heat oils to a high temperature there often appears a sticky yellow deposit on the pan which has to be scrubbed off. This is polymerisation of the oil and is why such oils are used to make varnish. Here are a few iodine values of some common oils and fats[12].

OIL	IODINE VALUES
Soy Bean	125 – 145
Sun Flower	120 – 145
Canola	105 - 120
Olive	79 – 95
Beef Tallow	42 – 45
Coconut	8 - 11

You can see from these values that the vegetable oils which have been heavily promoted for use in cooking and which fast food restaurants generally use, have high values and thus have high instability and polymerise easily. Coconut oil and beef fat have the lowest value and are therefore the most stable at high temperatures.

There has been much bad press regarding coconut oil because of its high level of saturated fat, around 92%; half the saturated fat in coconut oil is made up of medium chain fatty acids, C10 capric acid and C12 lauric acid. These acids are readily metabolised into ketones which are preferential sources of energy for the brain, they are not stored. Lauric acid is also converted to a substance called monolaurin which has antiviral, antibacterial, anti fungal and antiprotozoal properties[13].

More and more evidence is surfacing to show that medical science has been applying a false premise in which fat and normal cholesterol cause heart disease. I use the word normal because the deposits found in coronary arteries contain oxidised cholesterol which deposits on sites of inflammation. Cholesterol is a vitally important substance in the body, so important that it is manufactured in the liver and brain particularly and is why reducing cholesterol intake has little impact on levels because your body makes more if it needs it. Cholesterol is important in cell membranes where it helps maintain the cell's structural integrity; it is also involved with cell to cell communication. Cholesterol is the basis of all your steroid hormones, sex hormones, cortisol and of course 'vitamin' D. Too little cholesterol and all of these areas of function will be compromised. Around 25% of the body's cholesterol is found in the brain and is vital to the function of this organ. Just look how much mental illness we have in society; is this related? In the elderly it has been shown that those with the best memory capacity have the highest levels of cholesterol. It is well recognised that statin drugs which lower cholesterol can affect memory.

One big issue there may be with non-organic animal fat is that any chemical toxins the animals are exposed to, are likely to be concentrated in the fat. When you eat the fat, you get the toxins and this is why eating organic is important. Also if the animals are fed with grains high in omega 6 fats then there will be reduced omega 3 in the animal tissues. As you know omega 3 is heart healthy and omega 6 in excess is pro-inflammatory. This also applies to farmed salmon which becomes less healthy than its wild counterpart and also to eggs where hens are fed grains as opposed to a free range diet. The ratio of omega 6 to omega 3 fats in our diets has increased dramatically as vegetable oil consumption and grain fed animal products have increased. Omega 6 fats promote inflammation if they are out of balance. Heart disease is primarily one of inflammation like many of the diseases currently found in western society.

Two countries which eat the most fat and eggs are France and Japan, they have very low rates of heart disease. Science calls these anomalies! The Mediterranean paradox is an often quoted phrase. Do the French and Japanese have different metabolism to us? Maybe, maybe not; what they do have is a diet rich in phyto-nutrients, nutrients from plants. These nutrients are sadly lacking in the Standard American Diet (SAD), which is common in most western cultures. If cholesterol is an issue it is oxidised cholesterol that is the problem. Without adequate anti-oxidants in your circulation cholesterol can be oxidised and then it becomes sticky just like oil round the top of the bottle does. This is a problem, not the cholesterol but the lack of anti-oxidants. Damaged, oxidised cholesterol is what is found in artery plaque; the solution is to improve your diet and get plenty of colourful foods into your body, this is the idea behind 'The Rainbow Diet'

Dr Mercola discusses some of the issues here[14]. Again we must remember that thousands of jobs and careers rest on the current incorrect paradigm. It's not going to change quickly for the majority of people but you as an individual can change your habits when and if you choose.

So if animal fat is not the culprit; what is? From the previous chapter on diabetes you will know the answer, that's right, sugar. I mentioned earlier that cigarettes come with a health warning yet sugar in its many disguises both overt and covert comes with no health warning despite the epidemic proportions of diabetes in our society. Some of the following information may be a repeat of what I said in the diabetes chapter but it's worth repeating.

When we use the word sugar what we really mean is carbohydrate, particularly refined carbohydrates, sucrose and HFCS (high fructose corn syrup). All refined carbohydrates and starchy foods such as white flour, white rice, potatoes etc convert to glucose very rapidly during digestion. Blood glucose has to be maintained within a very narrow band otherwise you go into a coma and die. Too much (hyperglycaemia) or too little (hypoglycaemia) if sustained, will lead to death, no question. So, if you have a meal with a big dollop of carbs what happens to all the excess glucose? The body can only store a relatively small amount of glucose in the liver and muscles; to get rid of the excess, which it must, the glucose is converted in the liver to tri-glycerides and stored as FAT. If you are on a high carbohydrate low fat diet then you are still accumulating fat (tri-glycerides). Fructose, in sugar and high fructose corn syrup, is the worst as this metabolises to the Very Low Density fats found in VLDL cholesterol, the last L stands for lipoprotein. People get confused about cholesterol, the concept good cholesterol and bad cholesterol is very simplistic. There is only one kind of cholesterol; it is what it is combined with that differentiates it. HDL cholesterol equates to high density lipoprotein cholesterol, LDL equates to low density lipoprotein, VLDL as very low density lipoprotein. Lipoprotein is a fat combined with a protein; the cholesterol bit is exactly the same. There is no simple way to measure VLDL which is why it is not carried out and yet this is the most atherogenic type. There are no drugs which act on VLDL!

With regard to LDL it has been shown that there are several fractions and they are not all 'bad'. It is the small dense fraction, LDL2, that may be the issue and not the large buoyant fraction LDL1; to differentiate this is important yet how often is that done in medical testing? A total LDL figure is not as meaningful in this respect.

Dr Robert Lustig, among others, is a firm promoter of the message that it is sugar (50% fructose) and HFCS (55% fructose) not fat that is the cause of obesity, diabetes and related diseases.

This information naturally meets great opposition from the fast and convenience food industries and the sugar industry. Most fast and convenience foods would taste very bland without the sugar and salt in them and they may also contain hydrogenated fats to extend shelf life. They could use animal fat which has flavour and doesn't go rancid that's politically unacceptable at the moment as we've invested over 50 years in a false premise.

While animal fat consumption has gone down, sugar consumption and consumption of vegetable oils has gone up dramatically. In 1822 the average American consumed less than 10lbs of sugar a year; in 2005 it was up to 100lbs a year[15]. One of the main oils used in cooking is canola oil and demand in the U.S. has increased from around 300 million lbs in 1988 to almost 3000 million lbs in 2008, a tenfold increase in just 20 years. Canola oil was developed from rape seed oil which is high in erucic acid which is toxic to the heart muscle. Canola oil has much lower levels of erucic acid at <2%[16] and is given GRAS status. GRAS if you recall means generally regarded as safe; it probably also means no research has been done to confirm it!

 If erucic acid is cardio toxic, consuming a low level over a long period of time could possibly be harmful couldn't it?

Total vegetable oil consumption in the U.S. has gone up from 2lbs per person in 1910 to around 55lbs per person in 2010. Many of the oils are high in omega 6 polyunsaturated fatty acids which have an inflammatory reaction in the body, has this anything to do with the high incidence of inflammatory diseases: asthma, eczema, arthritis, heart disease etc., etc?

I have recently read an interesting article by Sally Fallon and Mary Enig PhD[17] which argues that canola is only dangerous if you do not have enough saturated fat in your diet. Asian Indian people used to use rape seed oil and mustard oil which are high in erucic acid without problems because they also used ghee from butter, and lard. However we do have to be aware that most canola oil is likely to be from GMO sources, which has its own issues.

We have been in the 'fat is bad' paradigm for over 50 years now. The heart disease burden hasn't changed during that time. Yes heart disease may have reduced from its peak but reduction in smoking and margarine consumption may have played a big part in this, not the reduction in butter consumption. If it takes 50 plus years to change a paradigm then if we wait for the government to act we'll be long dead!

What can you do?

- *You can vote with your wallet. You can choose to use healthy animal fats and coconut oil[18] and drastically reduce your use of vegetable oils in cooking and food preparation.*
- *Avoid anything that may contain artificial TRANS fats i.e. hydrogenated oils. These come in many guises: vegetable fat, margarine, hydrogenated vegetable oil, partially hydrogenated vegetable oil. Read the label and be aware.*
- *Eat plenty of sardines even if you don't like them. They are high in heart healthy and anti-inflammatory omega 3 oils; they are low down in the food chain which means they are lower in heavy metals which is an ever escalating problem in seafood.*
- *Eat wild caught salmon and trout and not farmed.*

- *Avoid fast and processed foods; it's easy to avoid processed foods in the supermarket, don't go down the aisles; all the fresh food is round the outside.*
- *Eat organic vegetables whenever possible.*
- *Eat plenty of berries, they are high in antioxidants.*
- *Ditch the microwave as it destroys your food[19].*

By avoiding poor quality nutritional food choices and eating real food you will find your health will improve.

This chapter is just the tip of the iceberg concerning the information that has been published on dietary fat. Science is very good at drawing conclusions from comparative data. If there is a reason in drawing those conclusions it may not be the reason that is promoted to the public and the conclusions may be omitting other factors. Sciences tend to look at things in isolation and draw conclusions from that. As I mentioned earlier when Ancel Keys 'picked' his data, that choice had a bias, he also looked at fat data in isolation as if it was the only factor in peoples' diets; he particularly ignored the amount of sugar (glucose, fructose) being consumed.

Whatever happened to common sense? When we were eating a high fat, whole food diet; when there were no processed foods, and when our toxic exposure was minimal, heart disease was much lower than it had been when it reached its 1970s peak. Saturated fat got the bad press but as we know correlation does not prove causation, especially when the data to prove the correlation was cherry picked and other parameters were not assessed (cigarettes, sugar and TRANS fat consumption).

References

1. http://www.nejm.org/action/showMediaPlayer?doi=10.1056%2FNEJMp1113569&aid=NEJMp1113569_attach_1&area

2. http://www.infoplease.com/ipa/A0908700.html

3. http://www.dairyinfo.gc.ca/index_e.php?s1=dff-fcil&s2=cons&s3=consglo&s4=tb-bt

4. http://www.humanesociety.org/news/resources/research/stats_dairy_eggs.html

5. http://www.webexhibits.org/butter/consumption-butter-fat.html

6. http://www.onlinestatbook.com/2/case_studies/graphics/sugar.jpg

7. http://www.sugar-and-sweetener-guide.com/consumption-of-sugar.html

8. https://www.ncbi.nlm.nih.gov/pubmed/22000650

9. http://www.vitamindcouncil.org/health-conditions/coronary-heart-disease/

10. http://www.vitamindcouncil.org/?s=hypertension&submit=Submit

11. http://nourishedkitchen.com/cla-the-good-trans-fat/

12. www.thesoapdish.com/oil-properties-chart.htm

13. http://www.naturalnews.com/026819_lauric_acid_coconut_oil.html

14. http://articles.mercola.com/sites/articles/archive/2011/10/22/debunking-the-science-behind-lowering-cholesterol-levels.aspx

15. http://www.businessinsider.com/chart-american-sugar-consumption-2012-2?IR=T

16. http://www.accessdata.fda.gov/scripts/cdrh/cfdocs/cfcfr/CFRSearch.cfm?fr=184.1555

17. http://www.westonaprice.org/health-topics/the-great-con-ola/

18. http://www.mercola.com/nutritionplan/beginner_fats.htm

19. http://www.mercola.com/article/microwave/hazards2.htm

Chapter 14 - <u>PROBIOTICS, PREBIOTICS AND THE IMMUNE SYSTEM</u>

If you were asked to describe where your immune system is, what would be your answer? Some might say it's in the blood; others might be more precise and say that it's the white blood cells, called leucocytes, which are produced in the bone marrow. Both would be partially correct.

For the most part, the immune system is contained within the lymphatic system which includes the spleen, thymus and a network of lymphatic vessels and lymph nodes. The lymphatic fluid drains into the blood stream and so immune cells enter the blood stream in this way. A large part of this lymphatic network of vessels and nodes is centred in your gut area. Your gut is also the site of what is called the micro biome, the tens of trillions of bacteria that inhabit the intestinal tract. It is becoming increasingly apparent that the health of our micro biome is of paramount importance to our overall health and wellbeing and much research is being done in this field.

Over the past 50 years or so many practices have been adopted which have contributed towards the decimation this army of beneficial bacteria. There is in fact a symbiotic relationship between them and us, which means we co-exist for our mutual benefit; we rely on these organisms for many things.

The immune system is highly complex and not easy to fully understand for professionals as well as non professionals; the experts are still working on it! You don't actually need to fully understand how everything fits together to take on board the fact that your gut health it so very important.

What has changed over the last 50-100 years to so dramatically affect these little friends of ours?

1. Chlorination of our water supply. Chlorine is very good at keeping our water free of harmful bacteria but when we drink chlorinated water our micro biome suffers. It is easy to take chlorine out of the water with a simple carbon filter, well worth the money and the water tastes so much better. Ozone is an alternative for water purification and doesn't have the down side of chlorine. Ozone is widely used in Europe for water purification.

2. Antibiotics. These chemicals are ubiquitous in our culture and food chain; they have been used so inappropriately over the decades. What was once a life saving discovery has become the feeding ground for so called 'superbugs'. When you take an antibiotic by mouth it wreaks havoc with your intestinal micro flora. A broad spectrum antibiotic is indiscriminate in the bacteria it kills and is why many people develop a chronic yeast (Candida) infection, that's another story!

3. Creation of a sterile world with antiseptic overload. There's an old saying that you have to eat a peck of dirt before you die (A peck is around 9 litres). There is an obsession with sterility in our modern culture yet if you have a strong immune system and good stomach acid then there is little to worry about. How can a dog dig up an old rotten chunk of meat, eat it and be O.K.? It has good stomach acid, strong enough to dissolve bones in a few hours. Cleanliness is certainly important to health but to overload with all these chemicals is unnecessary and it has an impact on our friendly bacteria within and the environment in general without.

4. Reduction of fibre in the diet. Having adequate fibre in the diet is essential to gut health. Fibre not only provides bulk for the intestines but also provides complex carbohydrates which feed the microbes in the gut; these are what can be called prebiotics.

5. Increased use of Proton Pump Inhibitors[1]. These drugs are used my millions of people and they have a deleterious effect on the micro biome, they also reduce stomach acid to the level where protection from ingested harmful bacteria is compromised. If you take these and decided to come off them then don't just stop. Wean yourself off them otherwise you may get rebound acid production and you want to avoid that.

6. Reduced consumption of fermented foods. These foods are natural sources of the bacteria which make up the micro biome. Which foods do I mean? Live yoghurt and kefir, kombucha, sauerkraut, kimchi, sourdough and loads of others[2].

7. Genetically Modified Organisms, GMOs. GMO crops have genes from other species. Bt crops are one example; they have a gene from Bacillus Thuringiensis and because of this they produce an insecticide. This gene can be transferred to your gut bacteria and then they will start to produce this insecticide. How is that going to affect our health[3]?

8. Roundup (glyphosate) exposure. Round up is a herbicide used on GMO, roundup ready, crops. Now it is purported by the manufacturers to be safe for humans because we don't have the biochemical pathway in our metabolism that plants have and we don't absorb much of it. Alas the bacteria in our gut do have the same biochemical pathway on which Roundup works and this may be having a detrimental effect[4]. This issue will be coming more to light as time progresses, meanwhile, the choice is yours.

A recent ruling in California means that Roundup is to be labelled as a potential carcinogen.

There are many other things which can affect your gut health, stress, alcohol and sugar to name a few. The point is if you want good health then you have to pay attention to the things detailed above.

This extract gives an indication of the importance of your gut bacteria:

> ***This bacterial genomic contribution is critical for human survival. Genes carried by bacteria in the gastro-intestinal tract, for example, allow humans to digest foods and absorb nutrients that otherwise would be undigested.***
>
> ***"Humans don't have all the enzymes we need to digest our own diet," says Lita Proctor, PhD, NHGRI's HMP program manager. "Microbes in the gut break down many of the proteins, lipids and carbohydrates in our diet into nutrients that we can then absorb. Moreover, the microbes produce beneficial compounds, like vitamins and anti-inflammatories that our genome cannot produce."[5]***

There is a great deal of interest in the scientific medical community regarding this vital area of health. A quick 'Google' of 'health micro biome' gives 900,000 results!

These bacteria not only enhance your immune activity; they are involved and implicated in many other areas. They are certainly vital for production of certain vitamins such as B12 and K; for more information check out this article[6].

Medicine is finally getting some understanding of the powerful nature of the interactions between the micro biome and the rest of the body; faecal transplants are being used to repopulate the colon of patients whose micro biome has been decimated by antibiotics and other causes. You might think that procedure quite disgusting but it is proving life changing to those who have had their intestinal flora destroyed; people with Clostridium Difficile infection which may be caused by the use of antibiotics may get great benefit from this intervention. Of course this can't be patented so the drug industry won't be investing any time or funds into it.

One of the main necessities in any health program is to repopulate your micro biome by consuming the sources of these bacteria listed previously. A foetus has no bacteria in the gut; the inoculation begins during birth as bacteria from the birth canal are introduced. Breast feeding then supplies a further inoculation and is one of the reasons why breast feeding is so important.

I previously mentioned that the immune system is focused within the lymphatic. The lymphatic system has a series of vessels like the blood system; the difference is that the system has no pump like the heart. Lymph flows only in one direction from the tissues to the neck where it enters the blood stream via the subclavian vein. The upward motion of the lymph is brought about by muscular contraction and motion of the body and is why exercise is so important. If the lymph is not flowing efficiently then toxins can accumulate in the tissues so lymphatic drainage can be an important protocol in regaining health. If you have a sedentary job then regular movement becomes very important.

A great portion of the lymphatic vessels lie just under the skin and skin brushing can be highly beneficial in stimulation lymphatic function. Skin brushing also has other benefits[7].

Endnotes

A strong immune system is of vital importance to your health; without this you invite all kinds of disease scenarios depending on your own susceptibilities which are influenced by epigenetic and environmental exposures. You can maintain a healthy system by avoiding all those things which may compromise it and by following the suggestions to augment immune activity. A class of compounds which are receiving attention are the beta glucans which are immune modulators found in such foods as, baker's yeast, shiitake mushrooms, oats and other grains.

After a century and a half of research, studies have shown that beta glucans act as immunomodulator agents, meaning they trigger a cascade of events that help regulate the immune system, making it more efficient. Specifically, beta glucans stimulate the activity of macrophages, which are versatile immune cells that ingest and demolish invading pathogens and stimulate other immune cells to attack. Macrophages also release cytokines, chemicals that when secreted enable the immune cells to communicate with one another. In addition, beta glucans stimulate lethal white blood cells (lymphocytes) that bind to tumours or viruses, and release chemicals to destroy it[8]

This is just another example of foods having therapeutic benefit.

References

1. http://www.sciencedaily.com/releases/2014/11/141125074656.htm

2. http://en.wikipedia.org/wiki/List_of_fermented_foods

3. http://www.greenmedinfo.com/blog/gmos-and-health-scientific-basis-serious-concern-and-immediate-action

4. http://grist.org/food/gut-punch-monsanto-could-be-destroying-your-microbiome/

5. https://www.nih.gov/news-events/news-releases/nih-human-microbiome-project-defines-normal-bacterial-makeup-body

6. http://articles.mercola.com/sites/articles/archive/2014/05/17/human-microbiome.aspx

7. http://articles.mercola.com/sites/articles/archive/2014/02/24/dry-skin-brushing.aspx

8. http://www.lef.org/magazine/2009/12/The-Immune-Enhancing-Benefits-of-Beta-Glucans/Page-01

Chapter 15 - COMMON CONDITIONS AND CONVENTIONAL MEDICATIONS

In this section I'll give some information on drugs or drug classes that are in common use. The general public is probably not aware that when a doctor prescribes a medicine and it doesn't 'do the job'; a common response may be to 'try something different' and prescribe a drug with a different name. That drug will often belong to the same class of drug as the first. It is fair to say that you may get a better response from the second drug especially if it's sold to you in a positive way, remember the placebo effect. The placebo effect if you recall is that nuisance effect that medicine doesn't like but which can nevertheless be a powerful contributor to positive therapeutic response.

Indigestion, heartburn, acid reflux

This group of symptoms is very common in the current climate of fast food, fast eating, alcoholic over indulgence, sedentary lifestyle, GMO foods, and stress in all its forms.

I mentioned in a previous chapter that doctors used to diagnose low acid or high acid conditions; on the whole this is no longer the case. If you have any of the following symptoms acid reflux, heartburn, burping, gas, bloating, or nausea after eating, then you are likely to have a stomach acid issue for which your doctor will more often than not prescribe a proton pump inhibitor (PPI).

Like most drugs, PPIs are big business and indeed they do reduce stomach acid, but what if your stomach acid is already low? Low stomach acid gives the same symptoms as high stomach acid and is likely to be more common, especially as you get older.

Proton pump inhibitors are so effective that they will reduce any stomach acid no matter what the level. A proton or hydrogen ion is a nucleus of a hydrogen atom; the very same hydrogen that you find in water H_2O, which is where protons come from. In the stomach there are specialised cells which pump out hydrogen ions and this is the site where the drug acts. Normal stomach acid is around pH 1.5-2. The pH scale is from 0 to 14 where 0 is the most acid and 14 the most alkali. So you can see that normal stomach acid is pretty strong.

Why do we have strong stomach acid? That is a very good question and one that medicine seems to have forgotten the answer to!

We have strong stomach acid because:

- *We need to digest the protein in our food. Acid is very important, along with certain enzymes, in splitting the proteins into their component amino acids, which can then be absorbed into the blood stream. The main protein splitting enzyme is pepsin, pepsin activity requires an optimum pH of 1.5 to 2.2. If you have insufficient acid then the process will be incomplete and if you have a leaky bowel problem, which many people do have, you can absorb chunks of partially digested proteins which can present a challenge to your immune system.*

- *A pH of 4 or less is sufficient to kill most bacteria which you ingest. If the stomach pH is more than 4 then bacteria are going to get to places they were never intended to go.*

PPI's generally cause the stomach pH to be greater than 4 ([1]). So in summary, if your stomach pH is over 4 you will not be properly digesting the protein in your food or killing off ingested bacteria.

You may ask; how does low stomach acid (achlorhydria) cause heartburn, gastric reflux and flatulence?

There is a valve at the top of the stomach called the Lower Esophageal Sphincter (LES) or cardiac sphincter as it is also known. This valve is sensitive to stomach acidity. As the acidity increases i.e. the pH falls the valve closes and prevents reflux. If the stomach acid is not sufficient then this valve will remain open and allow reflux. If the stomach acid is low then micro-organisms can become established in the stomach; these organisms ferment your food producing gas which causes bloating and belching. Does all this sound familiar? Reducing stomach acid further may compound the issues long term, even though there may be some symptom relief. Also long term consequences of achlorhydria can be more serious than the original problem[2].

The answer to low stomach acid and indigestion may be to supplement with *Betaine Hydrochloride* (BH) *and digestive enzymes.* How do you know if you have low stomach acid? You can get pH monitoring technology from your doctor or you can simply supplement with BH as detailed in this reference[3]. Just think a moment about what the word indigestion means; it means not digesting your food.

Some of the long term issues associated with PPI's may be due to their negative influence on vitamin and mineral absorption which rely on stomach acid[4].

As far as excess acid production is concerned there are some rare cancers and stomach ulcers which can be responsible and some other life style related causes[5].

The whole point is that before you can address the issue you need to know whether you have a low acid problem or high acid problem. Chances are if you are elderly it will be low and if you are young then lifestyle may be the issue. Taking drugs long term will have its consequences.

Drugs which fall into the PPI class are: omeprazole, esomepeprazole, lansoprazole and pantoprazole. They may have various trade names depending on country and source.

What are some of the potential side effects of these drugs? Diarrhoea, flatulence, nausea, vomiting, and stomach pain. The incidence of these may be low but isn't it interesting that these are exactly the symptoms you may be trying to treat.

PPI's increase fracture risk particularly if over 50 and may cause mineral depletion particularly magnesium for which supplementation may not be sufficient.

> *New research suggests that if you take the drugs long term — that's for more than a year — the risks can include infections, cancer and heart disease and a dangerous deficiency of some vital minerals and vitamins. – Daily Mail UK July 2012.[6]*

How does the body manufacture hydrochloric acid (HCl)? Hydrogen ions (H^+) come from H_2O (H^+, OH^-) and chloride ions (Cl^-) comes from salt (NaCl). So if you're not getting enough salt then your acid making capacity may be compromised. Also you need adequate Zinc. If you have poor digestion you may need to supplement with digestive enzymes and betaine hydrochloride. Seek advice from a suitably qualified natural health practitioner.

<u>Pain relief</u>

Pain is no joke and no one likes to endure it. O.K. there may be a few masochists out there so if you fall into that category you can skip this section!

The world market for pain killers is in the order of $68 billion[7]. With all that money being spent on pain relief we might ask; is it money well spent?

You have read about how effective pain killers are in a previous chapter. If you are fortunate you may get some pain relief and this would be highly desirable. Adverts for pain killers on T.V. give the impression that they work and they work for everyone. There may be something in the small print at the bottom of the screen, but who reads that?

You know from earlier on that pain killers will only work for some people and 'work' means a reduction in pain and not elimination of pain.

It might be acceptable to take pain relief for an acute condition but how many people take pain killers on a regular long term basis unaware of the consequences to their health. If you are aware of the consequences then you are making an informed choice. If you are not aware then are you blindly assuming they are safe?

Paracetamol (Acetaminophen, Tylenol) is a very commonly used drug, $6 billion in sales in 2011[8]. Paracetamol has been in use since the early 1900s and is generally considered safe, you wouldn't expect to die from it would you?

> *In the United States paracetamol is associated with more than 100,000 calls a year to poison control centres, as well as 56,000 visits to emergency departments, 26,000 hospitalisations, and 450 deaths.*
>
> *- U.S. national library of medicine 2002[9].*

Between 1970 and 2011, 3384 people died in acts of terrorism in the US; the majority of these deaths occurred on 11th Sept 2001. If you exclude 9/11, which is anomalous, then the number of deaths was 388 in a 40 year period[10].

150 people a year die from accidentally taking an over dose of paracetamol. The 450 mentioned above presumably includes purposeful over dose i.e. suicide. So, taking the accidental death rate from paracetamol poisoning, between 1970 and 2011 around 6000 people died; that's almost double the number of terrorist related deaths including 9/11. Why is this product still on the market? Is it anything to do with the $6 billion a year in sales?

Apart from its low safety margin for over dose, what other issues are there with the use of paracetamol?

- *The National Institute for Clinical Excellence in the UK has warned GPs against prescribing paracetamol in osteoarthritis because of concerns about toxicity to the heart, kidneys and gastro-intestinal tract.[11]*
- *Paracetamol for headache is a very common use, however over use, which means exceeding the dose or taking them on more than three days a week, can cause what is known as rebound headache; i.e. the drug is causing the headache[12].*

Ibuprofen is probably the second most common pain reliever sold over the counter and prescribed by doctors. Ibuprofen is a Non-Steroidal Anti-Inflammatory (NSAID); other drugs in this category include; diclofenac, indomethacin, naproxen, aspirin, flurpiprofen, ketoprofen, mefenamic acid, piroxicam, rofecoxib, celicoxib, etoricoxib and others[13].

All these drugs work in the same way; they inhibit an enzyme call Cyclo-Oxygenase (COX 1 or COX 2). This helps to reduce the level of pain causing substances in the body.

Where there is direct to consumer advertising as in US and New Zealand there are claims made such as 'treats the cause of pain' and 'targeted pain relief'. These are, in my opinion, misleading claims; an uninformed person may think that the drug ONLY goes to the site of pain, this clearly is not true.

There may be some justification in reducing inflammation in an acute situation but the inflammatory reaction due to injury is part of the body's healing process. Increased blood flow and temporary immobilisation i.e. you need to rest to allow healing to occur. That's the difficult one for most people, it's only when people become totally incapacitated and forced to rest that they actually do! The long term consequences of taking these products on a regular basis are not fully known? It is known however that there are potentially lethal side effects, some may be acute and others of a more chronic nature.

Would it not be better to support the healing process than to suppress it? Targeted pain relief with a picture of an inflamed joint may give some people the impression that the drug goes to the site of pain and only there. If you swallow a drug then it will be distributed throughout your whole body.

Because these drugs block COX enzymes they can and do have serious consequences for some people.

Vioxx (rofecoxib) was taken off the market in 2004 when it came to light that around 55,000 Americans had died as a result of taking it. A class action law suit resulted in almost $5 billion dollars of settlement claims. Many more may have died prematurely as a result of taking this drug[14] whose side effect potential was well known beforehand but ignored[15].

The reason this drug caused so many deaths was because of its primary mode of action, selective COX 2 inhibition[16]. COX 2 is involved in other areas of the body, importantly the cardiovascular system and heart attack and stroke was the outcome for those 55,000 unsuspecting individuals.

All NSAIDs have this potential, maybe not as profoundly as Vioxx, but nevertheless there is a risk. All NSAIDs block COX 2 to a greater or lesser extent.

COX 1 inhibition is associated with gastro intestinal bleeding and is why acid lowering drugs like omeprazole are prescribed with NSAIDs to reduce that possibility.

> *NSAID drug use is ubiquitous throughout the world, more than 60 million people in USA use them on a regular basis. 1-2% of users will experience serious upper gastro-intestinal events. Estimations of death from these drugs varies from 3200 to 16,500 annually in the US alone [17].*

If you take a middle of the range figure from the above quote say 9,000 deaths a year from Gastro-Intestinal bleeding this is equivalent to almost three 9/11s every year and yet is accepted as part of the medical protocol.

Opiates and opiods are being prescribed in ever increasing amounts. Over the last few decades there has been a war against illicit drug use which includes morphine and the morphine derivate heroin. While vast resources have been directed towards reducing the amount of these drugs in circulation the sad fact is that ever increasing amounts of opium like drugs are being legally prescribed and are finding their way on to the streets. These prescription drugs even have 'street names' for example. Oxycontin is called goodfella[18].

Other commonly prescribed drugs of this category include codeine, dihydrocodeine, oxycodone, pethidine, methadone, fentanyl, buprenorphine and others.

256 million prescriptions are written every year in the US for these drugs and 46 people die as a result of overdose every single day[19], that's 16,000 a year. Terrorism is starting to pale into insignificance in terms of people dying as a direct result of it; don't you think?

Lets recap; Vioxx deaths at least 55,000, NSAIDs 9,000 a year, opiods 16,000 a year. Why are we so afraid of terrorists? You're more likely to be killed by the medicine you are taking.

We know from earlier that pain killers only partially work in some people and opiods are no different. For neuropathic pain, which is probably one of the most difficult to treat the NNT is between 2.5 and 5. This means 60% to 80% of people will not get at least 50% pain relief[20].

Are there any alternatives to drugs? Sure there are but they are not likely to be offered by your average doctor.

My wife is a physiotherapist and she uses several modalities of treatment:

- Physiotherapy techniques
- Ultra sound
- Interferential
- APS therapy
- Acupuncture
- Bowen technique
- Scenar

I know for a fact that the vast majority of her clients have a positive outcome let's say 80%. That means she has an NNT of around 1.25. Why pop potentially lethal pills when safer alternatives are available? Later in the section on inflammation there is information on natural substances which can help reduce inflammation.

High Blood Pressure (Hypertension)

There are a few disease conditions which are known to increase blood pressure (BP) because of the disease process. This is possible with kidney disease, diabetes and the use of certain drugs (e.g. hormonal contraceptives, NSAIDs, recreational drugs)[21]; in these cases hypertension is classed as secondary, it is the result of an underlying identified cause.

By far the largest group of hypertensive patients, around 90%, fall into the category of primary or essential hypertension. This means there is no known cause and it has no overt symptoms unless it is extremely high. Let's qualify what 'no known cause' means. It means that the medical establishment in general cannot attribute a causative agent or disease process to account for the symptom of raised blood pressure and the only way it can be diagnosed is by measurement. Why can medical science not find an answer to this common problem from which millions of people apparently suffer and which has been around for a long time? Millions of people having a 'disease' for which the only treatment is drugs is big business. In the US:

Direct medical spending to treat hypertension totalled $42.9 billion in 2010, with almost half ($20.4 billion) in the form of prescription medications[22].

Let's do some investigation and see if some light can be shed on the issue. Firstly blood pressure is not a static parameter in the body. Normal blood pressure is often quoted as 120/80. For those of you who do not know what that figure means let me explain. The figures are the height of a column of mercury that the pressure in your blood vessels is able to hold up and is in millimetres (mm). The highest figure is when your heart beats (systole) and the lowest figure is when it is relaxing (diastole). Many blood pressure machines today use electronics rather than the old mechanical method of cuff and stethoscope so in practice the column of mercury may not be evident. 'Normal' blood pressure of course is not normal for everyone. Blood pressure like most bodily parameters has a normal distribution in a population. This means there will be a range of blood pressures which are evident in a 'standard population'. For an individual, how can you know if your blood pressure is raised unless you have monitored it from an early age?

A normal distribution range for diastolic blood pressure ranges from around 60 to 110[23]. So some people in this **normal** distribution will be categorised as having high blood pressure purely because of the definition. If you have monitored your blood pressure from an early age then you will absolutely know if your pressure is increased.

 Of course people who definitely have high blood pressure need to be aware of the consequences and if you haven't monitored it since say your 20s then may be the assumption is that there may be a problem.

Be aware that blood pressure increases as you age partly due to reduced elasticity in the blood vessels, so what is normal for a 20 year old won't be normal for a 70 year old. This reduction in elasticity is likely to be due to a life time of nutritional deficiencies, particularly vitamin C and other antioxidants.

Another thing about blood pressure is that it is not static throughout the day and goes up and down depending on demand. If you exercise vigorously then it will go up as your heart begins to beat faster. If you are stressed BP will increase as adrenaline released into the blood stream will constrict (narrow) certain blood vessels, this increases blood flow to the muscles ready for action! If we do not 'burn off' that adrenaline in a 'fight or flight' reaction then it will endure. After a meal BP goes up, at night in bed it goes down.

> *If normal blood pressure is defined then it is easy to see how people that fall within the normal distribution outlined above may be diagnosed as having hypertension.*

A well known phenomenon is that of 'white coat' hypertension. Most people, even the calmest, will have a level of stress reaction when they see a doctor; this is recognised and is why a doctor will not rely on a single measurement to give a diagnosis. What if you're stressed at the second, third and fourth measurement? The doctor by now will almost certainly be ready to make the diagnosis.

So now you know that for an individual BP varies throughout the day and your normal BP will be different from your neighbours normal BP. So what exactly is hypertension, the answer is that it is arbitrarily defined according to the following chart[24].

Category	Systolic (top number)		Diastolic (bottom number
Normal	Less than 120	and	Less than 80
Prehypertension	120 - 139	or	80 – 89
High Blood Pressure			
Stage 1	140 – 159	or	90 – 99
Stage 2	160 or higher	or	100 or higher

Comparing this chart with the previous normal distribution curve, it can be seen that the people at the high end of normal will have stage 2 hypertension and anyone over the mean value (around 85 DBP) will be defined as having pre-hypertension or hypertension. Even some people under the mean will be defined as pre-hypertensive!

Now assuming you do have high blood pressure and bearing in mind the previous arguments as to whether that actually is the case; what might be some of the causes that medicine generally is not recognising?

Low vitamin D levels due to lack of adequate sun exposure. It is known that the incidence of hypertension declines the nearer you get to the equator, i.e. the more sun exposure you get. People in this region of the world have vitamin D blood levels of between 60-100ng/ml. As mentioned in a previous chapter vitamin D is not actually a vitamin but a hormone and its functions are not fully understood but the knowledge base is continually expanding. The kidney is an important regulator of blood pressure and one of the ways it does this is via what is known as the Renin-Angiotensin System (RAS). This is the site of action of some anti-hypertensive drugs such as ACE inhibitors and angiotensin II inhibitors (ACE = angiotensin converting enzyme). Both these types of drug block the action of angiotensin II which may be one of the factors in high BP. It is now known that vitamin D down regulates the RAS[25] and so if you don't have enough your BP may go up.

Low magnesium levels because of insufficient dietary intake or excessive loss due to drug therapy. Drugs which deplete magnesium include:[26]

- Proton pump inhibitors such as omeprazole
- Fluoroquinolone antibiotics such as ciprofloxacin
- Diuretics such as furosemide
- Oral contraceptives
- Some chemotherapy drugs
- Some AIDS drugs
- Cyclosporin
- Alcohol

Magnesium has a relaxing effect on muscle. Your blood vessels are essentially a tube of muscle and as the muscle relaxes so the vessel widens and BP falls. The opposite occurs if there is too little magnesium and/or an excess of calcium. Magnesium is important in many areas of health; follow the reference for more information[27]. Many people are deficient in magnesium and since most magnesium in the body is inside the cells measurement is difficult and blood measurement only has any meaning if severely deficient. A more meaningful test is the sublingual epithelial cell test which actually measures the magnesium level inside the cells[28].

Calcium channel blockers are a conventional treatment for hypertension, low and behold, magnesium is nature's calcium channel blocker!

The best form of magnesium supplement is probably transdermal as previously discussed.

Dehydration causes the blood to be more viscous (thick) and this will then require more pressure to pump the blood around hence an elevation of BP. This is one reason to make sure your water intake is adequate; as a rule of thumb that would be 2 litres of good quality water daily.

Stress increases activity in the sympathetic nervous system and one of the consequences is a rise in BP. If you are constantly under stress then this needs to be addressed. Drugs are not the answer to this and will only create more problems further down the line. Meditation and relaxation techniques are well known to reduce stress[29].One of the conventional treatments for stress is Beta-blockers which reduce activity in the sympathetic nervous system.

Heavy metals including mercury, lead, cadmium and arsenic are known contributors to high blood pressure[30]. If you work in an industry that exposes you to these compounds or you have mercury fillings (silver) then this may be a contributing factor. Chelation therapy is one way to deal with this.

> *"Heavy metal toxicity, especially mercury and cadmium, should be evaluated in any patient with hypertension, CHD, or other vascular disease."[30]*

A blood test is no good on its own since the heavy metals are deposited in the bones and organs. Also fat tissue holds on to them as they may be in fat soluble organic molecules e.g. methyl mercury. A chelating agent has to be injected that will bind the heavy metals and transfer them to the blood stream and they are then eliminated via the urine. The urine can be collected and analysed.

Insulin resistance, seen in type II diabetes, can drive up blood pressure[31]. If insulin resistance is an issue then it has to be brought under control. Diet and lifestyle changes as discussed previously can assist with this and the plant preparation of berberine may be a useful adjunct.

> *'......berberine is a potent oral hypoglycaemic agent with modest effect on lipid metabolism. It is safe and the cost of treatment by berberine is very low.'[32]*

Vitamin C is involved with blood pressure regulation. At a dose of 500mg, well over the RDA, vitamin C has been shown to lower blood pressure[33]. As we've discussed earlier high dose vitamin C, and 500mg would not be considered a high dose in orthomolecular therapy, is beneficial for many reasons; one benefit is a strengthening of blood vessel walls reducing the possibility of rupture, which is a potential issue with high blood pressure. Vitamin C also chelates heavy metals allowing them to be removed from the body.

Fructose consumption in the form of sugar or high fructose corn syrup elevates uric acid which raises blood pressure.

Medication - if you are taking regular medication be aware that some drugs can increase blood pressure, for example anti-inflammatories (NSAIDs) can do this by affecting kidney blood flow.

Having read this far you must now be aware that the idea of primary, essential hypertension having no known cause is quite ludicrous; don't you think? The incidence and treatment of primary hypertension has been growing steadily over the time period that all the factors previously mention have been growing in importance.

<u>Conventional treatment of hypertension</u>
Drugs used to treat hypertension are classified according to their mode of action.

<u>Diuretics</u> reduce blood pressure by reducing blood volume, they cause you to lose salt and water follows on passively. They can cause mineral depletion particularly magnesium and dehydration.

The more common side effects of diuretics include: dizziness, drowsiness, fatigue, muscle cramps and thirst.

Commonly used drugs in this class include: furosemide, hydrochlorothiazide, chlorthalidone, chlorothiazide, indapamide, amiloride, spironolactone, triampterene, bumetanide, there are also combination products.

<u>Beta-blockers</u> as their name implies block beta receptors in the sympathetic nervous system. This causes a slowing of the heart and dilation (widening) of blood vessels; the result is a lowering of blood pressure.

Common side effects include: Dizziness, drowsiness, fatigue, abnormal dreams, cold extremities, depression and diarrhoea. Anyone who is asthmatic or has breathing difficulty should be wary of these drugs as they can suppress lung function.

Commonly used drugs in this class include: atenolol, propranolol, acebutolol, carvedilol, bisoprolol, metoprolol, nadolol, sotalol, timolol and others.

<u>ACE inhibitors</u> block the activity of angiotensin converting enzyme which converts angiotensin I to angiotensin II which has a vaso-constrictor effect i.e. it increases blood pressure.

Common side effects include dizziness and cough.

Commonly used drugs in this class include: captopril, enalapril, lisinopril, perindopril, quinapril, ramipril, trandolapril and others.

<u>Angiotensin receptor blockers</u> reduce angiotensin activity by blocking the receptor site where angiotensin II has its biological effect.

Common side effects include: dizziness, back pain, runny or stuffy nose and sore throat.

Commonly used drugs in this class include: candesartan, irbesartan, losartan, valsartan and others.

<u>Calcium channel blockers</u> block the calcium channels in the cell membrane which allow calcium into the cell. If you remember calcium causes the blood vessels to constrict. Unfortunately by blocking the calcium channel the site is also blocked to magnesium your natural calcium channel blocker!

Common side effects include: constipation, dizziness, nausea, vomiting, swelling (oedema), drowsiness, fatigue, slow heart rate (bradycardia), and shortness of breath.

Commonly used drugs in this class include: amlodipine, felodipine, nicardipine, nifedipine, verapamil, diltiazem and others.

I have just listed the most common types of drugs used in hypertension; there are more[34].

There are many drug information web sites where you can get more information on specific drugs. You can also ask your friendly pharmacist whom I am sure would be more than pleased to advise you.

With all these different types of drug available you would think we should have the handle on blood pressure; wouldn't you? Well, apparently not so.

If you are taking anti-hypertensives to prevent a heart attack or stroke then you would want to be sure they were going to be of benefit to you as an individual.

According to <u>thennt.com</u> with which you are now familiar you have to treat 125 people for 5 years to prevent 1 death, 67 people for 5 years to prevent 1 stroke and 100 people to prevent 1 heart attack[35]. In addition 1 in 10 people will be harmed by the drug treatment.

To repeat; your chance of anti-hypertensive treatment stopping you having a heart attack over a 5 year period is 1 in 100. Do you think that is an acceptable figure? 97% of people taking an antihypertensive will show NO benefit!

When treating mild hypertension 100% saw no benefit[36].

You can see from this data that this type of treatment strategy will provide benefit to a very small minority and yet it is surely prescribed with the intention that it will benefit the majority. Is this evidence based medicine? What about the morals and ethics of the situation?

On a positive side there are many foods that have been shown to reduce blood pressure, you can check some of them out here:-

http://www.greenmedinfo.com/blog/19-foods-proven-lower-blood-pressure

Cardio-Vascular Disease (CVD)

This is the number one killer in western society. It shows no overt symptoms until the later stages when the first symptom may be a heart attack with a high chance of death from that first attack.

The medical approach is prevention and in adopting this approach high levels of resources have been put into screening. There are several risk factors identified for CVD and each of these has its own screening tests. What are these so called risk factors identified by medical science?

- High blood pressure
- High cholesterol and triglycerides (fats)
- Diabetes
- Obesity
- Smoking
- Diet
- Physical inactivity
- Excessive alcohol intake

The first five of these risk factors can be targeted with drug therapy. The last four are lifestyle choices which influence the first four factors. If lifestyle choices are appropriate then all the risk factors can be addressed.

You know from the previous section that anti-hypertensive treatment has minimal benefit.

You have seen from previous chapters how animal fat has been greatly maligned and how excess sugar consumption, hydrogenated fats and excess omega 6 fats are greatly implicated. Also drug therapy can negatively affect lipid (fat) profiles.

'Diuretics, beta-blocking agents, progestogens, combined oral contraceptives containing 'second generation' progestogens, danazol, immunosuppressive agents, protease inhibitors and enzyme-inducing anticonvulsants adversely affect the lipid profile. They increase total cholesterol, low density lipoprotein cholesterol and triglycerides by up to 40, 50 and 300%, respectively, and decrease high density lipoprotein cholesterol by a maximum of 50%[37].

If you are not taking a statin already then you may be given one after starting on other medication. It's the old issue of try to fix one problem and create another.

You now know the problem with type II diabetes is sugar overload leading to insulin and leptin resistance. Diabetes and obesity are both part of the same issue, remember excess carbohydrate = sugar = fat storage.

You have seen how the reduction in the number of people smoking has had a marked influence on heart disease (and cancer).

Physical inactivity encompassed by a sedentary lifestyle is obviously an issue for some people and no drug therapy can compensate for sitting down all day! If you have a sedentary job it is good practice to get up regularly and move the body it will be highly beneficial.

It is well known that excessive alcohol intake like excessive anything is not healthy. Alcohol, just like drugs, is a toxin, drinking sensibly is obviously advantageous; denial can have its own issues! Being truthful with yourself is part of the change necessary on the path to health.

Homocysteine is often elevated in CVD yet is rarely evaluated. The jury is still out as to the clinical significance and yet high levels of homocysteine are associated with low intake of B vitamins, B6, B12 and folate. High homocysteine can cause damage to the lining of the blood vessels and to my mind would be something to avoid despite the current debate on the validity of the issue. Homocysteine is reduced by supplementing with these B vitamins or eat foods that contain adequate levels.

All the risk factors can be sensibly addressed through choices you make in full knowledge of the consequences. If you are relying on drugs to 'save' you from poor choices the odds of them helping you are not good; are they? You have seen some of the figures for CVD prevention previously and how effective, or not, they are.

Interestingly emotional disturbance is not considered a risk factor in the conventional model yet most people intuitively know how emotions affect the heart.

Inflammatory disorders
Arthritis is a group of disorders characterised by inflammation and pain; the drugs used to treat it target and suppress this inflammatory reaction, unfortunately the targeting is not precise and collateral damage often occurs. The drugs used include NSAIDs, steroids, DMARDs and immune suppressants.

Why is there so much inflammation in our western culture? Other diseases which have an underlying inflammatory process include asthma and eczema which are often closely linked. CVD has an inflammatory component which is in the blood vessels. There are increases in the prevalence of type I diabetes and autism, inflammation in the pancreas and brain respectively; inflammatory bowel disease (IBD), Crohn's, irritable bowel and stomach ulcers.

Inflammation that is not associated with a trauma injury is a sign of a body that is out of balance. There are inflammatory messengers called cytokines which have a powerful effect in the body and the question is; why are they being produced excessively? Does conventional medicine address this question? Treatments merely attempt to block the action of these so anti-inflammatories, cytokine blockers and immune suppressants become the mainstay of treatment options. None of these treatments will address the underlying cause but merely suppress the symptoms.

One theory regarding over activity of the immune system is that vaccines may be stimulating an excessive immune response[38] resulting in an attack on your own tissues. The immune system becomes confused between what is self and not self and starts destroying the host tissues.

Generally speaking you are not born with inflammatory disease yet inflammatory diseases are endemic in the population.

> **An estimated 52.5 million adults in the United States reported being told by a doctor that they have some form of arthritis, rheumatoid arthritis, gout, lupus, or fibromyalgia.**
>
> **By 2040, an estimated 78 million (26%) US adults ages 18 years or older are projected to have doctor-diagnosed arthritis[39].**
>
> **...the incidence and prevalence of IBD are increasing with time and in different regions around the world, indicating its emergence as a global disease[40].**

Why are there so many inflammatory conditions in western culture? What are people doing to create this havoc? They are:-

- *Consuming large amounts of vegetable oils high in pro-inflammatory omega 6 fats. Ancient diets had an omega 6 to omega 3 ratio of 1:1; most people have a ratio of 10 to 20 times that, even up to 25:1[41].*
- *Eating animals that are fed on grains and not grass which means the meat contains lower levels of anti-inflammatory omega 3 fats. Omega 3 fats are the precursors to anti-inflammatory cytokines.*
- *Eating less herbs and spices which have a natural anti-inflammatory, anti-oxidant effect.*
- *Consuming much, much more sugar particularly high fructose corn syrup. As we discussed in a previous chapter fructose metabolism, and sugar (sucrose) is half fructose if you recall, increases the levels of uric acid[42] which not only puts up blood pressure it also is involved with inflammation as in gout and gout like symptoms. Sugar triggers the release of inflammatory cytokines. Sugar and excess refined carbohydrate e.g. white flour, trigger the formation of what are called advanced glycation end products AGEs; these*

are pro-inflammatory and damage tissue particularly the capillary blood vessels and nerve endings.

- *Consuming more TRANS fats which are pro-inflammatory particularly to the lining of the blood vessels. TRANS fats are hydrogenated vegetable oils, margarine and the like.*
- *Consuming mono sodium glutamate (MSG), the flavour enhancer used in oriental cooking and many snack and convenience foods. MSG can have an inflammatory effect in brain tissue and in the liver.*
- *Consuming the artificial sweetener aspartame, aspartame has similar effects to MSG and is neurotoxic[43].*
- *Consuming gluten in large amounts. For most people gluten is not an overt problem but for those with celiac disease it obviously is. There is however evidence coming to light that most of us may be intolerant to other wheat proteins called lectins of which wheat germ agglutinin (WGA) is a major player. WGA lectin is a small molecule that resists digestion and can cause immune mediated reactions in the body leading to inflammatory processes[44].*

Apart from the things people are eating, there are other contributory factors:

- *Leaky gut is a common problem because of the abuse to digestive organs. Leaky gut will allow protein fragment to be absorbed with the ensuing immune response and inflammation[45].*
- *Heavy metals may be involved[46].*
- *Toxins in the food and environment may be involved[47].*
- *Genetically engineered foods may be involved [48].*

This list is not exhaustive, there may be other factors at play for an individual, it is a good starting point though. With any inflammatory condition, indeed with any health issue, it is important to clean up your diet. You can choose to do that or you can take palliative drugs; be assured that there is no drug that will cure your condition.

Drugs used as anti-inflammatories

Non steroidal anti-inflammatories (NSAIDs) work by reducing the synthesis of certain substances called prostaglandins. In the following list are a few NNTs for commonly used NSAIDs. Remember with pain relief the NNT is the number of people you need to treat to get 50% pain relief over 4 to 6 hours. Some of these are non selective COX inhibitors some are COX II inhibitors. COX = cyclo-oxygenase. The list is taken from the Oxford league table[49].

Drug	NNT	People getting < 50% Pain Relief	
Ibuprofen 800mg	1.6	38%	(Approximately 4 out of 10)
Rofecoxib 50mg	1.8	45%	
Diclofenac 100mg	1.9	48%	
Piroxicam 40mg	1.9	48%	
Diclofenac 50mg	2.3	56%	
Ibuprofen 600mg	2.4	58%	
Ibuprofen 200mg	2.7	63%	(Approximately 6 out of 10)
Placebo	18	95%	

On the whole pain relief for these drugs is very good compared to placebo; even so one in three people will not receive a 50% reduction in pain even with the most effective dose of Ibuprofen (800mg). Higher doses of drugs will of course carry higher risks of complications.

What's the down side of these drugs? NSAIDs:

- *Can interfere with the healing of fractures so may not be the best option for pain relief in those circumstances [50].*
- *Increase the risk of stomach bleeding.*

.........Many people don't know that NSAIDs can cause problems ranging from mild stomach upset and pain to serious stomach bleeding and ulcers (holes in the lining of the stomach) and even death. There is no medical test that can tell for sure if you will develop a problem, and in most cases, these problems can happen without warning. In fact, serious side effects of NSAIDs, such as stomach bleeding, result in more than 100,000 hospitalizations and thousands of deaths each year in the U.S.[51].

- *Increase blood pressure by their effect on kidney perfusion[52].*
- *Increase the risk of heart attack*

...... it is now clear what the COX inhibitors do in the body. Eight placebo-controlled, randomized trials, performed to find new uses of these drugs, showed that they posed a cardiovascular hazard, similar in magnitude to that resulting from being a smoker or a diabetic...... *53*.

- *Increase the risk of death!*

.........Conservative calculations estimate that approximately 107,000 patients are hospitalized annually for non-steroidal anti-inflammatory drug (NSAID)-related gastrointestinal (GI) complications and at least 16,500 NSAID-related deaths occur each year among arthritis patients alone. The figures of all NSAID users would be overwhelming, yet the scope of this problem is generally under-appreciated. - July 1998 issue of The American Journal of Medicine[54].

- *More people die from NSAID use that are murdered by firearms[54]; is anyone accountable? Apparently not, it's just accepted as part of the cost of doing business; whatever happened to the medical profession's oath to preserve life?*

<u>DMARDs</u> (Disease Modifying Anti-rheumatic Drugs) are a diverse group of drugs having different modes of action, some are immune suppressants and others are cytotoxic (used in cancer), there are antimalarials, antibiotics and drugs used to stop organ rejection. The term 'disease modifying' really means immune function modulation i.e. they affect or suppress certain activities within the immune system.

Some of these drugs are more potent in their immune suppressant activity. The newer (and most expensive) drugs inhibit Tumor Necrosis Factor alpha (TNFα).

Suppression of immune function has its consequences; increased risk of infection and cancer.

> *.......Patients must be advised about the risk of infections, malignancies, and various other potential adverse effects of anti-TNF therapy...... 55*

<u>Corticosteroids</u> are powerful anti-inflammatories and have a fairly rapid effect which is why they have become so popular for all sorts of inflammation. Using these for relief of an acute problem may be acceptable but what are the consequences of long term use?

Side effects are diverse and numerable.

Side effects of oral corticosteroids used for longer than three weeks can include: [56]

- *weight gain*
- *acne*
- *mood changes and rapid mood swings*
- *thinning skin which can bruise easily*
- *muscle weakness*
- *a combination of fatty deposits that develop in the face (moon face), stretch marks across the body and acne – this is known as Cushing's syndrome*
- *weakening of the bones (osteoporosis)*
- *the onset of diabetes, or worsening of existing diabetes*
- *high blood pressure*
- *glaucoma and cataracts delayed wound healing*
- *growth retardation in children*
- *increased risk of infection*

In view of the potentially serious side effects of anti-inflammatory treatments we may pose the question; are there safer alternatives?

First of all anyone with inflammatory issues must clean up their diet and lifestyle as detailed previously; if any one or all of the aforementioned toxicities are not removed then you may have what is known in the jargon as 'a maintaining cause'.

There are alternatives to drugs which are well proven to reduce the inflammatory response of the body. You can research these at your leisure; a good site for information is one you are by now familiar with http://www.greenmedinfo.com.

- *Turmeric, the yellow spice used commonly in Asian and Indian cooking is a well documented anti-inflammatory as well as having many other health promoting qualities.*
- *Other spices with anti-inflammatory properties include ginger, rosemary, boswelia (frankincense), black pepper corns, cardamom, basil, chamomile, celery, coriander, cinnamon, cloves, fennel seed, garlic, parsley, nutmeg. By incorporating these substances into your diet on a regular basis you will obtain the anti-inflammatory and anti-oxidant effects. It was Hippocrates who said 'let food be your medicine and medicine your food'.*

- *The ancient art of Tai Chi has been shown to be of great benefit to arthritis sufferers and information on this is readily available.*
- *Acupuncture is an alternative pain relieving modality.*
- *Electrical therapies - Scenar / TENS / APS / Interferential*

The role of the element Boron is important in bone health and may have a positive role in arthritis. Borax, a source of boron, used to be in wide use until it was branded as dangerous. Was this a plot to deter people from using it? You decide; http://www.health-science-spirit.com/borax.htm .

<u>Depression</u>

Is depression an illness which is diagnosed when nothing else can be found for the cause of your chagrin? People who suffered from fibromyalgia and M.E. were often diagnosed as depressed before these conditions were accepted as real problems. Around 1 in 10 Americans are diagnosed and treated for depression. Young children and adolescents alike are being treated for this ever increasing widespread phenomenon.

> *.......Between 1988 and 2000, prescriptions for antidepressant medications tripled for adults in the U.S., with 118 million prescriptions written in 2005 alone, according to the CDC.......*

Is anyone asking why so many people are experiencing depression? Is it anything to do with the pressures of modern life, the breakdown of family values and the lack of worldly and spiritual fulfilment? Something is certainly going on; and are drugs used to treat this condition effective or necessary?

The treatment of depression is based on a chemical imbalance theory which we've looked at previously but let's recap for clarification. One of the neurotransmitters in the brain is 5-hydroxy-tryptamine or serotonin as it's more commonly known. Other transmitters which may be involved include norepinephrine and dopamine. The chemical imbalance theory may have been promoted because drugs were discovered which could alter the levels of these chemicals and were presented in a positive manner indicating a benefit. It is only relatively recently that information released from GSK pharmaceuticals under the freedom of information act has shown that for most cases of mild to moderate depression SSRI antidepressants are no better than placebo. (SSRI = selective serotonin reuptake inhibitor; the most common type prescribed.)

> *....But analyses of the published data and the unpublished data that were hidden by drug companies reveals that most (if not all) of the benefits are due to the placebo effect[57].*

> *......In clinical trials, specific data was kept unpublished in order to build a strong case for the FDA approval of Paxil......[58]*

> *A total of 37 studies viewed by the FDA as having positive results were published; 1 study viewed as positive was not published. Studies viewed by the FDA as having negative or questionable results were, with 3 exceptions, either not published (22 studies) or published in a way that, in our opinion, conveyed a positive outcome (11 studies).*

> *The New England Journal of Medicine[59])*

If a doctor is unaware of this bias in the studies on clinical effectiveness how can he/she prescribe appropriately?

Many people go to their doctor when feeling low because of life's circumstances and are given antidepressant which for the most part will have no benefit over placebo. Life is much more demanding of us in the modern age with the pressures of earning money to buy all those things we don't need but are enticed into thinking we do. We are out of touch with our environment and our food sources; many people live in less than ideal conditions. There is a high rate of family breakdown and antagonism amongst people of different races or creeds. Is it any wonder we may feel we've lost our way and seek medical solace. Be assured drugs will not solve these issues but they are marketed well and people in a low state are easy prey; and anyway what other tools does a busy doctor have?

Even if anti-depressants did work for everyone they were only intended for short term use, so I learned at university, to help get you through a crisis, 6 to 9 months maybe. Many, many people are on these drugs long term and they are being prescribed more frequently in children; what are the consequences? Your brain chemistry will be affected and if you decide at some point to stop taking these drugs the process should be done in a controlled manner under medical supervision otherwise there is a strong possibility of withdrawal syndrome. Anti-depressants can increase the chance of suicidal thought particularly in children. In mass shootings over the last 20 years in the U.S., many of the perpetrators were taking antidepressants or other psycho-active substances[60].

Common side effects of SSRIs can include: [61]

- *feeling agitated, shaky or anxious*
- *feeling or being sick*
- *indigestion*
- *diarrhoea or constipation*
- *loss of appetite and weight loss*
- *dizziness*
- *blurred vision*
- *dry mouth*
- *excessive sweating*
- *not sleeping well (insomnia) or drowsiness*
- *headaches*
- *low sex drive*
- *difficulty achieving orgasm during sex*
- *in men, difficulty obtaining or maintaining an erection (erectile dysfunction)*

Often when we are low we just need someone to talk to, to offload. Starting on drugs is a slippery slope. If you get any of the side effects you're likely to be prescribed something to counter it and so the drug load progresses.

I have just talked about SSRIs here but there are older types of antidepressants which have a worse side effect profile and overdose danger, hence they have been largely superceded by the newer drugs. For a greater understanding of the serotonin myth read this article by

Dr Kelly Brogan; http://www.greenmedinfo.com/blog/depression-it-s-not-your-serotonin

Is the increasing use of powerful psycho-active drugs turning us into drugged up zombies? Major tranquillisers, are used in the treatment of schizophrenia; in high dosage they suppress motor activity and act like a chemical straight jacket. These powerful drugs are being used much more commonly in other conditions. Science is looking for the answer in chemical imbalances in the brain; theories abound with no scientific substantiation, only academic speculation. The assumption is that a chemical imbalance is causing the problem but maybe, if there is an imbalance, it is there because of the problem and is purely a manifestation of the disease.

The thought processes of science in general are based on physical observations, speculation and theory. This materialism is based in Newtonian philosophy, the world of so called physical reality. From this scientific perspective the concept of a 'spiritual self' or an 'emotional self' would be difficult to envision and yet this is where the imbalances may well be and is why meditation can be so effective in helping achieving inner calm which is paramount in solving many of our emotional problems. It is well accepted in alternative systems of medicine that the psycho-spiritual aspects of our being are intimately involved in our overall health.

Attention Deficit Disorder (ADD)

ADD and its related condition ADHD (the H stands for hyper-active) are modern day diseases; where do they come from?

Bringing up children is not an easy task and even more difficult when both parents are out at work and even when a parent is at home kids are often left for long periods in front of TVs and computer games. Kids may seem more demanding maybe because the time has not been put in to condition them into how their parents expect them to behave. If you do not train your dog, who is to blame if it doesn't do as it's told? Now I'm not suggesting children should be trained like dogs but they do have to learn to respect their elders and behave appropriately. When we were kids if we overstepped the mark we were sent to bed, had our pocket money stopped or were not allowed to go out and play. We soon learned to be more appropriate in our behaviour if we wanted to restore our privileges. We might ask, what is normal kids' behaviour? Since society has removed many of the disciplinary methods of old and some rightly so, they have not been replaced with appropriately effective alternatives.

Diets include high levels of sugar and food additives, colourings, MSG, aspartame all of which impact behaviour. My generation were fortunate that very little of this rubbish was around when we were young. Breakfast is an important meal to get right. If you have a high carbohydrate breakfast there is a tendency to get a dip in blood glucose later on this is likely to affect attention and concentration.

Children at school are being categorised as hyper-active or can't hold their attention. Some kids are naturally boisterous and others are day dreamers, some are downright difficult yet 'super nanny' is able to get a handle on them. How is giving them powerful psycho-active drugs going to help long term? It may calm them down but what of the future if these drugs are given long term; and they are. What happens to these kids when they become adult and are still taking these powerful psycho-active drugs?

Many of the drugs used to treat these conditions belong to the same class as amphetamine, the stuff teenagers were illicitly buying in the 60s in the discos. It seems that in ADHD the drug has a calming effect, it is not known why as they have a stimulant effect in 'normal' people. It is another theory of chemical imbalance which is still being worked on, meanwhile; are our kids being turned into future junkies?

In the US 11% of children are diagnosed with ADHD, a 41% increase over the past decade[62].

The situation is no better in UK where prescriptions for Ritalin have increased fourfold in a 10 year period and now stands at over 660,000 a year[63]. What does this bode for the future of our children, being chemically thwarted at such an early age? The medical experts prescribing these drugs are giving them to children as young as three. If the increase in the use of these drugs carries on at this rate; how long will it be before the majority of kids are taking them?

Eliminating toxins which affect the function of the brain, getting adequate essential fats and other nutrients into the system, drastically reducing low quality carbohydrate and sugar intake, getting adequate sleep and limiting exposure to inappropriate TV and video games will surely have a benefit in helping with behavioural issues.

Osteoporosis

Osteoporosis was investigated in some detail in a previous chapter. You discovered that osteoporosis for the most part is a manufactured disease and was created by defining osteoporosis. The definition being related to the bone density of a 30 year old, and then by definition even some 30 year olds will have osteoporosis because of the normal distribution in the population.

A doctor's skill is in diagnosis. Since osteoporosis is one of those silent diseases that show no symptoms, it can only be diagnosed by a machine. Once the diagnosis is made the solution is easily found in drugs (biphosphonates) that suppress natural bone turn over.

You have seen that in order to prevent one hip fracture around 80 people need to be treated for 3 years. Like most drugs, biphosphonates have potentially serious side effects particularly for long term use. They can lead to necrosis (death) of jaw bone tissue and increase the chance of fracture of the femur. They can have serious upper gastro-intestinal effects and is one of the common reasons for cessation of treatment. For a more complete review of publish data see greenmedinfo at this link[64].

Of course bone health like health in general requires that we get adequate nutrition. Doctors often give calcium supplements and vitamin D as if that's all you need for good bone health.

Bone is composed of a collagen matrix in which minerals are deposited to give it strength. The main mineral is hydroxyapatite which is made of calcium, phosphate and a hydroxyl (-OH) which can be replaced by fluoride. Fluoride weakens bones:

> *"One cannot help but be alarmed by the negative effects of fluoride on bone strength consistently demonstrated in animal models."*
>
> *- Dr. Charles Turner, Indiana University[65].*

Magnesium is needed for strengthening bones and also for the absorption and metabolism of calcium. The formation of hydroxyapatite requires magnesium and is one of the reasons when supplementing with calcium and magnesium they should always be taken together, in balance. Magnesium is involved in the conversion of vitamin D to its active form, very important. Low magnesium intake has been associated with osteoporosis particularly in women. Taking calcium without magnesium can increase magnesium loss and low magnesium can lead to calcium deposition in soft tissue, exactly where you don't want it. If this is deposited in joints then arthritis may ensue[66].

Other minerals and vitamins involved in bone structure and formation:

- *Zinc*
- *Chromium*
- *Silica*
- *Manganese*
- *Copper*
- *Boron*
- *Potassium*
- *Vitamin D*
- *Vitamin C*
- *Vitamin A*
- *Vitamins B6, B12 and B9(folic acid)*

Bone is a living tissue and two types of cell are involved in bone turnover. Osteoclasts break down bone and osteoblasts build up bone, the process is in dynamic equilibrium and as you can see bone health requires so much more than calcium, vitamin D and drugs. Drugs cannot replace nutrients. Nutrients cannot be patented and so are not likely to be offered by your doctor as he/she will not have been educated in such matters unless they have educated themselves of course.

Infections

MRSA – Methicillin Resistant Staphylococcus Aureus or 'super bug' as it's more colloquially known is largely a hospital acquired infection the prevalence of which increased threefold between 1999 and 2005 when there were around 180,000 cases in the US; deaths from MSRA may be up to 19,000 annually depending on which data set used[67].

Why is MSRA widespread? One simple reason is overuse of antibiotics.

Many more bacterial species are becoming resistant to antibiotics because by constantly exposing them to these substances they are able to overcome their effects due to a natural selection process. This class of potentially lifesaving drugs has been seriously misused; a class of drugs that were actually useful but are becoming less so as the days tick by.

Diseases like TB are re-emerging, according to the World Health Organisation there were 450,000 cases of multi-drug resistant TB in 2012. Bacterial antibiotic resistance in common infections of the blood and urinary tract and in pneumonia are now common place. Malaria and STDs like gonorrhoea are no longer responding[68].

All these diseases that were thought to be under control are no longer under control and the reason why? Yes, you know the answer; over use of antibiotics. I don't mean to labour the point but it is vital that people understand the seriousness of the situation.

So next time you go to the doctor's and you are offered antibiotics just consider whether they are really necessary. For most common infections your body can handle it if you are reasonably healthy. If a life threatening illness has been ruled out then discuss alternative support measures to help get you through.

By far the greatest quantities of antibiotics are actually used in livestock, in animal feed at sub-therapeutic doses to promote growth.

> *.....In 2005, 760 tonnes were used in human medicine and 1320 tonnes in veterinary medicine.....[69]*

Almost twice the amount used in humans is used in animals which means than even if you don't take antibiotics directly you will be exposed through the meat you eat. Another reason for buying organic! The bottom line is that antibiotics are rapidly losing their effectiveness and so staying healthy and avoiding all those things which have an immune suppressing effect is becoming more and more important. Immune suppressing 'things' include:

- *Sugar [70]*
- *Stress*
- *Lack of vitamin D[71]*
- *Lack of vitamin C[72]*
- *Lack of zinc[72]*
- *Malnutrition generally*
- *Heavy metals*
- *Other toxins*

- *Drugs*
- *Corticosteroids, oral or inhaled*
- *TNF inhibitors*
- *Interferon*
- *Cytotoxics – cyclophosphamide, hydroxyurea.*
- *Mycophenolate*
- *Prolonged use of opiods*
- *Cyclosporin and related drugs, tacrolimus and sirolimus (rapamycin)*
- *Anti-metabolites – azathioprine, mercapto-purine, methotrexate.*

Endnotes

The medical paradigm has lured us into a false sense of security. We think we can eat and behave how we like and modern medicine will fix us. This may well be true if you break a leg or have a life threatening emergency; doctors are in their element under these circumstances and very successful.

If you believe preventative medicine is going to help you to live a longer, healthier life, then the evidence does not support this for the majority of people.

You are most definitely what you eat and absorb. The absorb bit is interesting because many people are absorbing things they shouldn't be because of poor digestion and leaky gut; this is a contributing factor to the high incidence of inflammatory conditions seen today.

When you start to educate yourself you will become your own doctor (root of education, docere = to teach).

If you know the true worth of a treatment over placebo then that is surely empowering. People may often take a treatment because it is offered and they don't like to refuse. They may not know the full consequences involved because they are not given all the absolute facts to make an informed choice.

Children born today are being brought up in an environment where sickness and anticipated chronic ill health is almost taken for granted; yet with a little knowledge it doesn't have to be that way. The conventional wisdom about alternative choices is that there are no trials to validate these approaches and in the same breath they accept the clinical trials data which show poor benefit outcomes for many, as if these poor results validate their use.

Does the doctor give a disclaimer when a diagnosis is made or prescription is written? No, because they are protected by law; they, like James Bond, have a license to kill, even if unintentionally.

Surely we can do better; we have the technology to put a spaceship into orbit and yet we cannot cure the common cold. Diseases have been created which only need addressing by a change of lifestyle. Cigarettes have a government health warning; how long will it be before some of our common food items carry the very same warning?

References

1. http://onlinelibrary.wiley.com/doi/10.1046/j.1365-2036.17.s1.3.x/full

2. http://refluxdefense.com/heartburn_GERD_articles/stomach-acid.html

3. http://scdlifestyle.com/2012/03/3-tests-for-low-stomach-acid/

4. http://www.integrativepractitioner.com/article_ektid6418.aspx

5. http://www.healthguidance.org/entry/12512/1/What-Causes-Too-Much-Stomach-Acid.html

6. http://www.dailymail.co.uk/health/article-2177911/Heartburn-pills-uncomfortable-questions--They-help-millions--doctors-warn-long-term-effects.html

7. https://www.visiongain.com/Press_Release/682/%E2%80%9CThe-painkillers-market-will-reach-68-2-billion-in-2014%E2%80%9D-according-to-new-Visiongain-report

8. http://www.fiercepharma.com/special-reports/top-20-generic-molecules-worldwide

9. http://www.ncbi.nlm.nih.gov/pmc/articles/PMC1124220/

10. http://www.washingtonpost.com/blogs/wonkblog/wp/2013/09/11/nine-facts-about-terrorism-in-the-united-states-since-911/

11. http://www.pulsetoday.co.uk/clinical/more-clinical-/musculoskeletal/nice-warns-against-prescribing-paracetamol-for-osteoarthritis/20003979.article#.VMBWPi6sbb4

12. http://www.webmd.com/migraines-headaches/guide/rebound-headaches

13. http://www.green-lipped-mussel-oil.com/list-of-nsaids.html

14. http://cherryhill.legalexaminer.com/fda-prescription-drugs/vioxx-killed-half-a-million-the-facts-are-grim/

15. http://www.theweek.co.uk/us/46535/when-half-million-americans-died-and-nobody-noticed

16. http://www.wellnessresources.com/freedom/articles/vioxx_mechanism_of_heart_attacks_discovered_all_nsaids_may_have_risk/

17. http://www.nature.com/ajg/journal/v100/n8/full/ajg2005305a.html

18. http://www.drugfreeworld.org/drugfacts/prescription/opioids-and-morphine-derivatives.html

19. http://www.cdc.gov/vitalsigns/opioid-prescribing/

20. https://www.uspharmacist.com/article/neuropathic-pain-a-review-of-diabetic-neuropathy

21. http://www.nhs.uk/Conditions/Blood-pressure-%28high%29/Pages/Causes.aspx

22. http://meps.ahrq.gov/mepsweb/data_files/publications/st404/stat404.shtml

23. https://surfstat.anu.edu.au/surfstat-home/1-3-1.html

24. http://www.nhlbi.nih.gov/health/health-topics/topics/hbp

25. http://www.ncbi.nlm.nih.gov/pubmed/22075270

26. http://www.side-effects-site.com/magnesium-depletion.html#gallery%5BpageGallery%5D/0/

27. http://articles.mercola.com/sites/articles/archive/2004/08/07/miracle-magnesium.aspx

28. http://www.easy-immune-health.com/magnesium-level.html

29. http://www.nhs.uk/news/2007/October/Pages/Meditationreducesstressandimprovesmood.aspx

30. http://www.ncbi.nlm.nih.gov/pubmed/17405690

31. http://www.ncbi.nlm.nih.gov/pubmed/7512468

32. http://www.ncbi.nlm.nih.gov/pmc/articles/PMC2410097/

33. http://www.webmd.com/hypertension-high-blood-pressure/news/20120420/extra-vitamin-c-may-help-lower-blood-pressure

34. http://www.heart.org/HEARTORG/Conditions/HighBloodPressure/PreventionTreatmentofHighBloodPressure/Types-of-Blood-Pressure-Medications_UCM_303247_Article.jsp

35. http://www.thennt.com/nnt/anti-hypertensives-to-prevent-death-heart-attacks-and-strokes/

36. http://www.thennt.com/nnt/anti-hypertensives-for-cardiovascular-prevention-in-mild-hypertension/

37. http://www.ncbi.nlm.nih.gov/pubmed/11368251

38. http://www.globalresearch.ca/vaccine-induced-immune-overload-and-the-epidemic-of-chronic-autoimmune-childhood-disease/5431013

39. http://www.cdc.gov/arthritis/data_statistics/arthritis_related_stats.htm

40. http://www.gastrojournal.org/article/S0016-5085%2811%2901378-3/abstract

41. http://chriskresser.com/how-too-much-omega-6-and-not-enough-omega-3-is-making-us-sick

42. http://www.livestrong.com/article/485053-why-fructose-elevates-uric-acid/

43. http://articles.mercola.com/sites/articles/archive/2011/11/06/aspartame-most-dangerous-substance-added-to-food.aspx

44. http://www.greenmedinfo.com/page/opening-pandoras-bread-box-critical-role-wheat-lectin-human-disease

45. http://www.purehealingfoods.com/infoLeakyGut.php

46. http://www.ncbi.nlm.nih.gov/pubmed/24378456

47. http://chriskresser.com/how-toxins-are-making-us-fat-and-diabetic

48. http://articles.mercola.com/sites/articles/archive/2014/05/18/gmo-foods-inflammation.aspx

49. https://www.ncbi.nlm.nih.gov/pmc/articles/PMC1855338/

50. http://www.rheumatologynetwork.com/articles/do-nsaids-impair-healing-musculoskeletal-injuries

51. http://www.gastro.org/patient-center/diet-medications/nonsteriodal-anti-inflammatory-drugs-nsaids

52. http://www.ncbi.nlm.nih.gov/pubmed/9391772

53. https://www.pennmedicine.org/news/news-releases/2012/may/nsaids-and-cardiovascular-risk

54. http://americannutritionassociation.org/newsletter/deadly-nsaids

55. http://www.ncbi.nlm.nih.gov/pmc/articles/PMC3615849/

56. http://www.nhs.uk/Conditions/Corticosteroid-%28drugs%29/Pages/Sideeffects.aspx

57. https://www.ncbi.nlm.nih.gov/pmc/articles/PMC4172306/

58. http://mentalhealthdaily.com/2014/10/07/paxil-vs-placebo-2014-meta-analysis-with-unpublished-data-questions-drugs-efficacy/

59. http://www.nejm.org/doi/full/10.1056/NEJMsa065779

60. http://www.naturalnews.com/039752_mass_shootings_psychiatric_drugs_antidepressants.html

61. http://www.nhs.uk/Conditions/SSRIs-%28selective-serotonin-reuptake-inhibitors%29/Pages/Side-effects.aspx

62. http://www.nytimes.com/2013/04/01/health/more-diagnoses-of-hyperactivity-causing-concern.html?pagewanted=all&_r=0

63. http://www.theguardian.com/society/2012/may/06/ritalin-adhd-shocks-child-psychologists

64. http://www.greenmedinfo.com/toxic-ingredient/alendronate-trade-name-fosamax

65. http://fluoridealert.org/issues/health/bone-fracture/

66. http://www.betterbones.com/bonenutrition/magnesium.aspx

67. http://www.google.com/url?sa=t&rct=j&q=&esrc=s&source=web&cd=2&ved=0CCgQFjAB&url=http%3A%2F%2Fwww.cddep.org%2Fsites%2Fdefault%2Ffiles%2Fcounting20mrsa20cases1_6.pdf&ei=0QzYVPKeD9CB8QWf2wI&usg=AFQjCNG4Lf4mva0dQDAH2Dzsn2sWhpcZsQ&bvm=bv.85464276,d.dGc

68. http://www.who.int/mediacentre/factsheets/fs194/en/

69. http://jac.oxfordjournals.org/content/62/3/617.full

70. http://www.askdrsears.com/topics/feeding-eating/family-nutrition/sugar/harmful-effects-excess-sugar

71. http://www.ncbi.nlm.nih.gov/pmc/articles/PMC3166406/

72. http://www.ncbi.nlm.nih.gov/pubmed/16373990

Chapter 16 - LAST WORDS

'Knowledge is power'

'Who questions much shall learn much and retain much'.

Francis Bacon 1561 - 1626

In this book I have tried to present a lot of information in a short space, the reason being; to introduce you the reader to many ideas which ordinarily would take a long time to assimilate, as indeed it did me. I have tried not to overwhelm you with too much data but to supply enough information to create the arguments and instil curiosity. As I said in the introduction I claim no ownership to any of this information although I admit I may have allowed my own slant and emphasis at times. I think that this is valid in a free society and I encourage you to make your own interpretations of the data. Empowerment is not about being told what to do or being bullied into making hasty decisions, it is about having adequate knowledge and fortitude to decide for yourself with no fear of repercussions. Even if you make what might be considered by others a wrong decision, you should feel no guilt.

I have supplied many references, maybe too many, you have the choice to follow these up or not. Whether you choose to delve deeper and read the reference sources or not will not change the information extracted from them. For most readers I suspect they will neither have the time nor the inclination to follow the paper trail, so to speak, unless there is a personal issue in which case you may want to investigate further. If you need to make a decision about whether or not to take a specific drug for example then hopefully there is enough information and references to follow up which will help you to make such a choice or not. If there isn't then I hope you will be inspired to look further afield. In this day and age we are fortunate to have a whole library and reference works literally at our finger tips. When I was at university I, like others of my generation, had to spend hours in the library, no search engines in those days.

The purpose of this book is not to be a medical authority which it certainly is not, but to be a point of entry into the data pool of information and provide an enhanced insight which will allow you to have a more meaningful discussion with the appropriate health care practitioner.

If you ask a doctor a question and he/she doesn't know the answer then my view is that they should find out the answer, particularly if your health is dependent on it. The doctor's role is that of educator and health care adviser and to solely accept information from a biased source, the pharmaceutical industry, without question, might not be in your best interest. Of course not all medical practitioners are this naive, however, in a busy practice with thousands of patients it is not practical for most to question the paradigm in which they work; it is by far the easiest path to accept the status quo, not rock the boat and just get on with the job. Unfortunately that's exactly what medicine has become, a job; no longer a calling to serve fellow humans and uphold the main tenet of the ancient Hippocratic Oath of 'first do no harm'. This is an impossible tenet to uphold in the current medical paradigm where medicine has now been identified as the third leading cause of death in the US[1]. The death toll from medical error arrived at in the research is about 250,000 deaths in 2013, <u>N.B. medical error</u>. This figure does not take into account deaths from appropriately prescribed medication and is therefore a gross underestimation of the total deaths from the medical system. This is a huge indictment of our system of medicine; this fact has been known for a long time and this latest proclamation in the British Medical Journal of May 2016 just confirms it. Interestingly, if you access CDC information this third leading cause of death is not mentioned[2]; you might ponder on why that is? The reason I believe is that the recording of cause of death only has certain options and medical error is not one of the options and so the recording doctor puts something else. What do you think of that?

We live in a society in which we are continually exposed to the threat of terrorism, violence, influenza etc; how many people die from these events compared with 'death by medicine'? The US government and other governments spend large amounts of *your* money in the so called war on illicit drugs, presumably because they are considered dangerous and kill people and yet the deaths from such use is a drop in the ocean compared to deaths from medical error and legally prescribed drugs. We seem to have got something terribly wrong.

Most people have busy lives just trying to keep their head above water in the fast pace of life currently being experienced. We are so accepting of the information presented to us by the media, the experts and the government; it must surely be correct, we can trust the source, can't we? How many times have we been led down the garden path by official proclamations? There are many instances in history where information is given to the public as fact only to be discredited at a later date. An example in health care was the 'too many eggs are bad for you' public awareness campaign and now it seems they're OK. Eggs have always been a nutritious whole food and have very little effect on cholesterol[3].

The information presented in this book could be life saving; if it is taken on board and fully understood it will be life changing.

Whether drugs work or not is, as you've seen, dependent on the definition of the word work. You have enough information now to decide for yourself. You have seen that the benefit to an individual in many areas of drug use is purely a chance occurrence. Evidence based medicine in the treatment of chronic disease is purely a statistical construct; few people fully understand this, even practitioners. If medical practitioners really understood the <u>absolute</u> benefit of some of the so called preventative protocols and treatment options for perceived disease states; would they prescribe those medications? It is well known that 20-30% of prescriptions are never filled[4]; 50% of prescribed drugs are not taken as intended[5], much of it returned to pharmacies when the individual passes from this world. Why is this? Do people instinctively know that the medication is not appropriate for them?

What have you learned from reading this book?

- *If you want to be involved in your own health care then you have to take some responsibility for it.*
- *You have learned the difference between relative and absolute benefit.*
- *Drugs used to treat and prevent chronic disease only help a minority of people.*
- *Legally prescribed drugs and treatments contribute significantly to the annual death toll.*
- *Heart disease and cancer are still the biggest sources of ill health facing modern society despite the billions of dollars invested in research over the last four or five decades.*
- *There are other options for treating and reversing these conditions and yet they are not generally available via government funded health systems.*
- *Sugar, fructose and refined carbohydrates play an enormous role in the aetiology of the major diseases of western culture.*
- *We have been misled regarding 'the fat issue'.*
- *Toxicity plays an important role in determining our level of health.*
- *Toxins are lurking in the foods we eat, the air we breathe and the water we drink.*
- *Nutrient deficiencies are equally important.*
- *Genetically modified foods are a growing threat to our health and environment.*

If you get nothing more out of this book than a notion that something isn't quite right, then I will have achieved my purpose, because you will start to look at things differently. Information you once took for granted will be processed with a different mindset. You may start to question the validity of many things because as surely as our medical systems and food supply have many hidden aspects; this reality may be applied to many other areas of our modern world and which a little investigation may bring to light.

I sincerely hope you have reaped some benefit from the information contained within these pages and that you share that information with your friends and family. People have the power to effect change; there is no doubt about that. One of the biggest factors in effecting change is how you spend your dollars. When people start to choose differently the industry will respond, profits are their primary concern. One example of this is the new Coca Cola variety which is sweetened with stevia, a natural sweetener; stevia is even available on the table at my local cafe.

I hope you have enjoyed the journey and wish you well in your quest for health. There are many people out there who can help you on your journey.

When diet is correct there is no need of medicine.

When diet is incorrect medicine is of no help.

Ayurvedic saying

References

1. http://www.medscape.com/viewarticle/862832?nlid=104512_3901&src=wnl_newsalrt_160503_MSCPEDIT&uac=205868AN&impID=1084165&faf=1

2. http://www.cdc.gov/nchs/fastats/deaths.htm

3. http://authoritynutrition.com/how-many-eggs-should-you-eat/

4. http://www.reuters.com/article/us-new-prescriptions-study-idUSTRE61G3QX20100217

5. http://www.epill.com/statistics.htmlhttp://www.epill.com/statistics.html

<u>Addendum 1 – HPV vaccine</u>

I thought I had finished, again! However the HPV vaccine program came in to my field of awareness and I felt the subject matter was of sufficient importance to delay my finish and write this addendum.

Most parents with young children, particularly girls, are likely to be aware of this vaccine, what they may not be aware of is the controversy and dangers associated with it.

First, some background information from the Centre for Disease Control (CDC)[1].

HPV or Human Papilloma Virus is the generic name given to a group of *over 40* distinct viruses. HPV infection can be associated with cervical cancer and genital warts. The virus types which apparently give cause for concern are types 16 and 18 which are associated with 70% of cervical cancers and types 6 and 11 which are associated with 90% of genital warts. These virus type are the ones from which the vaccines are produced. There are two vaccines, a quadrivalent vaccine (Gardasil) which contains all four types and is licensed for use in both males and females age 9 - 26 and a bivalent vaccine (Cervarix) which only contains types 16 and 18 and is licensed for use in females age 10 - 25.

The vaccine has not been as popular as anticipated with only 57% of girls receiving one dose and only 38% receiving the then recommended 3 doses (2013). Vaccine uptake was much lower in boys.

Before the vaccine was introduced the prevalence of HPV of *any* strain was 42.5% in females age 14 – 59 (2003-2006). The prevalence was variable and peaked in women 20 -24 years old. Types 6,11,16 and 18 together were present in 11.5% of samples and post vaccine introduction this dropped to 5.1% in 14-19 year old (2007-2010). Among other age groups the prevalence of the four vaccine types *did not differ* in the two time periods. The figures in the 14-19 year old group represent a ***relative*** reduction of 56% but an ***absolute*** reduction of 6.4%.

The biggest concern with HPV is its association with cervical cancer and the goal of vaccination is to reduce the incidence of this form of cancer. Just what *is* the incidence of cervical cancer?

The following data is from the National Cancer Institute[2]; number of new cases per 100,000 of population and number of deaths per 100,000 of population.

YEAR	NEW CASES/100,000 POPULATION	DEATHS/100,000 POPULATION
1975	14.8	5.6
1985	10.2	3.8
1995	8.9	3.2
2005	6.9	2.4
2013	6.4	2.3

You can see from this data that the incidence and death rate from cervical cancer was falling quite markedly before the HPV vaccine was introduced in 2006 due to the introduction of the PAP screening test in the 1960s; the decline since then has been small.

Going back to the data on HPV prevalence and a 6.4% reduction in HPV incidence in 14 -19 year olds. Looking at the figures in a simplistic manner; assuming *all* cases of HPV infection in this group resulted in cervical cancer then the number of new cases and deaths might be expected to fall by 6.4% which equates to 0.4 and 0.15 per 100,000 of population. In comparison the number of road traffic deaths in the US from 2010 to 2015 was around 10 per 100,000[3] and the number of suicides in 2014 was around 10 per 100,000[4].

Of course not all HPV infection, even of the implicated strains, will lead to cervical cancer and the vaccine doesn't cover all the carcinogenic strains (there are around 13 in all classed as carcinogenic). So the reduction in new cases and deaths would be *less than* 0.4 and 0.15 per 100,000.

I know from a statistical view point this approach is very simplistic and probably full of flaws, however it does give a ball park figure and shows that the benefit is not that huge when the downside of HPV vaccination is considered.

Cervical cancer accounts for less than 2% of all type cancer incidence and death[5].

What is the downside of HPV vaccination?

Firstly, does HPV actually prevent cervical cancer? We don't know. HPV vaccine may reduce the rate of infection but the question of whether it works to reduce cervical cancer remains to be answered. There is a time lag between being infected with HPV and development of cervical cancer in the order of 20 years and so we won't know until 2026 or so and since the incidence was reducing anyway what will be the significance?

> *What other factors are involved? smoking; multiple sexual partners; long term oral contraceptive use; multiple births; weakened immune system; co-infection with Chlamydia or HIV; poor nutrition; heavy drinking and smoking and chronic inflammation are all risk factors which influence the development of HPV related cancer [6].*

A search of the VAERS database for HPV events gave the following results for the years 2006 – 2016: (VAERS = Vaccine Adverse Event Reporting System)[7]

Reported adverse events	37976
Number of serious reactions	5232
Number of hospitalisations	3891
Life threatening events	698
Number of deaths	115
Number disabled	1384

Why was the HPV vaccine introduced when cervical cancer rates had been reduced so much by Pap screening and treatment of identified lesions? This extract from a paper at Biomed Central – Infectious Agents and Cancer sums up the situation.

> *'Currently the benefit of the vaccine against the burden of cervical cancer in developed countries is unknown and there are risks of injury and death that have not been accurately determined. HPV vaccines are not demonstrated to be safer or more effective than Pap screening combined with surgical procedures. Hence it follows that implementing broad HPV vaccination programs is not cost-effective in countries where regular Pap screening programs are available and will still be required. HPV vaccines in vaccination programs in these countries are offering uncertain benefits in reducing the burden of cervical cancer and may cause more harm than good due to the lack of investigation of their long-term safety.* [8]

Each vaccine dose costs around $150, current guidelines are for two doses for 14 -19 year olds. I estimate there are in the order of 12 million girls in this age group; 12 million x $300 = $3.6 billion dollars of potential revenue in that age group alone if everyone had the vaccine. Surely that money could be spent more wisely?

In summary the HPV vaccine is of doubtful value and has definite potential for harm. The *fear* of cervical cancer is presumably the main motivating factor to be vaccinated. Yet cervical cancer account for only 2% of all cancers and can be prevented in the most part by Pap screening. Your chance of dying in a motor accident or killing yourself by suicide is much more likely. Why take the risk of an unproven vaccine which can potentially have serious side effects. I think it's time we stopped relying on science and start to use a little more common sense; what's is your gut feeling about this? Choose wisely for your children.

References

1. https://www.cdc.gov/std/stats13/other.htm
2. https://seer.cancer.gov/statfacts/html/cervix.html
3. https://en.wikipedia.org/wiki/List_of_motor_vehicle_deaths_in_U.S._by_year
4. https://www.cdc.gov/nchs/fastats/deaths.htm
5. https://www.cdc.gov/cancer/cervical/statistics/race.htm
6. http://www.nvic.org/Vaccines-and-Diseases/hpv.aspx
7. http://www.medalerts.org/vaersdb/index.php
8. http://infectagentscancer.biomedcentral.com/articles/10.1186/1750-9378-8-21

9.

Addendum 2 – More vaccine information

Having just listened to a very informative series of videos made by Ty Bollinger called 'The Truth about Vaccines'[1] I felt it important to detail some of the salient points. Some of this information may have already been given in the book, repetition is probably useful. I have just written these points in the order I originally wrote them down and I apologise for a certain lack of continuity. This addendum is just a matter of presenting extra information to augment what is already in the book.

We have to get over the concepts of pro-vaccine or anti-vaccine and develop the concepts of pro-information, pro-truth and pro-choice while we still have the opportunity.

When you are 'offered' a vaccine do you have true informed consent? For true informed consent you need to know;

- *The absolute benefit (remember absolute and relative explained earlier).*
- *All the potential risks both short and long term and the chance of experiencing them.*
- *The alternatives; there are always alternatives even if the only choice non-vaccination!*

If a government mandates that you or your child is to receive a vaccine then this is *paternalism* and not informed consent. It is a violation of the basic human right to autonomy over your own or your child's body. Paternalism is:

'The policy or practice on the part of people in authority of restricting the freedom and responsibilities of those subordinate to or otherwise dependent on them in their supposed interest.' – **Oxford English Dictionary.**

Antibiotics may reduce the ability of the body to detoxify mercury[2]. Vaccines may contain Mercury *and* antibiotics. And also antibiotics may be prescribed separately around vaccination time.

Vaccination and immunisation are often used synonymously however they are not the same. Vaccination is the process of introducing the vaccine material into the body, usually by injection. This may produce an antibody response which is seen as an indication of efficacy; this does not necessarily guarantee immunity; just because you have antibodies to the vaccine does not mean you are protected from the 'wild' disease strains. This has been shown on many occasions e.g[3].

When a clinical trial of *any* drug or vaccine is done it should be in comparison to a true placebo; sugar pills or saline (salt solution) injection. Often in clinical trials of vaccines true placebos are not used, instead what is used is an *active* placebo; for example when the current years influenza vaccine is tested it is often against the previous years, the quadrivalent HPV vaccine was tested against an Aluminum solution[4]. What this means is that some side effects will not show since both placebo and trial drug/vaccine contain toxic material.

Clinical trials carried out in healthy adult volunteers do not match many of the target groups; the elderly, children and infants for example [5].

A vaccine may contain egg protein and peanut oil residues; this may be a causative factor in food allergies particularly peanut allergy which was pretty rare before the vaccine era and is now common place[6].

Vaccines may contain foreign DNA[7]; do we know the negative consequences of this?

Aluminum, a vaccine adjuvant, is neurotoxic and accumulates in brain tissue. Polysorbate 80 is a detergent found in some vaccines and which enhances aluminum passage into the brain. For more information on aluminum and mercury see:

http://www.nvic.org/Doctors-Corner/Aluminum-and-Vaccine-Ingredients.aspx

and

https://www.amazon.com/Thimerosal-Evidence-Supporting-Immediate-Neurotoxin/dp/1632206013 .

It is difficult to obtain true information from vaccine companies because they cannot be sued in USA. They are not likely to volunteer information that would be detrimental to their business; are they?

In the US newborn babies are given Hepatitis B almost immediately; why? The main indication for this vaccine is in sexually active people and IV drug users. If the parents are HepB negative then there's no reason to give it *and the vaccine contains aluminum.*

Doctors are given financial incentives to vaccinate; is this ethical?

Vitamin K is given at birth by injection to prevent a rare haemorrhagic disease. Why not give oral vitamin K or even make sure the mothers diet is adequate? This injection contains Aluminum so that's the second dose of aluminum shortly after birth(in the US). The following is from drugs.com [8].

> *'WARNING: This product contains aluminum that may be toxic. Aluminum may reach toxic levels with prolonged parenteral administration if kidney function is impaired. Premature neonates are particularly at risk because their kidneys are immature, and they required large amounts of calcium and phosphate solutions, which contain aluminum.*
>
> *Research indicates that patients with impaired kidney function, including premature neonates, who receive parenteral levels of aluminum at greater than 4 to 5 mcg/kg/day accumulate aluminum at levels associated with central nervous system and bone toxicity. Tissue loading may occur at even lower rates of administration.'*

Are new born babies routinely tested for kidney function?

And this from Medscape[8].

> *'.......Only when the GI barrier is bypassed, such as by intravenous infusion or in the presence of advanced renal dysfunction, does aluminum have the potential to accumulate. As an example, with intravenously infused aluminum, 40% is retained in adults and up to 75% is retained in neonates.......'*

'.......If a significant aluminum load exceeds the body's excretory capacity, the excess is deposited in various tissues, including bone, brain, liver, heart, spleen, and muscle. This accumulation causes morbidity and mortality through various mechanisms......'

'........Aluminum causes an oxidative stress within brain tissue. Since the elimination half-life of aluminum from the human brain is 7 years, this can result in cumulative damage via the element's interference with neurofilament axonal transport and neurofilament assembly......'

'.......It has also been linked to vaccine-associated macrophagic myofasciitis and chronic fatigue syndrome, thus highlighting the potential dangers associated with aluminum-containing adjuvants as described recently.......'

Vaccines may have a role to play in human health but the way they are being given along with toxic adjuvants is causing problems in the health of our children. In the US autism spectrum disorder is officially at 1 in 68 children although it may be nearer 1 in 45[10]. This is up from 1 in 150 in 2000 and around 1 in 2000 back in 1985. What is going on? There are most likely other factors influencing this increase but neurotoxins in vaccines must be implicated along with pro-inflammatory diets and poor micronutrient nutrition. At this rate how long will it be before the majority of our children have this disorder?

<u>*References*</u>

1. https://go.thetruthaboutvaccines.com/
2. https://www.ncbi.nlm.nih.gov/m/pubmed/6524959/
3. http://www.digitaljournal.com/article/323187
4. http://www.nvic.org/nvic-archives/pressrelease/gardasilgirls.aspx
5. https://www.researchmatch.org/trials/trial/NCT02918006
6. http://www.nytimes.com/1964/09/19/peanut-oil-used-in-a-new-vaccine.html?_r=0
7. http://cbcd.net/?p=1600
8. https://www.drugs.com/pro/vitamin-k1.html
9. http://emedicine.medscape.com/article/165315-overview?pa=WPBJ9aKseBTP8XrV1fmW%2BUS0I7o2HCl2dZyJEtyZVMu9Y8PDCLzGGpO0jtcG%2BRRCzIDseXjgHHeg6nhLb1vahmdDnIu908wGp6AYmWKHBoY%3D
10. https://www.autismspeaks.org/science/science-news/new-government-survey-pegs-autism-prevalence-1-45

Addendum 3 – Another cancer treatment option.

We all have potential cancer within us at any moment of time; we only produce a tumour mass when the ability of the immune system is compromised to such an extent that the rogue cells can no longer be removed. One of the main defences against rogue cells and foreign invaders is class of cells within the immune system called *macrophages.* Macrophages are activated by a protein which we make in our bodies called GcMAF. GcMAF is *Vitamin D binding protein macrophage activating factor.* From its name you can see that Vitamin D is important and that this complex activates macrophages which then carry out their role of removing rogue cells and foreign invaders.

GcMAF is a natural substance and as such cannot be patented and hence is unlikely to received research funding from the main stream. There are however some doctors using this (and a newer compound called Rerum) as part of a protocol to treat cancer and other immune disorders including neurological diseases like *autism and Alzheimer's.* The protocol involves the use of GcMAF/Rerum, a probiotic supplement called Bravo and the ketogenic diet mentioned earlier in the cancer chapter. As you may recall the ketogenic diet starves cancer cells of glucose; glucose being the primary fuel for cancer cells. This halts cancer cell growth. The probiotic replenishes the microbiome in the gut which is tremendously important for health and particularly immune health. The rerum stimulates macrophage activation to attack tumour cells.

Professor Marco Ruggiero, a leading authority on GcMAF has much to say see this youtube video. https://www.youtube.com/results?search_query=marco+ruggiero+gc maf

This protocol is likely to be met with a lot of resistance by the conventional system which is mainly funded by the pharmaceutical industry. If a treatment is effective but cannot be patented then this means great financial losses to the industry; they will not take it lying down! Consequently there is likely to be much propaganda to dissuade the public from using this treatment. As with any new treatment find an appropriately qualified practitioner and follow the treatment protocol. **Do your own research, make up your own mind.**

If there was a screening test for cancer that was non-invasive and could *detect cancer several years before it was able to be detected on a scan* and also indicated the type of cancer you'd probably think that was a useful test.

There is such a test called *the Oncoblot test;* you can read about is at http://oncoblotlabs.com/ .

It is very new so your doctor may not know about it. In my view this is a test which should be offered by our medical systems. If we can detect cancer when it is a small ball of cells then we can take remedial action in terms of diet, lifestyle and supplementation to reverse the situation.

Medical doctors always talk about screening to reduce the incidence of disease; this truly is a useful screen unlike some you have studied in this book.